Bantam Books by David Reuben, M.D.

EVERYTHING YOU ALWAYS WANTED
TO KNOW ABOUT SEX
ANY WOMAN CAN

Any Woman Can!*

LOVE AND SEXUAL FULFILLMENT
FOR THE SINGLE, WIDOWED, DIVORCED
...AND MARRIED

David Reuben, M.D.

* BY THE AUTHOR OF "EVERYTHING YOU ALWAYS WANTED TO KNOW ABOUT SEX ...BUT WERE AFRAID TO ASK"

BANTAM BOOKS
TORONTO · NEW YORK · LONDON

A NATIONAL GENERAL COMPANY

To BARBARA,
who is truly the perfect Wife,
the perfect Mother,
and the perfect Woman.

*This low-priced Bantam Book
has been completely reset in a type face
designed for easy reading, and was printed
from new plates. It contains the complete
text of the original hard-cover edition.*
NOT ONE WORD HAS BEEN OMITTED.

ANY WOMAN CAN!
LOVE AND SEXUAL FULFILLMENT FOR THE SINGLE, WIDOWED, DIVORCED
. . . AND MARRIED
*A Bantam Book / published by arrangement with
David McKay Company, Inc.*

PRINTING HISTORY
*McKay edition published August 1971
2nd printing ... September 1971
3rd printing ... September 1971
Condensations appeared in* PSYCHOLOGY TODAY,
PHILADELPHIA INQUIRER, HEARST MAGAZINE *and* MACFADDEN-
BARTELL WOMAN'S GROUP
Bantam edition published October 1972

Back cover photo of the author by Charles Moore, Black Star

Published simultaneously in the United States and Canada

ACKNOWLEDGMENTS

I would like to thank my friend and agent, Don Congdon, for lending me his wisdom, encouragement, and enthusiasm—qualities which he has in abundance. I am deeply grateful to Kennett and Eleanor Rawson who went far beyond their roles as publisher and editor to help me in every way possible. Carolyn Anthony provided professional assistance in many ways. Max Geffen deserves my thanks for always being there when I needed him. Oscar Dystel and Marc Jaffe amply displayed their confidence in me and my book. Attorney Michael Greer supplied vital legal expertise and attorney Richard Munks contributed legal research on common law marriage. Vivienne Miller, my personal secretary, continued to demonstrate her loyalty, dependability, and devotion—rare and much appreciated attributes. Dr. Joseph Kwint and Dr. Louis Schlom helped by reading and commenting on material in various chapters. Melecia Cranny of the San Diego Medical Society-University Library was helpful in many ways. John Pridonoff was untiring and persevering in typing the manuscript. Finally my wife, Barbara, made the book possible by reading every word as it was written and contributing her expert judgment. Her tact, insight, and intuition are unsurpassed. Finally, my son, David Jr., made it all easier by taking his daddy out to play when the words started to pile up.

Spring Valley, California
April 16, 1971

CONTENTS

THE SEXUALLY
MAROONED WOMAN

What is a sexually marooned woman?

Any woman who is unwilling or unable to fulfill her destiny as a full-fledged female and thereby enjoy a lifetime of gratifying sexual experiences is sexually marooned. (After all, the only real distinction between men and women is their sexuality—in every other respect they are virtually identical.) A woman who is not completely expressing her womanliness in its most direct way is emotionally and sexually cut off from the rest of the world—*marooned*.

How do some women get that way?

Somewhere, somehow, something goes wrong. In America, the single woman is by far the most liberated member of society. Usually unfettered by children or family, often earning an excellent salary, glowing with good health, she has an abundance of free time to indulge her every whim, yet she often suffers under a terrible burden.

Which one is that?

The greatest of all human pleasures—*sexual fulfillment*—is officially denied to every adult female who is single, widowed, or divorced. A woman is free to practice law, perform brain surgery, work on the hydrogen bomb, even travel to distant planets. She is morally—and in many cases *legally*—forbidden to merge her vagina with a penis until and unless she marries.

Before a modern woman is allowed to use the equipment she was born with, she must, in effect, find a man to sponsor her, obtain a copulation permit—diplomatically known as a marriage license—and officially file her intention to have sexual intercourse. Any woman who won't, can't, or just doesn't feel like doing it this way finds herself in an unbelievable position. Other men and women actually expect her to pack up her sexual equipment and store it until she gets married (maybe in the hope chest with the pillowcases and the mothballs?).

In our erotically charged environment where naked sex is used to sell cigarettes to high school seniors and full-page ads offer spray-on vaginal perfume in strawberry flavor, the healthy well-developed unmarried woman isn't supposed to notice. In an era where fashion expects her to wear hot pants, a see-through blouse, and no bra, she has a hard time keeping her mind off the reason she's wearing them.

To tantalize her further, the same arrangement that rules out sex for her rules it *in* for every man, married, single, or in between. As a constant confirmation of his manhood, he is supposed to stalk the social scene impregnating as many women as he can. Every resource for persuasion is at his disposal, every technique for sexual stimulation is at his fingertips. If the woman follows her normal feelings and has sex with him—without mariage—she loses. All the coercive pressure of society is marshaled against her. If she resists and remains aloof—she loses. She passes up another chance to be a vital natural woman, as Nature intended her to be.

What does this mean to the average single woman?

Nancy knows how it feels. She is twenty-six and an assistant buyer for a department store chain. Tall, slender, and blonde, she speaks intensely: "Doctor, I've had this conversation with myself a thousand times. I know what sex is, I know how you do it, I want to get started, but I'm afraid. I mean, what would I have to look forward to? I'm going with this guy, we get along all right but I'd never want to marry him, and he wants me to move into his place and start sleeping with him."

"How do you feel about that?"

"Oh, I think it's great for openers. But what do I do for an encore?" Nancy threw up her hands.

"He doesn't want to get married, I don't want to get married, and I'm sure one day I'll come home from work and find a note instead of a boyfriend. I just don't happen to think it's worth it." No more smiles.

"What's the alternative?"

"The alternative, Doctor, is what I've been doing for the past four years—waiting, saving, and getting older —*all of me*. I'm sure I'll get married someday but what am I supposed to do until then? Stay home crocheting a quilt for my wedding night?"

Nancy belonged to that large group of women who are rebelling against the hypocritical demands of society and demanding to live their lives in more realistic terms. It is a difficult venture. There are no landmarks, the path is dark, few women have ventured there before. Those who are too timid are left behind—the ones who are too bold are trapped and cut off from the rest of society. Unwilling to regress to the role of the desexualized babysitters nodding before the television set and ill-equipped to work out a better solution, many sexually marooned women are destined to congregate on small isolated emotional islands of their own. From time to time, they dip a toe into the sexual waters, then quickly pull back awaiting the romantic rescuer who never comes.

Does "marooning" show up any other way?

Sexual marooning may wear many disguises—sometimes it even masks itself as sexual freedom. That's what Wanda called it, anyway. She was thirty-one, well-developed, and articulate:

"You know, Doctor, I never believed that a person had to settle for whatever crumbs fate cared to toss their way."

"What do you mean by that?"

"Well, I wasn't really supposed to go to college— my parents didn't have the money. I worked like crazy and won a scholarship to a first-rank woman's college. Then I found out women aren't supposed to be stockbrokers. I cracked that barrier. The toughest obstacle of all was sex, but I managed to beat that game, too."

"How did you manage that?"

"I just think like a man. I find the fellow I like, I go after him, get what I want from the relationship, and then when the fun's over, I look for someone else. It's that simple."

"Then why are you crying?"

"You can't call it crying until tears actually come out!"

"That's fine, Wanda. I concede. Let's say you are in the pre-crying stage. But at least tell me how I can help you."

"Nobody can help me!" There were real tears now, plenty of them. "It was supposed to work. It should've worked! It was so sensible! What went wrong?"

"With what?"

"With my life, that's what. I get whatever I want from men. They take me to the places I want to go, they treat me the way I want to be treated. I don't have any sexual problems—I mean, just the same as every other woman."

"What do you mean, 'just the same as every other woman'?"

"Well, you know. Everything's fine at first. I never have trouble reaching a climax, and I just can't seem to get enough sex. But then after a while when the novelty wears off, I—I guess I still enjoy it, but it's just not the same."

"You mean after a while, no orgasm?"

"Yes. Isn't every woman like that?"

"Fortunately not. Do the orgasms start to fade toward the end of your relationships?"

"No, I've thought a lot about that. It's before the end—say the end of the middle. As if something inside of me knew that the whole thing was going to turn sour."

"That could very well be. Sometimes the unconscious mind can see it coming before a person is really consciously aware of it."

Wanda considered herself a sexual freedom-fighter. Actually she was more of a sexual outlaw, or as she described herself later on in treatment, "a sexual bandit."

How was she a sexual outlaw?

Her reaction to being sexually marooned was to ignore the rules of society (or at least try to ignore them) and do as she pleased. Her descriptions were accurate. She slept with any man who appealed to her, discontinued her relationships when she grew bored, and, according to her description, acted in general like a "totally liberated woman." She worked her way through four or five major sexual liaisons every year with a few one-night stands in between. Everything looked good on the outside, especially to her girl friends, who envied her freedom. As Wanda described it later, she paid a high price for her emancipation:

"I guess the cards were stacked against me from the start—I just didn't know it. Everybody was against me—the men I went out with were just looking for a good time. 'Good old Wanda' never had her hooks out for marriage. My girl friends who 'admired my courage' so much were putting me down behind my back. And I didn't even realize that my own body was trying to tell me something."

"What made you think so?"

"Well, as you said, sex without orgasm isn't really sex. I just didn't realize that there was more to it than getting into bed with a groovy guy."

As a sexual outlaw, Wanda did whatever she wanted with whomever she chose whenever she liked —almost. But she paid for her liberty at extravagant rates. First there was the constant and intense social disapproval, even at work. Promotions always seemed to go to men (Wanda was ready for that) or women who were more conventional about sex. (Wanda didn't expect *that*.)

Are there any other disadvantages to being a sexual outlaw?

Yes, there is also a social problem. Women who seize their sexual rights often lose their social rights. When Wanda was around, her unmarried female friends felt uneasy, married women felt threatened, and older women were positively hostile. The only group who applauded her were men—and then, as she put it, "only between the hours of 8 P.M. and 2 A.M. Before sundown they didn't want to know I existed."

Like most outlaws she was considered fair game for bounty hunters. In her case the bounty was collected in the bedroom. Her boyfriends considered her more a sexual object than a human being. Because she was willing to seek sexual happiness unprotected by the armor of society—marriage, alimony, property laws —her male companions tended to forget that she was also a human being. That sort of thing can be hard on a girl.

Isn't there another solution?

Maybe. But just as hard in a different way is the role of sexual exile. For some women the pressure is just too much. Those who lack the courage to challenge society's rigid prohibitions against sexual subsistence for single women put their emotions on the shelf— for good. For them the struggle is over before it begins. Their femininity slowly fades and their personalities become paler and paler as they withdraw into themselves. It is almost as if their emotional engines were gradually running down. Diane went through it and describes it best:

"I know I look better now, Doctor, but last year at this time I couldn't have taken second prize in an Ugly Contest!"

It was hard to believe. Diane was wearing long white leather boots, a dark green suede miniskirt, a semitransparent pale yellow safari shirt, and accessories to match. She was thin, graceful, and, to say the least, dynamic.

"I was only twenty-five, but I felt like my own grandmother. Here's a picture to prove it!"

She was right. The picture showed a dejected woman with stringy hair. A loose print dress hung below her knees. Skinny legs ended in sagging bobby sox encased in platform shoes. In line with the costume, the woman's facial expression was one of utter despair.

"It's hard to believe that's really a picture of you."

Diane became serious. "The way I look at it, it's not really me. That's a picture of some old lady whose body I was using as a hideout."

Diane was from a prominent New York family. Her parents were rich, tense, and always in the limelight. They excelled in each of their many activities and expected their daughter to do the same. But Diane wasn't ready or able. Overwhelmed by the tremendous, sexual and emotional demands of her high-pressure existence, she fled into sexual oblivion. The girl in the picture was Diane in her most neutered form. As she said later on, "It didn't work, and I knew deep inside it wouldn't work, but I was desperate and it was all I could think of."

Her new costume didn't really mean she had solved

her problem—it was only her way of signifying that she was ready to try again. Back from exile, she was in the uniform of her social group and ready for action—or trying to be ready, anyhow.

"I don't know, sometimes I tell myself it's going to work out, and other times I just get panicky. I know sex is right and all that, but when it comes to *doing it* I get terrified. My solution is to cop out. I have intercourse but I don't feel anything. It's the same as doing my laundry. If I don't enjoy it, why do I do it? And if I have to do it, why can't I enjoy it?"

Diane and millions of other women like her are victims of a prehistoric conspiracy that started when the first woman trod the earth. This particular conspiracy has two jaws that sometimes tend to crush a woman like a gigantic vise.

How does it work?

The first jaw hinges on the fact that the human female is a biological weakling. Reproduction in women is an ovarian pinball game. Barely twelve eggs per year roll out of the ovaries to await collision with a lucky sperm. Whether intercourse takes place or not, the lonely egg sits around in the fallopian tube for forty-eight hours or so each month. If no spermatozoa show up, it simply bursts like a soap bubble and is seen no more. (In cats the system is much more efficient. Ovulation only occurs *after* intercourse. The egg encounters eager sperm almost immediately.) With this wasteful method there are barely two dozen days a year when a woman can become pregnant; for reproductive purposes the other 341 are a total loss. As a result, the average woman has sexual intercourse about 288 times before impregnation occurs.

(Some women will disagree, citing unfortunate experiences in the back seat of a convertible or a terrible weekend at the lake, but statistically the figures are accurate.) Even if pregnancy does result, about twenty percent of the time it terminates in a spontaneous abortion known as a miscarriage. To make matters worse, human reproduction is painfully slow. Gestation time is almost a year, and new people are usually manufactured one at a time. (By contrast, kittens appear twice a year in bunches of five or six.)

What's the other part of it?

The other jaw of the conspiracy depends on the fact that women have the primary responsibility for the survival of the human race. The environment of our planet is decidedly hostile to humans. Most of it is too hot, too cold, too dry, too wet, too hard, or too soft for their ideal development.

There is never enough food for everyone. A minority of people die from the effects of overeating; most are suspended between chronic malnutrition and slow starvation. Mankind is prey to a thousand crippling diseases that hasten death. Those who survive are assailed by floods, earthquakes, hurricanes, tidal waves, and a dozen other natural disasters. Even those men and women who live in civilized (industrialized) societies and are sheltered from the worst ravages of Nature have begun to poison their own surroundings. Polluted air, contaminated water, cigarette smoke, toxic chemicals in food, and other by-products of progress are beginning to take their toll. Left to his own designs, man long ago would have wiped himself from the face of the earth. Fortunately for all of us, Nature has provided the ultimate survival weapon. It has sustained *homo sapiens* through the Ice Age, the Black Death, fifty thousand years of war, and a million epidemics. With a little luck it may even ensure his survival through the era of the Space Age. The name of that all-powerful weapon is: SEX, and its custodian is woman.

The only half of the human race capable of reproduction is the female. In spite of his wit, his dazzling technical achievements, and his boundless pride, no man can produce another man. Only women have the ability to create a new being from the raw material of their own bodies. To make sure that every woman devotes herself unceasingly to this vital task, Nature has infused her with a sexual energy unsurpassed in the animal kingdom. From the instant of conception onward, the primary thrust of every woman's being is to be fertilized, to conceive, and to reproduce. No force on earth can stand in her way.

Why is that?

Even in embryonic development the sexual organs have top priority and the female genitalia get all the attention. By some curious twist of genetics, according to some experts, *every human embryo starts out as a female*. As time passes, about fifty-one percent of the tiny beings have their genitalia remodeled (men like to think of this as an improvement) and emerge as males. For the other forty-nine percent things begin to happen much faster. At the very moment the sperm glides lazily into the depths of the egg, the fuse is ignited on a sexual time bomb and a whole chain of events begins which culminates in a dramatic climax two decades later.

The female genitals develop rapidly, aided by sex

hormones that pour from the mother's bloodstream into the fetal circulation. These powerful chemicals prime the tiny ovaries so that they themselves can produce massive amounts of hormone when the time for action comes. At the very moment of birth, the female sexual organs have their first full-scale test in anticipation of their future use. The girl baby emerges from the uterus with a dramatically enlarged vulva. Her tiny breasts are swollen and rounded and even secrete a clear fluid (known as witch's milk) for several days. Once the reproductive organs have proved their ability to respond to hormonal stimulation, the amount of hormone in the blood recedes and the genitalia regress to baby size. But a significant fact remains: *the sexual parts of the female body are so important they are developed and tested at the very moment of birth even before the heart and lungs are functioning fully.*

For the next fifteen years or so the reproductive system *seems* to lie dormant. Under the surface, however, the sexual time bomb ticks away silently and relentlessly as the body and the mind mature.

Which are more important, the physical or emotional changes?

At the time of puberty the girl undergoes many dramatic physical alterations. But even more important are the subtle and profound emotional changes that evolve and accelerate during the next few years. The final result is a *woman*—a young adult female who is bursting with life and overflowing with emotion. She is sentimental and affectionate, wistful and charming. The combination of youthful exuberance and surging sex hormones gives her a radiance and dynamism unique to the human race. Love in every form, romantic and sexual, pours out of her. Until the door gets slammed in her face. Not once, not twice, but over and over again, our society tells her there is no room for her feelings. It tells her there is no room for her as a human being unless she fits into a rigid, archaic, irrational pattern hammered out a thousand years ago deep in some Teutonic forest. Iris is just feeling the first stifling pressure of the social system under which she lives. With long chestnut-brown hair and large sensitive eyes she looks younger than her twenty years:

"Doctor, what are they trying to do to me?"

"What do you mean?"

"Either I'm completely out of my mind, or everyone else is crazy and I'm going sane! Take this job I have. I graduated at the top of my class in high school and this bank was knocking themselves out to get me to work for them. Everything started out fine, and for the first month or so it was great. I caught on to everything right away and even got promoted. Then *it* started."

"What started?"

"I don't really know, but they began to put me down. Like first it was the flowers I kept on the counter in the teller's cage. No one could see them, but the manager said it was against the rules. Like my skirt. A couple inches above my knees. Just like ten million other girls wear. Are the bankers afraid the customers will get so hung up on the lewd thrill of peeping at my kneecaps they'll forget to put their last nickel in the crummy bank? And the real joke is I stand behind a solid oak counter so thick I could be naked from the waist down and none of our senile customers would know the difference. And talking about clothes, someone should point out to the manager that it's positively obscene for him to wear brown loafers with his shiny blue suit—and with white socks! Ugh!"

"But why does that bother you so much, Iris?"

"Because I'm not really a dope, Doctor. I know why they're doing it. All these Mickey Mouse rules and regulations are designed to keep men on the top where they think they belong. This job has been an education for me—you never saw so many sheep in your whole life. In the ladies' room when we're getting ready for work in the morning, all the girls are chattering away at each other—you know, making jokes and fooling around. As soon as the bell rings—I didn't believe it at first, but they really have a bell—everything changes. Instead of twelve female human beings, you have twelve zombies. In the ladies' room, it's people; out on the floor, it's the Girls' Detention Home."

"But that's just at work, isn't it?"

"Just at work? Eight hours a day, five days a week for fifty weeks a year is a lot of time. After a couple of years in that Formica convent it blows your mind. And if you want to get ahead, you have to make the final sacrifice."

"The final sacrifice?"

"Yes, sir. Our great bank has two hundred branches. There are exactly seven women managers. Fourteen little ovaries have been sacrificed to advance their careers. They still wear skirts, but deep inside these ladies are more masculine than Joe Louis. They haven't beaten the system—they've just gone over to the other side. I can't do it that way. I just don't want it that way."

Iris slumped in her chair. She was in no danger of being masculinized at that moment. Vulnerable, frightened, confused, she was feeling intensely the frustration of dealing with a demanding and hypocritical society.

Do many women have the same problem?

One of the greatest paradoxes that confront our culture is the position of working women. More than three-quarters of single, divorced, or widowed women must work to support themselves. Theoretically, these thirteen million women have equal job opportunities. In reality (with rare exceptions) only the lowest-paying and most menial work is open to them. Not one of the twenty-five leading occupations of women, as listed by the U.S. Census Bureau, is among the eighty-five top-paying job classifications in the nation. By virtue of a thousand gentlemen's agreements most of the good jobs are closed to women. A woman is welcomed as a bookkeeper, rarely as an accountant. She is employable as a school teacher, unwanted as a professor. Male employers practice tokenism with gusto; there are always a few female engineers, executives, and a lady pilot or two (but never for a major airline). They are usually trotted out from time to time for ceremonial purposes and then put back in storage so they will be handy to refute the next feminine complaint.

On the other hand, most states have special work laws for the protection of women. They usually require a higher minimum wage for women, special rest periods and facilities, and prohibit heavy work and dangerous tasks. Frequently these laws also protect women from getting the job, since it becomes much cheaper to hire a man.

What about women owning property?

When it comes to property rights, things get even more bizarre. In most areas of the country, property laws are strongly biased in favor of the man; during marriage he usually acquires all his wife's worldly goods. Even in so-called community property states, the management and control of the community property remains with the husband, no matter what kind of idiot he may be. In a few places the laws seem to have a particularly masculine twist. One Western state gives a man the absolute right to *kill* another man if he discovers him having sexual intercourse with his wife. (The statute implies expert marksmanship, since annihilation of the wife is not tolerated, no matter how closely involved she may be.) Characteristically the wife does *not* have equal privileges. If she sends a female competitor to her great reward, she must be prepared to take the full legal consequences.

Of course, there are some areas of absolute freedom available to women these days. They are free to run for office, but even freer to be defeated. In 1920, after 144 years of democratic government, the other half of our population, women, were finally given the right to vote. It hardly seems to have been worth the trouble. Although women voters outnumber men sixty million to fifty-two million, women make up only ten out of 435 Congressmen, one out of 100 Senators, no state governors, and about one half of one percent of the nation's mayors.

Don't women have some rights?

The one exclusive right of every American woman is the right to get pregnant—unless, of course, she doesn't happen to be married. The unwed mother, no matter what the circumstances, is relegated to a social position combining all the attributes of a child molester and Typhoid Mary. Linda is in the middle of such a pregnancy and knows exactly how it feels. She is twenty-three, and worked as a ticket agent for a large airline until her "condition," as the supervisor called it, became too obvious. With honey-blond hair and pale blue eyes she seemed almost child-like as she slid herself sideways into a chair:

"Another two months and I'll be singular again instead of plural, Doctor." She laughed, then went on: "Well, it's been an education any way you look at it. The baby's father is a co-pilot for the airline where I used to work, and in the last six months I think I've heard all the wisecracks about pilot-to-co-pilot I can stand. Although I must say some of them were pretty funny." She laughed again. "Really, I think the only thing that's kept me from going out of my mind with this pregnancy has been my sense of humor. There are times when it's been pretty gruesome." She didn't laugh this time.

"What do you mean?"

"Well, take for example how it all happened. Jack, that's the co-pilot, was a wonderful guy. During his lay-overs in Chicago—and please, no more jokes about *that* expression—we got friendly. We were both lonely and started spending weekends at my apartment. One night, about three months later, we got careless and I got pregnant. Now don't ask me why I didn't get married!" Linda's voice became a little shrill.

"I'm not going to ask you anything—unless you want me to."

"I'm sorry, Doctor, but this has been more of a strain than I was willing to admit. I never realized that pregnancy was against the law. I mean, I've been treated like a criminal. The first thing that happened was I lost my job. I started putting on weight—not much—but just enough to show. The supervisor called me in and asked me point-blank if I was pregnant. I admitted it—by then I couldn't hide it, anyhow. He asked if I was married. I told the truth about that, too. Then he asked me to resign. I refused. I told him I didn't do anything wrong and I asked if he could show me where it was against company rules to act like a human being. Well, things got a little tense right then and the interview was over. The next day I got a letter saying I was discharged for being overweight. What a joke!"

"In what way?"

"Well, first to get fired for being pregnant. It just wasn't fair. Then the alibi they used—overweight. The dum-dum supervisor weighs in at 240 pounds, and nine months from now he isn't going to lose any of it, either." The smile was back again.

"Besides, they pay an obstetric allowance to the married girls who get pregnant, and let them continue working. Why shouldn't they do the same for me? It's been such a fight!" After a few minutes Linda recovered her cheery good humor—at least on the surface.

"I suppose you're waiting for me to tell you why I didn't get married."

"Only when you're ready to talk about it, Linda."

"Well, it's simple. I just wasn't in love. Jack is a nice guy and I guess I could have forced him to marry me if I wanted to, but he was nice for an occasional weekend—not for a lifetime. Anyhow, he transferred to another route when he found out I was pregnant. That's about it. Just because of a thirty-second mistake, we don't have to be chained together for good."

"I'm sure you're right."

"Then you're probably the only one. My parents have turned against me, the phone doesn't ring on Saturday nights any more for dates, and it's like I have a nine-month case of bad breath. I couldn't even find an apartment until I told them my husband was overseas. The worst part of the whole business is I love my baby—I want to have it. In this crazy world some sick woman who hates her kids—including the one she's carrying—is considered just fine, as long as she's married. I don't get it."

"What are you going to do?"

"I suppose I'll muddle through for the next few months, but it's all so unfair. Why don't they just leave me and my baby alone?"

Understanding and sympathetic psychiatric treatment helped Linda over the rest of her pregnancy and helped her to make the adjustments after that. She gradually realized how she had unconsciously created her own problems and began to do something about it. She found a job with another airline and began a new life. She stopped by a year or so later:

"Well, Doctor, I'm pregnant again, but this time things are much better."

"In what way?"

"Actually in two ways. First, I've gotten married. I can't fight the whole world for another nine months. Second, I married a pilot this time—no more co-pilots for me." She laughed.

"Why are you laughing?"

"I'm laughing because I married Jack! He was so

wonderful, after all. After I got pregnant he stopped coming around because he thought I didn't want to have anything to do with him after what he 'did to me.' I met him by accident after I got out of the hospital and—I guess it sounds corny—we fell in love. He got promoted, adopted the first baby, and we're as happy as can be."

Don't other girls work out their problems like Linda?

Linda was one of the few lucky ones. The moral indignation of our entire hypocritical society is pointed like a gun at the head of every unmarried mother. The fact that no woman in the entire history of the human race ever got pregnant without the eager cooperation of a man is conveniently overlooked. (The only possible exception to this rule was the Virgin Mary—and even *she* was married at the time.) Of course a woman doesn't have to get pregnant.

What can she do?

She can choose from many methods of birth control. The worst techniques have a failure rate of about seventy percent and the best devices are about ninety percent dependable. The exception is the contraceptive pill. It is virtually one hundred percent effective in preventing pregnancy. According to the manufacturers it is also capable of causing blindness, paralysis, and sudden death in certain cases. Of course, men don't take birth control pills. As long as women are willing to take the drug—and the risks—they don't have to.

Clearly our society is aligned against those of its members who happen to be born with a vagina instead of a penis. Because of a genetic accident occurring at the precise microsecond of conception, half of all embryos are destined to develop as females and committed to do their best in a world created by man.

Aren't married women better off?

The plight of a woman in a masculine society is a thousand times worse if she happens to be unmarried. Married women obtain at least some protection by association with their husbands. Even though they are not accorded equal status, they live under a sort of masculine umbrella. The occasional man who does stand up for the rights of women is nearly always a married man. He usually speaks out after some rather intensive nagging by his wife, and then he generally defends only the rights of married women. Few people stand up for the single girl. Presumably the assumption is that if she is ever going to amount to anything she will get married. That is something like saying that if a chicken is going to amount to anything she will learn to crow like a rooster. Making marriage the ticket of admission to the equal enjoyment of the good things of life doesn't seem fair. Besides, there are millions of women who did as they were commanded by society and got married but via divorce or the death of their husbands find themselves single again. Even the Internal Revenue Service discriminates against them, by denying them important and justifiable deductions.

Women in general are used to absorbing more punishment than men, and single women are experts at it. For the most part they remain well-mannered, attractive, refined. They are the great silent minority, the gentle victims.

Does it take long for most women to adjust to their role?

Sometimes they have to do it almost overnight. It was that way for Anne. She is thirty-seven, still slim and attractive. Divorced last year after ten years of marriage, she has the custody of her two children.

"I still don't know if I did the right thing, Doctor." She shook her head slowly from side to side.

"The right thing about what?"

"About divorcing Tom." There was a note of dismay in her voice. "You don't know what I've been through this past year. I'm almost beginning to think the only thing worse than being unhappily married is being divorced. At least when I was married, I *existed.*"

"I understand, but can you be more specific?"

"Well, I was *Mrs.* Spencer. Now when I go somewhere and introduce myself as *Anne* Spencer, it's like I'm a cheap imitation. I get the feeling people think of me as 'Brand X' or something like that. The thing is so subtle that it's hard to describe, but the whole atmosphere changes when they find out I'm single. I mean, if a woman's married, to the world at large it's like the Good Housekeeping Seal of Approval—you know, she's stamped ACCEPTABLE."

"Can you give me an example?"

"I guess the first three months were the hardest— it seemed to hit me from all sides." Anne breathed a deep sigh and then went on. "Well, like the time I went out to dinner—or I should say, tried to go out for dinner. I guess I was feeling sorry for myself—I'd been divorced about a month—and I decided to take myself to a nice place to eat. I was hoping it would sort of cheer me up—you know what I mean. I made reservations like always—Tom and I used to go there a lot—and got dressed. When I arrived, the hostess said, 'Will someone be joining you?' Now that I think back on it, it was a rotten thing for her to say. Divorced four weeks, eating at a place where I used to go with my husband, and she wants to know if someone will be joining me. It's like asking someone on her way to the electric chair where she's going to spend her vacation! But that wasn't the worst part. When I told her I was alone, she smiled one of those smug little smiles that only a married woman uses on a girl who isn't married and said, 'I'm sorry, but we don't allow unescorted ladies.' I just fell apart. I cried all the way home in the cab, took two sleeping pills, went straight to bed, and didn't get up until one in the afternoon the next day." Anne looked into the distance.

"What's wrong?"

"Nothing." She shook her head slowly from side to side. "I just remembered what happened after that. I finally got up, fixed some coffee, and had a little talk with myself. I told myself that this was just a fluke, that I was really the same person I had always been and that there was nothing to get upset about. I felt much better, so I put my clothes on and went down to get the mail. There was only one piece of mail. It was a form letter from the Credit Bureau. It said, 'Since a change has occurred which may affect your credit standing, effective immediately all your department store charge accounts have been closed.' I felt like jumping out the window. They wouldn't let me into a restaurant, they took my charge accounts away—what were they going to do for an encore, ship me to Devil's Island?"

The contrast between the life of a married woman and the plight of a single girl was particularly painful for Anne because she had to make the transition in the space of a few weeks. But whether the rejection descends on a woman suddenly or gradually, it always hurts.

Why does it happen that way?

As part of our punitive concept of dealing with criminals, a convicted felon loses his civil rights. He is prevented from voting, holding public office, and owning certain types of property. As part of our punitive concept of dealing with women, those who don't happen to be married lose their social rights. Things that the average American takes for granted, like eating in the restaurant of his choice, having charge accounts and credit cards, borrowing from the bank, are often hard to arrange for a single woman. For the girl who is determined enough there is, of course, always a way out. Penny is one of these women. She is twenty-nine, and according to her, "just doesn't feel like getting married yet."

"I used to get mad when I got the 'back-of-the-bus' routine. I figured I'm entitled to the same as everyone else. So I started fighting back. When I want to go to a restaurant, I make reservations for two in a man's name and just go. After I get to my table I wait about fifteen minutes and then order. I guess they assume my boyfriend didn't show up and I'm left to suffer on my own. Sometimes they even feel sorry for me. Once the manager came over and said, 'Your date let you down tonight, didn't he, honey?' I felt like saying, 'No, it's dopes who run restaurants like this one who let me down by making me tell lies to get in.' But I didn't do it because it wouldn't have made any sense. You know, sometimes I wonder if it's worth it. I used to do it a lot to break down barriers, but for the past year or so I don't even feel like trying any more."

Of course, the worst part about being single, widowed, or divorced in our culture is the subtle but relentless social pressure that wears away the resistance of the toughest and most determined woman. Let Anne continue:

"Well, I survived the early days, I suppose, but then just when I thought the worst part was over, it really hit me. There was no way for me to pick up my life where I left off. I slowly began to realize that there is simply no place for an unmarried woman in a married society. Those who are married gradually give us the message that we don't fit in. The girls I used to have lunch with when I was married kept inviting me just like before, once a month. But then after three months or so, they skipped a month. I met one of them downtown the next week and asked her about it. She got kind of flustered and said, 'Oh, Anne, I'm so sorry! We changed the day we meet and everyone must have forgotten to tell you!' Well, I caught on. I couldn't help catching on. When the Lunch Club, the Bridge Club, and the girls you've been shopping with for ten years all forget to tell you they've changed their schedule, you really have to be stupid not to realize you're not in demand any more. The only group I didn't get kicked out of was Little League, and for a while I was afraid they weren't going to give me green stamps at the supermarket any more just because I was single. When I got a divorce from Tom, I didn't know I was getting a divorce from the rest of the world!"

Why do unattached women stick together?

The basic reason is that there is no other place for
them to go. They have been pushed out of normal
society as surely as toothpaste is squeezed out of the
toothpaste tube. Instead of going down the emotional
drain, the ones who can save themselves cluster in
little knots on the fringes of our culture. Unfortunately,
this sort of emotional quarantine doesn't make their
problems any easier. It is the equivalent of telling a
hunchback, "Stand up straight! Do you want to ruin
your posture?" If the single woman were able to function perfectly in married society, she wouldn't have
her problem in the first place. In effect she is rejected
for being single and then denied the opportunity to
do anything to make herself acceptable again.

Is it really that serious?

Yes. The best source of social relationships is within
the framework of already existing contacts—friends,
neighbors, in-laws, fellow workers. As a single woman,
through divorce, widowhood, or simply remaining
single, is dropped from the social network, her range
of friends and acquaintances narrows sharply. She becomes socially marooned, and unless she is rescued
quickly, she rapidly becomes sexually marooned. For
most women the loss of social contacts inevitably
means the loss of sexual opportunities.

Marcia had a unique experience. She is forty-seven
and a well-known sociologist. Four years ago her husband died and Marcia was able to observe, first-hand,
as an expert, what a sexually marooned woman has
to go through:

"Doctor, it was like presiding at your own funeral! I mean, I knew exactly what was happening to me, but there was nothing I could do about it! And the worst part about the whole thing was I should have seen it coming, but when it happens to you personally, you're never really prepared. For the first month or two after Frank died, I had almost too many people around me. I was so unhappy I just wanted to be alone. I finally got rid of everybody—or so I thought."

"What do you mean, you thought *you* got rid of everybody?"

Marcia laughed. "Well, I may be slow to catch on to some things, but when I look back on it I realize that they were delighted to get away. They were busy with their own lives and I was just taking up their time. Even if I hadn't asked them, they would have drifted off by themselves in a few more weeks."

"Then what happened?"

"I found myself spontaneously initiated into a new caste. As you know, in sociology, the term *caste* applies to a social group from which there is no exit. Once you are in, you are locked in and usually stay there for life. You are only allowed to associate with other members of the same caste. Intermarriage with other castes is strictly prohibited. There is also an interesting and rather devastating technicality to this caste system. Sexual intercourse is forbidden between members of different castes. The only exceptions are furtive and limited contacts which are always punished when they are revealed."

"Was it really like that?"

"Doctor, I spent four years in India studying their society, and I never believed anything like that could exist here. It does. But the most unbelievable part is that it happened to *me*. As you mentioned before, I was 'socially marooned'—I had no friends, no social contacts, and no chance to make any. It was just a matter of time before I became sexually marooned, and that made me feel even more hopeless. It was a choice between nothing to do, no place to go, and no one to go with, or associating with members of my new social caste."

"What was wrong with that?"

Marcia smiled. "I try not to think of myself as a snob, but after twenty years of teaching at the University I find it hard to spend an evening with a man whose major interest in life is chrome-plating or making sausages. It was terrible for a while until I put on my thinking cap and worked out a solution."

"What did you do?"

"I found myself brooding too much about what was happening to me, so I decided to forget the whole business—that is, *try* to forget it. I went back to India on a fellowship, and I met a man whose wife had just died a few months before. He was an anthropologist and we started a mutual research program—we really did. You know, correlating social customs with evolution of the society. As time went by we began developing our own social customs and—let's say our private society began to evolve. About a year later we got married and I rejoined my old caste—married women. It's good to be back!"

What about women who never marry?

Our society has many blind spots, and one of them blots out the woman who, for one reason or another, never married. She is always the object of derision and good for a few laughs. The point that everyone forgets is that she is not a special kind of unusual being—she is simply a woman who, willingly or unwillingly, remained single. Ironically, a lady of sixty-two who is unmarried is laughed at if she is a spinster, treated with reverence if she is a nun, pitied if she is a widow, and often secretly admired if she has been divorced four times. Yet deep beneath the surface, all four women are basically the same and in fact have many emotional characteristics in common. Most of them are hampered in achieving a solution to their problems by the rigid and unrealistic attitudes of the society in which they live.

What can be done about the problem?

The dilemma of the sexually marooned woman can be resolved in one of two ways. First, our society can become aware of the injustices it has inflicted on more than fifty percent of its members and, in a burst of contrition, accept women in general and single women in particular as full-fledged members with equal privileges. From a practical point of view it would be much easier to make Niagara Falls flow uphill.

The only workable solution is for the woman to take the initiative herself. She must understand in detail the prejudices of society which caused her to be marooned and defend herself against them. She must *honestly* admit the ways in which she contributed to her own problem, and change her approach. She must learn a dozen separate emotional survival techniques, and rescue *herself*. The key to happiness for the sexually marooned woman is knowledge and understanding. With the detailed information in the following chapters, with determination, and with the tiniest bit of luck, every woman who is sexually marooned (or in danger of becoming sexually marooned) can find her way back to civilization. She might even return in better condition than when she left.

2

MYTHS OF FEMALE SEXUALITY

Where do women learn about their own sexuality?

From those who are least able to teach them. Ninety-nine percent of "experts" in the sexual problems of women never had a menstrual period, a hot flash, or a baby—and never will. In fact they will never have any female sexual experiences at all—because they are men.

What makes these men qualified to explain female sexual responses to women?

Nothing. Scholarly books on women and their sexual behavior began to be written about five hundred years ago, during the Dark Ages. At that time women occupied a social position somewhat higher than cattle and somewhat lower than male lunatics. Just as no self-respecting scientist would think of asking a cow how she felt, no medieval scholar would stoop to interviewing a woman. The next generation of sexologists prepared for their projects by reading the books written by their forerunners. They piously pored over the questionable revelations they encountered there and mumbled something like, "Hmm, that's just what

I suspected. I knew it. I knew it all along." Fortified with the ignorance of the Dark Ages, they sallied forth to further muddy the sexual waters. No one ever took the time to ask the ladies what they were feeling (or not feeling) in the sexual department. They didn't have to—after all they had the word of a whole generation of experts—all of whom would be more likely to interview a cow than a woman.

Did these experts do any harm?

Only to women. Most of the early "facts" about female sexual behavior consisted entirely of male wishful thinking. Little things about women not really being capable of enjoying sex and men being sexually superior to women began to appear in medical textbooks with monotonous regularity. As the same misconceptions and misunderstandings were repeated over and over again, they began to take on the veneer of facts. As one expert repeated some scientific gossip to another, the errors took on an aura of authenticity. Gradually the platitudes found their way into magazines and newspapers and became part of American sexual folklore. By relentless repetition they finally achieved wide acceptance as facts.

How did this affect women?

Because there is such a lack of honest authoritative information about female sexual functioning women are the most avid seekers of knowledge about their own sexual lives. They devour every scrap of information about their sexual selves. Although what they read was mostly bad news, it was (or so they thought)

better than no news at all. As they were bombarded
again and again with the same dubious information
about female sexuality, they began to believe it. Even
worse, they gradually developed the "cops and robbers
syndrome."

What's the "cops and robbers syndrome"?

Policemen and criminals, in their spare time, watch
television. They see how their video counterparts operate and, like the rest of us, tend to imitate (consciously or unconsciously) the behavior depicted on
the screen. Subsequently, when a TV producer wants
to film a show about police and crooks, in a bid for
realism, he bases his research on the actual responses
of real individuals. Unfortunately for him, the subjects
already have adopted the characteristics of the actors
who portray them on television. The resulting show
only succeeds in perpetuating the stereotype it was attempting to avoid.

How does that pertain to women?

As women are deluged with apparently reliable accounts of how they behave (or should behave) sexually, they gradually adapt their sexual responses and
expectations to correspond with the accounts they
have read. It becomes a case of reality imitating fantasy—with the woman coming out on the losing end.
Not only do women act as if all the myths written
about them were true they pass the bad news on to
their daughters who make it part of their own lives
and in turn inflict it on *their* daughters. Carried to its
ultimate absurd conclusion, the result is a generation

of women who have accepted as facts a tremendous collection of sexual rumors, misconceptions, misunderstandings, and just plain old masculine wishful thinking.

"Masculine wishful thinking"?

Yes. Each man has his own private sets of fears and anxieties about sex. Part of it is the result of the tremendous burden of guilt that our society imposes on every child—boy and girl—long before they have their first sexual stirring. The other factor that works against men is their relentless attempt to deny their unquestionable *functional sexual inferiority*.

How are men inferior sexually?

Unfortunately, the standard penis is simply not a sexual organ. As issued, it is too short, too thin, and much too flexible to mesh with the vagina. A dozen complex emotional and physiological events must take place before erection occurs and the penis becomes a phallic projectile. Even after intercourse begins, the erection must be maintained, ejaculation must be delayed, and orgasm must be coordinated to succeed in gratifying the woman. It is by no means an easy job. In fact every man at one time or another in his lifetime finds his sexual potency either absent or significantly impaired. For most, failure of erection is occasional and transient—for others it is the cause of a major sexual impairment.

Every male over the age of puberty suffers from the same uncertainty—will he be able to achieve and maintain an erection that night? By contrast, inter-

course for the woman is simplicity itself—at least from
a mechanical point of view. Every woman is capable
of copulation virtually anytime. She may not enjoy it,
she may not reach orgasm, but at least she can engage
in intercourse. Virtually no woman has ever had this
experience:

SHE: What's the matter?
HE: Nothing. I mean, I just can't seem to—you know,
it won't, it won't . . .
SHE: How come?
HE: How should I know how come? I just can't seem
to get ready.
SHE: Is there anything I can do?
HE: God, I wish there was something *somebody*
could do.
SHE: Maybe we should wait until tomorrow?
HE: Actually I don't think we have any choice—unless
of course you can figure out a way to go ahead with-
out me.

No matter how understanding the woman may be,
the man always feels that he has failed. More important, as with every human being, he needs a reason
for his failure. The most attractive and most tempting
explanation is the sexual deficiency of his partner.

How does that help him?

It doesn't. From a rational point of view, proving that
all women are sexually impaired would seem only to
make the man's problem more difficult to resolve. But
misery loves company, and shifting the blame to his
partner takes some of the sting out of a man's predicament. If the man with sexual anxiety happens to be a

professor or sexual researcher, often the temptation to pass the emotional buck is irresistible.

How does this work in practice?

Let's say, for example, the professor who helps establish sexual standards suffers from premature ejaculation. In this condition erection proceeds on schedule, the penis enters the vagina without difficulty, and ejaculation occurs almost instantaneously. (According to the severity of the problem, the exact timing of orgasm can vary from half a minute before insertion to two minutes afterward, but a man with premature ejaculation who can last thirty seconds is doing well.) No matter how it's spaced, extra-early orgasm in the man is no fun for anyone. Since he is a man first and a professor second, he is not anxious to admit his sexual defect to his students, who hang on his every word. Usually he is not even willing to admit it to himself. Selecting the only way out of his predicament (besides overcoming the underlying *emotional* problem that causes his *potency* problem), he first invents, then rationalizes, and finally proves, the first myth of female sexuality: *Women are slower to reach orgasm than men.*

Isn't that true?

It depends on which side of the bed you occupy. Every man with prematurity cherishes this fairy tale. As long as he can find enough women to believe him and accept a return match of sex without gratification, no one is the wiser. But when women begin thinking for themselves, things begin to change. In recent years women have been studying psychology, medicine, and psychiatry; some of them have started to analyze sexual problems from their own points of view. They are even beginning to ask embarrassing questions like:

"If a man ejaculates before his partner reaches orgasm, instead of proving that she's too slow, doesn't it prove that he's too *fast?*"

That question intrigued Nita, and not simply from a theoretical standpoint. A research assistant at a major medical center, she has been divorced about five years. She is pale and blonde and speaks with quiet intensity:

"As a researcher, I'm trained to think for myself. We're not supposed to accept things just because everybody else does. I only wish I'd had the sense to apply it to my own life!"

She bit her lip.

"In what way?"

"The only way that ever really mattered—my marriage! I was married to a math professor for six years and we never had one decent night of making love. I figured it out once—in about eleven hundred attempts at intercourse, I reached a climax a dozen times. That works out to twice a year—maybe I should have scheduled one on Christmas and one on my birthday." Nita didn't smile. "And the worst part is, all the time I thought it was my fault. In those days I believed everything I read in the books and everything my husband told me. He was an expert in math so I thought he was an expert in sex, too. Boy, was I wrong!"

"What do you mean?"

"Well, it was always the same. Whenever we had sex, just as I was getting started he ejaculated and everything was all over. Half the time he'd ejaculate even before we got together and it was all over *me!* At first he felt sorry and apologized, but then as time went on he started to get self-righteous. He would bring home books and scientific papers to prove he was 'normal' and it was all my fault."

"What kind of books?"

"Oh, you know, the usual old-fashioned books on sex—the ones that say the more normal a man is, the faster he reaches a climax in intercourse. I only wonder why they don't have an International Ejaculation Olympics every year and select the *most* normal man in the world—anything over three seconds wouldn't count. Of course there's only one problem—where would the winner find a woman who was interested in that kind of supersonic sex?"

Nita thought a moment. She continued:

"The biggest objection I have is the way books like that reach their conclusions. For example, they say because male monkeys reach orgasm fast, it's normal for human males to do the same. By that comparison, the ideal husband should climax in a flash, live on peanuts and bananas, wear a red velvet suit, and work for an organ grinder. I just don't feel that way!"

Is Nita right?

In a real sense, yes. Many of the women who have been solemnly diagnosed as frigid are simply understimulated sexually. Under the old rules, once a man delivered an erect penis into the vagina, the responsibility for reaching her orgasm shifted to the woman. It just isn't that way. No woman deserves to be labeled sexually frigid unless her sexual partner provides her with at least enough mechanical stimulation to trigger the orgasmic reflex.

How much stimulation is that?

For the average couple, about eight minutes of actual intercourse or seventy-five to eighty pelvic thrusts. This assumes of course a reasonable amount of foreplay—enough to start vaginal lubrication—and an emotional atmosphere of mutual affection. Under these circumstances the average woman should be able to reach orgasm a good part of the time.

What if she can't?

Then she may be suffering from some degree of orgasmic impairment (a more descriptive term than *frigidity*) based on an underlying emotional conflict. But if her partner furnishes her with a rapid entry, a few half-hearted thrusts, a quick spurt of sperm, and a mumbled apology, it is more likely his problem than hers. Tragically, the man who cannot delay his orgasm and thus prolong his erection long enough to satisfy his partner expends a tremendous amount of time and energy trying to convince her that *she* is to blame. Even if she is convinced, that doesn't really solve his dilemma—he still has the problem of premature ejaculation. It would seem much more sensible for him to undertake the cure of his own disease rather than invent a new one—delayed female orgasm —to prove he's normal.

Can premature ejaculation be cured?

Yes. It is basically an emotional problem—men with this condition try to fight their battles with their penis, and always end up losing. Since the basic conflict is always an unconscious one, the victim is rarely aware of what is happening to him. He knows only that most of the fun is taken out of sex—for him and for the woman. What should be the most rewarding and delightful of all human experiences is converted into a short interlude of mutual disappointment. Let Nita continue:

"It wasn't until a year after the divorce that I even began to understand what premature ejaculation was. And really the only way I learned about it was to research it myself. Even now that I understand it, it all seems so stupid. If women had the problem of reaching orgasm too soon—and I know some who would love to have it—they'd be at the psychiatrist's office in an hour trying to get over it. You wouldn't find them trying to convince everybody it was normal.

"If it's any consolation, all men aren't that way. After the divorce I met a wonderful man, Roger. The only drawback was he had the same problem as my ex-husband—you know, slam-bam-thank-you-ma'am. I just plain told him I wasn't ready to spend another six years counting the cracks in the ceiling. I packed him off to a psychiatrist that week."

"What happened?"

"It's too long to go into this afternoon but he found out a lot about himself—and how the mind controls the body. He was in treatment about six months, and when I saw what a different person he was, I made an appointment with you to try to get the same kind of results myself."

"Did he get over his sexual problem?"

"Judge for yourself. After his last treatment he came over to my place to celebrate. He had a few drinks and said, 'You know, Nita, if I could have three wishes, this is what they would be: I would be eighteen again, I would already know everything I learned about sex in the past six months—and I'd have six straight uninterrupted months with you, right here in this bedroom!' You can't ask for a better testimonial than that, Doctor."

Do men have any other misconceptions about women's sexual responses?

Unfortunately, quite a few. The places where most men get their sex education—the back seat of a car, a motel room, a girl friend's apartment—are really not the ideal surroundings for scientific study. Since life-long sexual attitudes are often based on these early experiences, it is vitally important to get the record straight. The second most common myth of female sexuality and the one that all too many women sincerely believe about themselves is:

Women are more slowly aroused sexually than men.

This misconception grows out of the on-the-scene observations that women usually fail to respond to the kind of sexual stimulation that drives men out of their minds. With characteristic masculine conceit men have concluded that anyone who isn't turned on by the same thing that turns them on just isn't turn-on-able.

Is that true?

No. Men, unfortunately, for them and their partners, ignore a basic biological fact that is glaringly obvious to every woman who has smiled indulgently at the masculine ego: the mechanism of sexual arousal in the female is completely different from that in the male. There are few (if any) accounts of women being whipped into a frenzy by peeking at a set of hairy male breasts or watching a chubby male dancer slowly wriggle out of his tuxedo to music.

On the other hand most men are strongly stimulated by the more forbidden aspects of sex. For example, in topless shows, the emphasis is on secondary sexual characteristics such as breasts and buttocks. These are the parts of the female anatomy that were rarely (until recently) exhibited in public. Watching an almost-naked woman dance has a dual fascination to a man. First, and most obvious, is the direct erotic effect. But just as important (and *more* important to some men) is the forbidden aspect of the situation. Looking at female breasts is not socially acceptable in our society, and getting a peep at the forbidden glands intensifies the sexual excitement. Once that part of the body is displayed openly and without feelings of mutual guilt, it loses much of its ability to excite men sexually. Just as burlesque was a victim of more mature attitudes about sex, topless shows and even totally naked performances will self-destruct in time. Those things that suggest sex and are related to sex without being sexual in themselves, like black net stockings, long hair, and lacy underwear, also are stimulating to many men. They provoke intense sexual images and fantasies that the viewers are motivated to act out in reality.

Visual images and fantasies are much less important to women. Connie learned all this the hard way. She teaches third grade in a suburban grammar school—with her reddish hair and freckles she looks too young to be anything but a schoolgirl herself:

"Doctor, I almost made the biggest mistake of my

life. Up until three months ago I'd made up my mind never to get married. And all because I was so stupid!"

"What happened?"

"Well, I started going out when I was fifteen and I've known a lot of boys, and let's be honest about it, I've had sex with most of them. But I never reached a climax—not until recently, anyway. It was the same with all of them. We'd start to make out, they'd get all excited, we'd take off our clothes, and before I knew it, it was over. Sometimes I felt a little something toward the end, but most of the time it was just to please them. And what I did to please some of them!"

"What do you mean?"

"After I graduated from the fumbling stage and had my own apartment, things were a little less hectic, but I still had to do all the work. I dressed up in long sheer gowns, short sheer gowns, black negligees, white negligees, black and white negligees—anything they asked me to do just to get them excited. I even learned to dance—you know, special little dances that men like."

"Why did you go through all of this?"

Connie wrinkled her brow. "Looking back on it, I don't really know. Maybe I hoped if I excited them enough some of it would rub off on me. All I can say is, if it did, I didn't notice it."

"Then what happened?"

"Oh, the fellows would get undressed—most of them showed off their magnificent physiques for a minute or two and then they expected me to fall passionately into their arms. It was great for them but honestly it did nothing at all for me. I had just about decided that if sex had nothing more to offer me, there was no point to getting married. Then I met Carl."

Connie's problem was a common one. Her boy-friends had demanded two types of stimulation from her—visual, requiring an assortment of negligees, rapidly followed by direct physical contact. It worked fine for them and they took it for granted it would have the same effect on her. They overlooked one little detail—they were men and she was a woman.

"How was Carl different?"

"It's hard to explain, but I'll tell you one thing—I sure could *feel* the difference! The first time we were together I had a climax, and that was only the beginning of bigger and better ones. And I didn't have to trot out my collection of nifty nighties either. Carl seemed to just get close to me—just being with him was so *intimate*. He had a kind of sexiness—as if you knew what he could do to you and you were just waiting for him to do it. To me that's a thousand times more exciting than being treated like the target for tonight, if you know what I mean."

Women are often aroused by "sexy" men—but the feminine definition of "sexy" is a lot different from the way men ordinarily use the word. To a man, a woman is sexy if she has large breasts, a small waist, firm buttocks, and an attractive face. With no other qualifications, she emerges as a sexual object. Women are much more selective. Once they emerge from junior high they demand more from a man than big muscles and symmetrical features.

To be sexy a man must be distinctive—something that he-man types find hard to understand. (Often a man who is short and dark—particularly if he has an atmosphere of mystery or tragedy—is most sought after by women.) Women seem to search for the quality of maleness itself rather than the superficial trappings. At best sexiness in a man is an elusive quality, but certain things about it are clear. It has little to do with the stereotype of a "man" and it is hard to simulate—either a man has it or he doesn't.

Even more vital, some men may be very sexy to certain women and not at all to others.

What makes a man "sexy" as far as women are concerned?

There are millions of men in this land who would gladly give their entire fortunes for an exact answer to that question. The precise explanation is locked deep in the unconscious mind of fifty million American women. However there are some clues.

Most men approach the question of sexiness the same way they approach the question of sexual stimulation—strictly from a masculine point of view. They try to imagine what qualities in a man would attract them if they were women, and proceed from there. The result is usually slightly comical. The average man who sets out to attract women radiates confidence and strength. He constantly asserts his mastery of the world and is supremely self-assured. As one female patient characterized it, "To me a man like that is interesting but not exciting. I always like to have a few of them in reserve just in case I want to trade romance for security. But they never really turn me on."

The kind of man who does turn women on is completely different. Usually he is anything but a he-man in external appearance. Most men try to impress women as lions. Their deception is doomed before it even gets underway because women know that men are much more closely related to puppy dogs.

How do women know that?

When it comes to the relations between the sexes, every woman has a secret weapon that no man will ever possess. In this world it is the female who raises the male. The young lady who dates a football hero may have a brother at home only a few years younger. She has helped change his diapers, watched him cry when the doctor gave him shots, and has seen him pace the floor for hours before getting up the courage to call a girl for a date. Instantly and often without being consciously aware of it, she recognizes that her football player and little Tommy at home are brothers under the skin. As tough as a man may pretend to be, every woman knows that underneath the tough guy is a tender little boy.

How does that affect sexual attraction?

Sex, like every other basic human feeling, thrives on honesty. The basic deception of male "toughness" and omnipotence clashes with the full and free expression of love, affection, and their constant companion, sexuality.

On the other hand, most women are almost irresistibly attracted by a man who acknowledges, at least in part, his vulnerability. The man who projects the image of a sincere but imperfect human being who fights against life's adversities with good humor, charm, and a certain flair is the one most likely to achieve happiness with the opposite sex. The typical hero who sails through every encounter without a blink of his steel-blue eyes or a furrow in his ivory brow may be the delight of all the boys in the seventh grade, but most women will respond to him with a surge of apathy.

The ultimate clue lies in the magic of Hollywood. Over the past thirty-five years the major studios made millions by thrilling the ladies with somewhat awkward heroes. James Stewart, Charles Boyer, Cary Grant, even Clark Gable, in their most popular roles always emerged as charming, engaging, slightly bewildered human beings. Any man who wants to be "sexy" has only to learn what every woman already knows: the most delightful thing about human beings is not necessarily their perfection—often it is the grace with which they acknowledge their imperfect human state.

What is the most common myth of female sexuality?

Not by coincidence, the most widely circulated myth is the one that is most attractive to men:

Men are somehow sexually superior to women.

This bold tribute to male vanity is usually based on hasty observations of three-year-old girls by four-year-old boys. These juvenile sex researchers peek at themselves, then at the little ladies, and draw the obvious (and incorrect) conclusion: boys have a lot and girls don't have anything so boys must be better. This is reinforced later on by noting that girls don't play baseball so well, and that most of them are afraid of snakes. To the grammar school intellect this is conclusive proof of male superiority. When the same little boys grow up and become professors of anatomy they smugly announce that "The clitoris is nothing more than a penis that failed to mature!" By then they should know better.

Isn't that true?

No. The facts are quite different. Actually the female sexual equipment surpasses the male in every possible way—design, function, complexity, and endurance. Take the design, for example. The most primitive animals have one common channel for urination, defecation, and reproduction. It is called the *cloaca*—appropriately enough, the Latin term for *sewer*. Human males are somewhat more refined, having a separate arrangement for defecation but combining one pathway for reproduction and urination. The human female, however, boasts the most elegant arrangement of all: absolute segregation of the three functions. Male superiority? Not from the standpoint of design, anyway.

The female genitalia are far more complex than the male in every other way. The male has two sex hormones—women have three major hormones and at least three subsidiary sex hormones. They also have breasts that are functional in contrast to the rudimentary male appendages. Most sensational of all—and most often overlooked by men who are arguing sexual supremacy—is the ability of women to create new people. Once a man lends his services for a few moments the entire awesome process of reproduction centers on the woman. Literally from the raw material of her own body she produces a brand-new, unique human being. She converts a few drops of seminal fluid into a neurosurgeon, a bishop, or a Nobel Prize winner. (More often she just produces another happy,

healthy member of the tribe *homo sapiens*—which
isn't so bad either.)

*But what about the function of the female sexual
organs?*

As far as function is concerned, no man was ever born
who can compete with a woman for sheer sexual capacity. Women can begin sexual intercourse sooner, do
it more often, continue it longer, and probably enjoy
it more. *The female capacity for orgasm is so great
that it has never been fully measured.* Most researchers who have studied female sexual reactions allow
their female subjects to reach about fifty consecutive
orgasms and then discontinue the project in amazement. If a man can ejaculate five times in one colossal
night he is considered sensational—the woman he
looks down on can reach five climaxes in a minute,
take a sip of water and go on to forty-five more.

The only reason most women do not begin to approach their real sexual potential is the relentless and
sometimes ruthless suppression of their sexuality by
men. Since most men are at least *unconsciously* aware
that their own sexual prowess is microscopic compared to women's, they conduct a constant campaign
to downgrade and minimize female sexual capacity.
This kind of thinking may do something for the male
ego, but the effect on women is devastating. Judy
learned the hard way. She is a school psychologist in
her early thirties. Tall and well-developed, with a
deep tan and blond hair bleached by the sun, she
looks like the kind of girl who does shampoo commercials:

"Doctor, I'm a two-time loser—or at least I'm going
to be if something doesn't change. But I'm not going

to go down without a fight." She set her pretty jaw grimly.

"Sounds pretty serious. What do you mean?"

"I'm thirty-four and I've had two marriages fall apart—I can't stand to have it happen again. It's taken so much out of me I don't have any more to give." The tears rolled down her cheeks.

"Why don't you start at the beginning?"

"I'm so mixed up I don't even know where the beginning is any more. I suppose it started with my first marriage—no, it was earlier than that. I had four brothers and a father who thought girls were good for nothing. As long as I can remember I always wished I could be a boy.

"As you can imagine, I never had any trouble attracting men, but I never got anything out of it. Really. When it came to sex I never felt *anything*. The whole business made me feel so inferior I guess I thought I didn't deserve to feel anything. It was that way all through my first marriage—all two years of it. I had it both ways. For me, there were two kinds of sex—a lot of intercourse and no feeling and no intercourse and no feeling. It all came out the same— nothing. I was desperately searching for something somewhere that would let me be a woman—something that would let me feel what a woman feels!"

"Did you find what you were looking for?"

"Yes, I did. But sometimes I wish I'd never even started!"

"What do you mean?"

"I think it's honest to say, Doctor, that after three years of reading everything that has been written on the subject of female sexuality *and* attending all the seminars I could find *and* being an observer at more than a dozen research projects not to mention a few experiments I've carried out on my own, I can consider myself somewhat of an expert on the subject."

"I'm sure you're right."

"Well, it hasn't helped. If anything, it's gotten worse, but in a different way."

"In what way?"

"First of all, let me tell you a few things you probably know already, but I want to go over them anyway. You know how men consider the clitoris to be a miniature penis? Well, the real story is quite different. Actually the clitoris and its related structures are much larger than the male organ. The only difference is that the penis is almost entirely external while the part of the clitoris that can be seen is just the very tip. That's only the beginning. The nerve and blood supply to the clitoris and the rest of the female sexual organs is about thirty times as great as the blood supply to the penis. I can give you a hundred more facts, but they all add up to the same thing—the female sexual apparatus and female sexual functioning are superior in every way to the male. But so what?"

"What do you mean, 'so what'?"

"Well, it hasn't done anything for *me*. As soon as I began to realize that women weren't some kind of sexual freaks, my whole sexual life changed. I began to have orgasms, I really started to enjoy sex for the first time in my life, and I felt like I had been dead and suddenly come back to life. So I got married."

"And then?"

"And then everything was fine for six months or so. I mean, sex was so wonderful I just had to have it—I couldn't get enough. But apparently for my husband the novelty began to wear off, and he lost interest in sex. Instead of every night, it was every other night.

Then it became twice a week, then twice a month. After that it wasn't even worth keeping track."

"When your husband couldn't keep up with you, what did you do?"

Judy laughed. "No, I didn't look elsewhere. I figured as long as I'm married to a man, he deserves all my business, however infrequent that may be. I may be unhappy, Doctor, but I'm not cruel."

Judy had fallen into a trap of her own construction. In a desperate attempt to rescue herself from a lifetime as a sexual cipher, she had single-handedly exposed the myth of male sexual superiority. It was an impressive feat, but like many pioneers she had gone too far. In her second marriage she had determined to make up for all her previous lost opportunities—unfortunately for her new husband most of those had occurred in bed. Judy's account left out a few details that her husband filled in. Actually she was determined to fill her newly discovered orgasmic quota of fifty at every opportunity. Her husband was game to the end but at orgasm number four or five he dropped by the wayside.

Judy's brief psychiatric treatment was aimed specifically at helping her deal with the reality of her sexual problems. As she came to understand it was not her obligation to prove the doctrine of female sexual supremacy all over again every night, she came down to earth. Step by step she worked through her early conflicts with her father and brothers and became aware of her determination to convince them—at any cost—that she was really good enough to deserve their love. Her first marriage was one long apology to her family for having been a woman. There was only one problem—none of them were listening. It was no accident that her first husband was equally indifferent —unconsciously but deliberately she had chosen him for that reason. A month or so after her treatment was concluded, she stopped by the office:

"I just wanted to tell you, Doctor, I have a new project."

"What's that, Judy?"

"I've given up trying to prove that women can do it more than men—we all know that by now, don't we?"

There was still a touch of the old crusader in her tone of insistence.

"Yes, we certainly do."

"Well, what I'm working on now is a way to help my husband achieve *his* full sexual potential. I know he'll never work up to fifty times a night like us girls, but in the meantime he's enjoying the practice."

3

MORE MYTHS
OF FEMALE SEXUALITY

Are women more realistic about sex?

Fortunately for men, even when women begin to realize their colossal orgasmic capabilities they are usually satisfied to work for quality, not quantity. The endless quest of the male Casanova or Don Juan is not a role that appeals to women—most of them reject the idea of a lifetime of Sexual Olympics—they recognize it as a losing game.

Did Sigmund Freud clear up some sexual misconceptions about women?

For the most part women have come to rely on men for information on how their bodies work; the results have been good and bad. Sigmund Freud was one of the major (though certainly not the first) researchers who pointed out that the brain was inseparably linked to the genitalia. That helped bring a lot of sexual problems into clearer focus. Regrettably Dr. Freud was not aware that the clitoris was inseparably linked to the vagina. He can be considered the father of modern psychiatry for his first discovery; he must be considered the father of the next myth of female sexuality for his related omission. He forced at least two generations of women to pay the penalty for believing: *There is a difference between vaginal and clitoral orgasm and vaginal orgasm is somehow superior.*

Didn't Freud know any better?

As a scientist he *should* have known better. His early studies in psychoanalysis led him to the awareness that little girls masturbated. Academically this was a dramatic discovery but realistically it was something that other little girls and mothers of little girls had known for centuries. He also observed that most female masturbation in this age group (and though he didn't realize it, in *every* age group) centered around the clitoris. As the girls matured and grew into young women they began to replace masturbation with sexual intercourse and showed *apparently* less interest in the clitoris and more interest in the vagina. Freud then leaped to the conclusion that there were two types of orgasm. The clitoral variety was childish and only suitable for the Viennese equivalent of teenyboppers. Any mature women immediately relinquished all clitoral sensation and felt everything she was going to feel exclusively in the vagina. It was a magnificent theory, at once profound and dazzling. There was only one problem—it was completely wrong.

If it was wrong, why didn't someone set the record straight?

Unfortunately the only people who knew for sure that Freud was in left field were women—and no one listened to them. Psychiatry in those days was exclusively a man's domain (and things haven't changed that much since then) and all important decisions relating to how women were supposed to feel were made by men. But there was another more compelling reason for the myth of vaginal-clitoral orgasm—it was flattering to men. Many psychiatrists lost their objectivity when they put on their pajamas and every theory that made them more comfortable in bed was greeted with eager delight. The traffic from New York to Vienna took on rush hour proportions and every American analyst who could afford passage made the pilgrimage. They returned with the new and exciting revelation that American women were copulating all wrong and if things didn't work out, it wasn't the man's fault. According to the psychoanalytic smoke signals at the time, all a man had to do was get an erection and ejaculate—if a woman wasn't satisfied, it was her own fault. There was also a subtle suggestion that she had brought it all on herself by masturbating. This combination of blame and guilt made millions of women unnecessarily miserable.

Nina was one of them. Nina is forty-four, though she looks somewhat younger. She is a widow and works as a court clerk. Her dark hair drawn in a tight chignon and her tweed suit made her appear serious but the mischievous twinkle in her green eyes made it clear she was only dressing for her day in court.

"This isn't the way I usually dress, Doctor, but I had

to come straight from court—I hope you don't mind. I really prefer my blond wig and miniskirt but somehow at work it doesn't seem right."

"You know by now the motto of this office is 'come as you are.' Just make yourself at home."

"Somehow it's good to hear you say that. For the last twenty years I haven't even felt at home with my own body."

"What do you mean?"

"I guess my story is different from the ones you usually hear. I was married at eighteen, I loved my husband, and I didn't have any sexual problems at all —at least I didn't think I did. I enjoyed sex from the start and after a few months of getting used to each other, I had an orgasm about ninety percent of the time. Even when I didn't have a climax it didn't bother me because I knew I'd make up for it the next time or the time after that. I'd been married about five years when one of my girl friends gave me a book —I don't even remember the title now—but it was something like, *Seven Sexual Problems of Women*. I started to read it and I was amazed to find it was all about me."

"All about you?"

"It might as well have been. It talked about masturbation and described what had happened to me in detail. It talked about early sexual adjustment and that was the way it went with me."

"Didn't you realize it might also have applied to a lot of other women?"

"I was so amazed at what I was reading I didn't stop to think about it. What really got to me was the way it played down the kind of sex I was having. I was having clitoral orgasms just the way it said in the book. You know, 'sudden, intense, localized feelings and then relaxation.' "

"What's wrong with that?"

"According to that book, everything. Why, it was supposed to be the same as masturbation, and you know how 'terrible' that is. The final result, Doctor, was I got so upset I stopped having climaxes. No matter how hard I tried, nothing happened. After about six months of sweating and straining and driving my husband out of his mind, I went to a psychiatrist." Nina frowned.

"What did he have to say?"

"Well, he carefully explained that I had never experienced anything approaching a 'mature sexual experience' and went on to describe a 'true vaginal orgasm.' According to him, it was a profound sensation of fulfillment which began deep in the vaginal and pelvic area and rapidly diffused over the entire body. The way he went into detail it sounded only slightly less dramatic than an eruption of Vesuvius. I knew one thing—I never experienced anything even close to that unless you count the time I drove my car off the road and fell twenty-five feet into a ravine!" She smiled but her heart wasn't in it.

"What did the psychiatrist suggest?"

"He told me that the only way to finally achieve a vaginal orgasm was to recognize the emotional immaturity that prevented me from growing up sexually and becoming capable of true orgasm. I started to protest that I was having orgasms already and then I remembered I wasn't—anymore."

"Then what happened?"

"I went through about three years of treatment with two different psychiatrists without having anything approaching a vaginal orgasm."

"How about the old style orgasm?"

"Not much luck there. Once in a while, maybe, but nothing like before. In the meantime my husband was killed in an accident which didn't make matters any better."

"What happened then?"

"Then I came to see you."

What was Nina's real problem?

Nina's problem came in two parts. The part that projected above the surface was her frigidity—the inability to reach a sexual climax. Actually frigidity is a bad word to describe this condition because it accuses and convicts the woman simultaneously. Any woman who fails to attain an orgasm during intercourse is immediately tagged as The Ice Queen. It just isn't true. Usually the woman who finds orgasm out of her reach has the same deep feelings and needs as any other human being—sometimes even more. Unfortunately she also has an unconscious emotional barrier which prevents her from finding real sexual satisfaction. To label a person in this situation "frigid" is really unfair.

Is there a better term?

Yes. Orgasmic impairment (or O-I for short) is more descriptive—and more honest. There is no moral judgment attached: it just describes what's happening (or not happening). It also implies that there is hope. If a woman's orgasmic capability is merely impaired, it can be restored. If she's *frigid*, she's *frozen*.

Did Nina have that?

Yes, but her O-I was a very special kind. It was *iatrogenic.*

What does that mean?

Iatrogenic, like many medical terms in English, is manufactured from two Greek words, in this case *iatros,* meaning "physician" and *genos* meaning "caused by." *Iatrogenic orgasmic impairment* means that Nina's sexual problem was caused by her doctor. More precisely, it was brought on by the misguided good intentions of the physician who wrote the book that she read and the two psychiatrists who treated her.

Then it was all their fault?

No, only about ten percent. The other ninety percent of Nina's problem was hidden deep in her unconscious. Without being consciously aware of it, Nina welcomed the bad news. Like every other emotional symptom, her sudden orgasmic impairment was a desperate attempt to resolve an unbearable conflict. It worked but in the process she had to sacrifice most of her enjoyment of sex.

What was really going on?

Like many people with emotional problems, Nina didn't tell the whole story the first time through. As she went over the details of her sexual experiences again, some interesting facts emerged. In describing the early days of her marriage, she had said, "I loved my husband and I didn't have any sexual problem at all—at least I didn't think I did." That was true—up to a point. But Nina later recalled that after about five years of marriage her husband started seeing other women—on the side. It was that development that impelled her to do her own research in the area of sex and she started by reading the book, *Seven Sexual Problems of Women.*

The misinformation about clitoral versus vaginal orgasm was just what she had been looking for. It brought all of her old feelings of guilt about masturbation rushing back to the surface and gave her the excuse she needed to give up orgasm. She had also neglected to mention that her husband's sexual problem was impotence and when she stopped having regular orgasms, he stopped having erections. (In her own words, "After about six months of sweating and straining and driving my husband out of his mind. . .") His punishment for seeking out other women was loss of the ability to copulate and Nina's revenge was complete—except that she had to give up virtually all sexual gratification in exchange. At that stage she needed official approval of what was going on. It was easy to find two psychiatrists who went along with her little plan by agreeing that "clitoral" orgasms didn't count and encouraging her to give them up.

But it wasn't her fault that these psychiatrists felt that way, was it?

Not exactly, though many patients select the psychiatrist who tells them exactly what they want to hear.

If she really didn't like what they were telling her, and more important if she wasn't improving, Nina didn't have to stick around for three years. As things turned out, it probably wasn't an accident that as soon as her husband died, she *immediately* dropped her current psychiatrist and switched to one who looked at things differently.

Differently in what way?

Instead of telling Nina why she shouldn't have orgasms, it made more sense to tell her how to go about having them again. And the first step was to explain the mechanics of orgasm in the female. It goes something like this:

The clitoris is directly connected to the spinal cord and brain by the same plexus of thousands of nerve fibers that supplies the vagina. Stimulation of either organ immediately affects the other. In addition, the extremely sensitive roots of the clitoris extend deep into the walls of the vagina itself. As the penis rubs against the vaginal wall it applies exactly the same pressure to the internal part of the clitoris and to the vaginal lining. The third factor is probably the most important. The labia minora, those two thin curtain-like membranes that extend over the vaginal opening, are attached above to the body of the clitoris. Even though the shaft of the penis may never actually come into contact with the *tip* of the clitoris, as the penis slides in and out of the vagina it successively pulls and releases the lower ends of the labia. This causes constant and rhythmic friction against the head and shaft of the clitoris and if everything else is right, orgasm is rapid and inevitable. *Every orgasm that occurs in a woman is basically clitoral.* Orgasms occur-

ring by sexual intercourse may be clitoral *and* vaginal
—which only means that the penis is stimulating the
vagina and clitoris simultaneously. But for Nina—and
every other woman—that part was academic. The only
real question was whether or not she was able to enjoy
sexual intercourse.

The answer wasn't long in coming. Once she clearly
understood that all orgasms were identical and were
basically dependent on stimulation of the clitoris,
things began to improve. First of all, she had no more
excuse for being a copulatory wallflower. Secondly,
with her husband gone, there was no necessity to use
her sexuality as a weapon. After a few months of nail-
ing down all the emotional nuances, as Nina explained
it, "Now having an orgasm is just as easy as taking a
shower—and a lot more fun! It doesn't really matter
to me how it happens, just as long as it does happen.
And now it's happening again."

*But isn't a vaginal orgasm better in some way than
just a clitoral orgasm?*

Nope. From a sexual point of view, there is an Orgasmic Bill of Rights—all orgasms are created equal.
Every orgasm, whether produced by intercourse, foreplay, or masturbation depends on the same sensory
triple play—clitoris to spinal cord to brain, instantaneously followed by a reverse explosion—brain to spinal
cord to clitoris. Every other part of the body—vagina,
heart, lungs, skin—also participates, but the center of
attention, as always, is the clitoris.

Does a woman really need to have an orgasm to enjoy sex?

It depends on who does the talking. Some well-meaning but misinformed students of sexual problems bypass the whole question of vaginal versus clitoral orgasms. Their approach is unique—it consists of first stating, then trying to prove the next myth of female sexuality: *A woman doesn't need to have an orgasm to enjoy sex.*

This concept is based on the idea that simply being close, touching bodies, and sharing the mutual experience of sexuality is fulfilling enough. Some of them even condemn female orgasm as "spoiling the serenity and tranquility of the sexual act." It doesn't take a genius with a computer to figure out that one hundred percent of these "experts" are men.

Most of these men—and some of them are physicians and even psychiatrists—are leading spokesmen of the "I-never-experienced-it-myself-but-I-can-imagine-how-it-feels" school of sex. By *imagining* the dozens of complex sensations and responses that make up a woman's part of sexual intercourse they readily (sometimes a little too readily) conclude that women are already getting enough of what sex has to offer and orgasm for them is an unnecessary frill. One observation that may lead them to this judgment is that most women are capable of prolonged intercourse—extending for an hour or more. Many men, unfortunately, are unable to sustain their sexual responses for more than a minute or two. Therefore they conclude that the ladies should make up in quantity what they miss in quality.

Does anyone really believe that?

That, of course, is the problem. The experts who offer this solution can't find many takers—among women anyway. Peggy is typical of the skeptics. She is thirty-five and unmarried. As assistant to the president of a large corporation, she is sophisticated and knowledgeable in the world of business—nobody can fool her there. When it comes to her personal life and particularly her sexual life, like every woman, she is more vulnerable. She describes it well:

"The thing that gets me, Doctor, is how do you really find out who is right."

"What do you mean, Peggy?"

"Well, in business there's always a reliable reference. If we want to check on a person, there's Poore's Register. If we want to check on a company, there's always Dun and Bradstreet. But if you want to find out if someone's telling you the truth about sex, where do you go to look up his version? This isn't just a theoretical problem because that's exactly the kind of spot I've been in for the past six months. And I'm still not out of it."

"Why don't you tell me about it?"

"Okay, I might as well—this is one subject they never taught in business administration. I've been going with Jess for almost a year now. I don't know—he doesn't want to get married and I don't blame him. His first marriage was such a mess and he's only been divorced a few months. I guess I wanted to marry him at first but since this thing's come up, I'm not so sure." Peggy clasped her hands together.

"I wish I could just tell it without getting upset."

"Sometimes there's nothing wrong with getting upset—especially if it's about something really important."

She nodded. "There's nothing more important than this. You see, Jess and I have been having sex together for almost a year. Rather *he's* been having sex and I've been watching from the sidelines. I never have a climax. He just goes ahead and has his fun and then he's through and it's over until the next time."

"Have you had orgasms before?"

"You mean before Jess? Sure, almost all the time. Well, let's say about half the time."

"How come you don't have them now?"

"I don't get the chance. Jess believes it isn't necessary for a woman to have a climax to enjoy sex so he just does his part and that's it."

"How long does it take for Jess to 'do his part'?"

"Gee, I don't know. About a minute or two I'd guess."

"Why do you go along with this sort of thing?"

"I didn't want to at first but Jess convinced me it was normal. He said his psychiatrist had proved that women don't need to have an orgasm to enjoy sex and that a lot of women who had accepted it that way were much happier. Something about not always having to worry about whether they reach a climax or not."

Was Jess right?

In part. When he said women shouldn't have to worry about whether they were going to have an orgasm, he was on the right track. But the solution is not giving up orgasm once and for all. A better goal is to solve the orgasm problem by having an orgasm every time (or almost every time) without having to worry about it. Actually Jess was a sexual swindler. As Peggy found out later, his first marriage had been "such a mess" because his wife insisted on being included in his sexual plans. She was understandably disappointed when her husband brought her to a high level of sexual excitement and then wriggled away mumbling, "I guess that's it for me. Maybe it'll work out tomorrow night." Instead of facing his own problem, Jess concocted a new theory of female sexuality which made female orgasm superfluous. When his wife objected, he looked for a psychiatrist to reinforce his ideas. It wasn't easy. Peggy described it:

"So anyhow, he went to about a dozen psychiatrists trying to find out who agreed with him. He finally came across a doctor. It was as if they had been made for each other. He stayed there for three hours and even had dinner with the good doctor. He finally got home about eleven P.M. and he was really happy. He kept me up until midnight raving about this wonderful psychiatrist who really understood women. He said, 'My doctor says that there is no reason for a woman to have an orgasm during sex. All of her emotional needs can be met simply by the presence of her husband and the knowledge she is satisfying him. Orgasm for females is obsolete!' I got pretty mad and told him, 'That's wonderful. I'm so excited to know your doctor feels that way. I hope you two will be very happy together.' That was the end of the conversation."

Didn't Jess have a sexual problem of his own?

Yes, and it soon became evident. He suffered from premature ejaculation. In this combination physical-emotional condition, he was unable to have intercourse for more than a minute or two without reaching a climax. Instead of admitting that he *had* a problem he desperately tried to shift the blame to the entire female half of the human race. He couldn't admit that he, because of his own sexual disability, couldn't bring a woman to orgasm. The real answer was that women were not intended to have orgasm. When his wife wouldn't go along with his bright idea, he searched until he found first a psychiatrist and then a woman who joined his new club. But Peggy had paid her dues and was ready to resign. After a few months in treatment she had some new ideas on her own:

"What an idiot I was! But it makes sense the way you explain it. In spite of being 'liberated' I suppose I still felt guilty about living with Jess. When he came up with his new theory, it was tailor-made for me. If I had sex but didn't enjoy it, why should I feel guilty about it? I guess I was trying to say, 'It's about the same as not having it at all'. And that is only too true. Now that I think back on it, it was all so crazy. I don't even know why he needed me—he could have almost done as well by himself. I remember what the famous doctor used to say, 'Simply explain to the woman that participating in intercourse without an orgasm is no worse than having an egg without salt.' Somebody should explain to that genius that it's more like having salt without an egg."

Why is it so important that a woman have an orgasm during intercourse?

Every modern woman is entitled to enjoy the greatest sensory experience available to human beings—sexual orgasm. It is the ultimate "trip." The "highs" and "freak-outs" so desperately pursued by drug users are like a weekend in a drafty turkish bath compared to the sense of absolute exhilaration produced by one good orgasm. To deprive a woman of this experience —one which is rightfully hers—is something no man would deliberately do. Only lack of knowledge and misunderstanding could encourage a woman to voluntarily give up her greatest chance at sexual happiness.

Are there any sexual misconceptions which are particularly hard to erase?

The most deeply ingrained myth of female sexuality is also the one that has the stamp of medical approval. Sometimes by indifference, rarely by ignorance, the family doctor and even the gynecologist (both of whom are almost always men) encourage women to cash in their sexual chips long before the game is over. The last and perhaps most pernicious myth of female sexuality goes: *For a woman, the menopause means the end of sex.*

The truth is that the menopause means the end of menstruation—and nothing else. As some women have learned to their dismay, even after menstruation has ended, reproduction may linger on. A change-of-life baby is convincing proof that many a woman's life hadn't changed as much as she thought it had. Becoming pregnant again at forty-five can be a bit of a shock to the mother of teenagers who has been eagerly anticipating a few years of peace before taking on grandchildren. However it is convincing biological evidence that the reproductive and sexual capabilities of a woman may extend well into the fifth decade and beyond.

What really goes on during the change of life in a woman?

An understanding of the menopause requires some knowledge of a woman's glandular makeup, especially in relation to hormones. A substantial part of female sexuality (but not all of it) depends on tiny twin organs buried deep in the pelvis, the ovaries. By a quirk of nature they are the only truly disposable glands in the human body. It happened in a strange way.

About a hundred thousand years ago, the average woman's life expectancy was twenty-five years or less. Ovaries designed to last forty years provided an ample margin of safety. These days human life expectancy has more than doubled and a forty-year guarantee on an ovary is much less impressive. The ovaries wear out at age forty while the rest of the woman goes on. In effect modern women are outliving their reproductive systems by at least three decades. The resulting problems are not restricted to the reproductive department. By the age of forty most women are willing (if not eager) to leave childbearing to others. They are not quite so anxious to renounce sexual gratification.

Unfortunately reproduction and hormone production are tied together. At the same time those little ovaries stop hurling monthly eggs toward the uterus the production of sex hormones also slows to a dribble. While the eggs may be expendable, continued femininity depends upon the daily drops of hormone being fed into the bloodstream. As the supply of estrogen (the major female sex hormone) falls off, the woman's body is affected in several important ways.

Specifically, what happens?

First to feel the shortage are the sexual organs themselves, with the changes being most obvious in the external genitals. The vagina becomes narrower and shorter, the clitoris decreases in size, the uterus and ovaries begin to shrivel up. Even the breasts sag and lose their firmness. As the deficiency of estrogen becomes more acute, the woman loses most of her interest in sex. The brain itself suffers estrogen lack and sexual intercourse becomes "too much trouble." In a real sense the woman who loses her hormones becomes defeminized. At the same time the rest of her body is suffering too.

It happened to Rachel. She is fifty-one and the chief buyer for a chain of department stores. She was tense and agitated as she spoke:

"Doctor, I know you hear this all the time from neurotic women like me but I think I'm losing my mind."

"What do you mean?"

She picked a gray hair off her jacket. "Maybe I waited too long—maybe there's nothing you can do for me—maybe there's nothing anyone can do for me!"

"Why don't you tell me how it started?"

"When you hear my story you'll really think I'm crazy! But I might as well tell it. I stopped having periods when I was forty-two. Let's see, that was nine years ago. Anyhow I started feeling funny—not sick but just not right. Headaches, trouble sleeping, backaches—that sort of thing. You know, I work hard at my job—buying for three stores, eight-thousand items, a budget of four million dollars—it's a big responsibility. And with those discount stores cutting prices all the time—but I'm getting off the track. That's another thing—my mind keeps wandering. Look at how I'm dressed." Rachel got up and took a step or two. She was wearing a gray tweed suit a size too large, a white blouse and simple black shoes.

"It doesn't look bad to me."

"Oh, Doctor. I'm a buyer! Fashion is my career! I'm supposed to set the example and here I am dressing like somebody's grandmother! How long do you think I can keep this up!"

"Why do you dress that way?"

"Because I don't care. I don't care about anything. Everything seems to be too much trouble. I don't even wear makeup anymore!" She began to cry, then after a moment she smiled weakly. "That's the only advantage to not wearing makeup. When I cry, there's no touching-up to do." Rachel wiped her tears quickly. "Where was I? Oh yes. Well, I've felt bad for about the past eight years, but a few months ago something happened that made me sure I was going out of my mind.

"I was getting dressed one morning and I noticed my skirt seemed to be getting longer! I checked my clothes and discovered that *all* my skirts were longer! I measured myself and found I was an inch shorter! What's happening to me?"

A quick check with a tape measure showed Rachel was exaggerating. She had actually lost only about a half inch in height—but that was enough. She was experiencing one of the more dramatic effects of a hormone deficit. Besides maintaining the sexual apparatus in top form, estrogens also stabilize the calcium and phosphorus concentrated in the bones. In Rachel's case the bones of the spinal column had lost much of their mineral content over the past eight years; finally one of the vertebrae collapsed, causing her to lose a fraction of an inch in height. This made her skirt appear longer and finally brought her to seek treatment. A careful examination also revealed wrinkled skin, dry hair, and excessive fat deposits on her legs and hips. Since the onset of the menopause she had gained about thirty pounds.

"How has this affected you sexually?"

"Sex? What's that?" Rachel laughed. "Doctor, for the past four years, sex has just been a word to me."

"And before that?"

"Now you're talking about something different. When my husband was still alive—he died about ten years ago—I thought I had the most perfect sex life in the world. I mean, it was at least five times a week and I almost always reached a climax. But then . . ." Rachel was crying again.

"Do you see what I mean? I cry maybe six or seven times a day and if I didn't control myself I'd be crying all the time. Anyhow, after my husband died I couldn't see giving up sex completely. I went out with men and after a while I started enjoying it again. It wasn't the same as with my husband but I had to do something. But about four years ago, I lost all interest in the whole idea. I've tried maybe half a dozen times since then but it's reached the point where it's actually painful. I don't know." Rachel sighed.

Further tests showed Rachel had virtually no sex hormones circulating in her body. She had been having hot flashes ever since the end of her periods. (She hadn't mentioned those because she thought they were "normal.") Her sexual organs were about half their normal size—this explained the discomfort when she tried to have intercourse. The mental changes—depression, withdrawal, and feelings of futility—were another consequence of estrogen deficiency.

Her gynecologist immediately started her on estrogenic hormones by three separate routes—tablets to take by mouth, injections, and a hormone cream to be placed in the vagina. Two months later she came in for a visit. The change was dramatic. At least thirty pounds lighter, she appeared ten years younger. No more tweed suit and black shoes. No more gray hair. She was dressed in a pale beige pants suit, short brown leather boots, and over-size sunglasses. Her gray hair was now honey-blond. More important was the way she spoke:

"I don't know what you did, Doctor, but I feel like I've been swimming in the fountain of youth. The whole world looks different and it's not just these groovy glasses." She laughed and took off her sunglasses.

"You're feeling better then?"

"Better? I wish I'd felt this well when I was twenty-five! I mean, I still have a few wrinkles and I can't stay up all night—every night, that is—but I'm a completely new person."

"How are you getting along sexually?"

"That's the best part of it. I feel kind of embarrassed to admit it, but sexually I'm an adolescent again." She lowered her voice and leaned over. "Do you know that my breasts are actually getting bigger? I had to get all new bras. And as far as sex is concerned, it's not so simple anymore. I mean I have real sexual feelings now and—and, I have to do something about them. They aren't the kind that go away by themselves. I'm even thinking of getting married again."

Rachel was experiencing the dramatic reversal of virtually all the symptoms of the menopause. The hot flashes disappeared, the aches and pains vanished, the sexual organs filled out again, and as Rachel mentioned, the breasts regained their previous size. But most important of all estrogen supplied her with vitality and enthusiasm that is available from no other source. What meant the most to Rachel was the return of her optimism and her zest for living that made everything worthwhile.

Is there any way to avoid the menopause entirely?

Unfortunately not. The ovaries ultimately give up the ghost and stop producing their hormones. At the same time, sex hormone production from the adrenal glands declines considerably. Reproduction grinds to a halt about the age of forty-five, give or take five years, and the breasts lose their ability to produce milk. *But that's about as far as it has to go.*

The undesirable physical and mental changes of the menopause are almost entirely preventable. For the cost of a hormone tablet a day or an injection every month or so, *every woman over the age of forty can virtually maintain herself biologically and emotionally in the thirties.* (With the proper hormone combination she can even continue a monthly flow similar to menstruation, if she prefers.) Most important of all, if she enjoyed sex before the menopause, she can enjoy it as much or more after the change of life. Even those women who have never experienced total sexual gratification until then, have the opportunity to achieve sexual happiness at the time when they have been led to believe their chance is over.

Why is that?

By the age of forty or so most of the sources of sexual anxiety have disappeared. There is little risk of pregnancy, no more of the cutthroat competition for men that existed in the twenties and thirties, and much less of the social disapproval for the honest enjoyment of sexuality than existed before. In addition, all of a woman's sexual energy no longer needs to be devoted simply to attracting men. In a more diffuse way, the expression of her sexual feelings can be used to make her relationship with men deeper and more meaningful. She has the time and inclination to add the fine nuances so often missing from the high pressure competitive sex of the second and the third decades. The change of life is another name for the menopause but if the woman deals with it realistically the *change of life* can mean a *change for a better life.*

Physically and emotionally the human female is the most complex organism on the face of the earth. She has a potential for sexual and emotional happiness unparalleled by any other creature. The only means of ever achieving that potential is the understanding and acceptance of the truth about her mind, her body, and her own unique sexuality. If the facts are presented to her honestly and she is willing to accept them realistically, she will have made great progress toward arriving at her goal.

4

HOW SEX GOT
A BAD REPUTATION

How did sex originate?

Sex, as we know it, started with the crocodile. This scaly cold-blooded distant cousin of man was the first animal to develop a penis. Before then, life was much simpler. All the earth's inhabitants had about the same type of sexual equipment and used it about the same way. The male and female simply backed up to each other, wiggled their sexual equipment into contact, and oozed primitive sperm into contact with primitive eggs. There wasn't much to see, hardly anything to feel, and in many species if a couple turned on like this once a year, it was sufficient. Twice a year was oversexed and many animals copulated only once in a lifetime.

What difference did the penis make?

For one thing it was visible. Secondly it revolutionized sex by fitting *inside* the female body. In those days there was no such thing as a vagina. The female sexual equipment was a cloaca consisting of a common channel for urine, feces, and semi-annual eggs. (Things have improved a lot for women since then.) Obviously the crocodile penis too has undergone major design modifications as it was handed down over the years to *homo sapiens*. From an evolutionary point of view the modern American male sports the latest in phallic equipment. But problems still remained.

What kind of problems?

Men equipped with this wonderful organ quickly developed a lively interest in the female sexual apparatus, by then improved and expanded into a closely-coupled vagina, labia, and clitoris. Like the crocodiles before them men and women discovered that combining their sexual resources resulted in immense pleasure for both contributors. For the next 50,000 years all went well. Sex was a normal physiological function as routine as swimming had been to the crocodile and as essential and enjoyable as eating was to early man. Then came the Dark Ages.

What happened during the Dark Ages?

About 400 A.D. Western civilization abruptly lurched in a different direction. Suddenly sex was out and guilt was in. As some long-forgotten genius in the field of medieval motivational psychology discovered, *men and women are unbelievably responsive to the linking up of sex and guilt.* From that moment on, the fate of society (and most of its members) was sealed. The most efficient means of controlling human behavior had been put into effect: focus on an activity which everybody must engage in—*sex;* select its most en-

joyable aspect—*copulation;* finally provide the threat
of severe and relentless punishment for its enjoyment.
As the machinery of sexual repression creaked into
action, the power and influence of those in control
grew enormously. There were, to be sure, a few
hitches at first but all resistance finally yielded to the
crushing force of sexual repression.

One of the major early problems was that the moralists actually underestimated the potential of their
new weapon to change the destiny of the Western
world. Apparently the original idea was to make sex
only a minor transgression. However all levels of society almost immediately succumbed to the irresistible urge to feel guilty about perfectly normal sexual
feelings. In effect this was the "new morality," Dark
Ages version.

What form did the new morality take?

In some ways a most frightening form. Sex rapidly became an emotional commodity to be consumed under
the strictest prohibitions, if at all. Like the famous insurance policy that pays off if the insured is killed by
a cable car on the Fourth of July while carrying an
Easter bunny, sexual relations came to be allowed only
under the most rigid restrictions. According to these
forerunners of our modern moral guardians, sex was to
be limited to married couples in bed, in the dark, fully
clothed, ideally involving an impotent man and a
frigid woman with just enough sperm dripping onto
the lady's private parts to bring on a joyless impregnation.

What about the Bible?

That was another challenge for the moral reformers. Since it sets a liberal tone toward sex, a major hatchet job was in order. The Good Book was extensively distorted and misinterpreted to make It appear to endorse sexual repression. Genesis was reinterpreted to make Adam and Eve seem like sinners who were evicted from the Garden of Eden for daring to engage in sexual intercourse. Later versions were further sanitized and Adam's penis was replaced by the ever-present serpent hovering greedily around Eve's pubic fig leaf. The sexual purifiers smugly ignored reality: if God had not intended His first man and woman to copulate He would simply have molded their mortal clay a bit differently and left them nothing to work with.

Some of the changes were downright silly. In the Revised Version of the Bible of 1881, the word "whore" was changed to "harlot" and the term, "whoremonger" was replaced by "fornicator." No exact figures are available to the number of souls saved by these semantic gymnastics.

The Bible was only the beginning. After emasculating this once lusty and vital Scripture, every other possible work of man, artistic and literary, was purged and distorted to eliminate any mention of rational human sexuality.

How does that affect us today?

Fifteen hundred years ago the single most enduring principle of Western society was forged: SEX IS

BAD. From that moment to the present, hundreds of millions of innocent people have been brainwashed into believing a silly bit of nonsense: sex is synonymous with sin. Regrettably, no force on earth has been able to turn back the emotional calendar and the misconception goes on, constantly reinforced. For more than a dozen centuries every persuasive force available has been harnessed to desexualize the most highly-sexed animal this planet has ever known—the human being. Their message is always the same and always untrue: *sex, except under nearly impossible circumstances, is wicked.*

Is our society really against sex?

Every social institution in our country has cooperated in rigorously and systematically suppressing any reference to sex, and above all, sex as desirable and enjoyable.

The public schools lead the way. Instead of guiding school children toward the rational fulfillment of their sexual destinies, most schools have decided not to get involved. With regard to sex, our educational system is pre-Columbian in many cases. The official version is that the sexual organs haven't been discovered yet, so why give the kids any ideas. This is somewhat behind the times in an era when third graders engage in heterosexual touching and thirteen-year-olds go all the way. The average high school freshman knows more about orgasm than the superintendent of schools. But the school continues to enforce a grotesque moral code designed to crush developing sexual awareness in young minds. Teaching materials are swept clean of any sexual contamination; guilt-ridden "experts" prepare "student editions" of well-known books which are totally sanitized and contain only the tattered remnants of the author's original message. Classical literary works are often arrogantly butchered by simpletons who never wrote a complete sentence in their lives but can sniff out a reference to reproduction without opening a volume.

The legal system (which should know better) has jumped on the moral bandwagon. It is grimly trying to protect people from their own natural biological impulses. An American, living in the freest nation in the history of the world, may be sentenced to up to twenty years in prison for copulating with a willing married person (adultery), having sex with a willing single person (fornication), and possessing images of other humans either without their clothes on or engaging in sex (pornography). Ironically the punishment for these desperate crimes can be more severe than that decreed for murderers and rapists. In some jurisdictions even masturbation is a crime. Since everyone masturbates at one time or another, are the police supposed to arrest themselves? What about the judge?

But isn't that silly?

It seems that way. Actually, this campaign by a small number of misguided misanthropes to seize absolute control of man's most intimate and personal function would be no more than a tasteless joke if it were not for one thing: *the project has been an almost complete success*. Moving relentlessly, generation by generation, guilt has fought sex to an almost complete standstill. Utilizing the advanced techniques of mass communication and indoctrination perfected over the past fifty years, the human sexual urge has finally been blighted. Although people in our society continue to copulate, during every sexual act guilt also lies between the sheets. Every act of intercourse carries with it the conviction that there is something wrong about bringing penis and vagina together. Most physicians and certainly every psychiatrist knows of scores of young and otherwise vigorous men and women who are impotent and frigid. At the precise moment when they should be enjoying their full genital potential they sit on the sidelines—virtual sexual cripples.

But aren't there clinics for this kind of thing?

One of the most tragic developments of modern times is the sex rehabilitation clinic. At these centers groups of experts in sex, who presumably have escaped the effect of sexual brainwashing, solemnly receive dozens of forlorn couples who are unable to accomplish what every orangutan in Borneo can do without even thinking about it. These unhappy folk must swallow their pride and submit to a series of copulation lessons utilizing, ironically, the most advanced teaching techniques. These include tape recordings, closed circuit television, and live demonstrations. No grades are given but presumably there is a final exam. After twenty years of being taught how *not* to be human, with difficulty many of the victims regain their sexual powers. The need for resexualization of healthy adults is just another example of the end result of suppression of normal sexual feelings. This is the harvest of the lunacy of self-appointed "moral guardians" who, in their infinite wisdom, have decided that men and women must surrender control of their own sexuality. What they have taken away, the sex clinic tries to put back.

Don't they help some people?

Maybe. But sex clinics are primarily for those with a license to copulate—married couples. The unmarried members of our society have to make it on their own. For single men, the sexual situation is difficult; for single women it is almost impossible. The female libido is supposed to lie dormant for twenty years until it is instantly defrosted by a two dollar marriage license. Girls just aren't built that way. Sue speaks from experience:

"Doctor, I'm almost twenty-five now and I feel as if I'm being suffocated. I don't know what to do. I work in an ad agency as an assistant copywriter and we're supposed to be sophisticated people. But when it comes to sex, men are all the same." Sue pushed her pale blond hair away from her eyes and brushed away a few tears at the same time.

"I mean, if I go out with a man and *won't* go to bed with him, he gets angry, calls me a prude, and I never see him again. If I sleep with him when he wants me to, we have a great time as long as I'm just a swinger."

"What do you mean by swinger?"

"Pardon me for being cynical, Doctor, but most men that I know use that term to distinguish their girl friend from a human being. A swinger is always there when you want her—her body, that is. She doesn't have any feelings, doesn't make any demands, and never never thinks about *marriage*. That, Doctor, is a *dirty* word."

Suddenly Sue clenched her fists.

"I can't go on living like this! I'm a woman and I need sex! I'm going to climb the walls if I can't find someone to make love with but it all ends up the same way! 'It was sure nice while it lasted, Sue, but we don't want to get serious, do we?' You're darn right *we* want to get serious, somehow, with somebody!"

Now the tears came in a flood. After a cup of tea things were a little better.

"I'm sorry, Doctor, but you can see what a terrible problem this is for me. I'm not going to go through this for another twenty-four years—you can bet on that. Any single girl who's honest will admit what I just admitted to you—sex is the biggest problem in her life. Can you help me?"

Fortunately there was help for Sue. Her willingness to face her problem frankly was the starting point. It made her treatment much easier. Every single woman who is as honest with herself as Sue will admit that sex is the biggest problem in *her* life. Wedged between society's hypocritical prohibitions and her own powerful sexual strivings, the single woman has little room to maneuver. A prime factor working against her is the unique nature of the female sexual drive.

Why are women so complicated sexually?

Female sexuality is determined by a series of interlocking glandular mechanisms of almost unbelievable complexity. Compared to a woman, the male sexual apparatus is as simple as a fountain pen. To further complicate things, the sexual attitude of every woman between puberty and the menopause is tossed on the tides of the menstrual cycle. Within this roughly twenty-eight day period, which mysteriously corresponds to the phases of the moon, every female goes from a de-sexualized uninterested bystander to a hormone-primed amazon whose entire physiology is aimed (usually beyond her awareness) at instant re-

production. It is literally a sexual roller coaster and
women take the whole ride every month.

It all starts with the ovary. The two major female
sex hormones, estrogen and progesterone, are produced there and march arm-in-arm through every cell
of the body to make it uniquely feminine. Estrogen
always paves the way, beginning at puberty. At that
time the basically unsexualized girl-child is precipi-
tously transformed into a woman. Without warning,
tremendous amounts of estrogenic hormone flood her
bloodstream, and womanhood is on the way. The
bones of the pelvis are rebuilt and the hips widen
dramatically. The breasts enlarge, pubic and axillary
hair appears, the vagina, clitoris, and labia are suddenly functional and responsive, and reproduction becomes a possibility. Progesterone is following close behind. Its job is to put the finishing touches on the
estrogen-triggered changes. (For example, estrogen
enlarges the breasts; progesterone produces prolifera-
tion of the milk-producing glands within them.) The
most important part of female sexuality is the one organ which shows no detectable changes at puberty but
which is most drastically affected by the sexual hormones—*the brain.*

*Exactly how do hormones influence a woman's sex-
ual feelings?*

For thousands of years philosophers have searched in
vain for that subtle quality called femininity. Hundreds of thousands of careful examinations of male
and female brains have failed to detect any structural
difference which might account for the obvious fact
that women think and act and respond differently
from men. Only within the last thirty years has the

answer begun to emerge—hormones. The subtle
chemical influence of sex hormones is what makes the
brain and the thoughts of a woman profoundly different from those of a man. Every moment of every
day every cell of a woman's brain is bathed in sex
hormones. Awake, asleep, cooking, watching television, or just day-dreaming, estrogen and progesterone are diffusing through every brain cell. Every reaction, every thought of a woman is under the direct
influence of these hormones.

As if this influence were not enough, the effects of
sex hormones are also directly distributed throughout
the body by a network of endocrine glands. At the
base of the brain itself is a strange hybrid organ called
the *pituitary gland*. The front part of this structure is
similar to the other glands and secretes its own hormones. The posterior portion of the pituitary is unique
in that it is directly connected to the brain by thick
nerve fibers. As the pituitary is bathed in concentrated sex hormones, powerful nerve impulses from its
posterior portion bombard the brain. These combine
with the direct chemical effect of the sex hormones to
exert an even more powerful sexualizing influence on
the feminine mind.

Do women have male sex hormones too?

Yes. The pituitary gland sends impulses simultaneously to the adrenals, two small glands lying atop the
kidneys. These structures produce a wide variety of
secretions including cortisone and adrenalin, vital to
maintenance of the body. In addition, the adrenal
glands of every woman produce *testosterone*, the same
male sex hormone produced by the testicles of adult
males. In men, testosterone produces a beard, strong

muscles, a deep voice, and an all-pervading interest in sex. In women, testosterone has one primary function —it intensifies sexual drive. By a delicate regulatory mechanism, the masculinizing influence of testosterone is precisely balanced by an equivalent amount of estrogen. If all goes well, the end result for the ladies is no whiskers, no muscles, no baritone voice, nothing more than a strong healthy interest in sex. Should the regulatory machinery break down and testosterone prevail, the unfortunate girl develops a beard, a booming voice, big biceps, and an obsession with sex that overwhelms her personality. The cause may be a tumor of the ovary or adrenal gland and needs immediate medical attention. If the secretion of the male sex hormone is precisely balanced by an equivalent amount of estrogen, the woman remains feminine but retains her interest in sex.

Do sex hormones change during menstruation?

Definitely. As if this complex equilibrium between masculine and feminine hormones weren't enough, a girl has to contend with the constant ebb and flow of hormones during the menstrual cycle. As the cycle begins, the ovary starts to secrete estrogen in small amounts. With each passing day, the concentration of estrogen in the blood rises until about the fourteenth day after the onset of the menses. About that time ovulation occurs and shortly afterward, the ovary pours out a steadily increasing supply of progesterone. This hormone is designed to prepare the uterus and other parts of the reproductive system for impending pregnancy. By about the twenty-eighth day if fertilization has not occurred, the whole operation simply collapses. The secretion of both hormones stops abruptly, the lining of the uterus dies and menstruation begins.

Are there any other changes during menstruation?

Yes. Not only are the uterus and breasts exposed to the entire range of hormone concentration every twenty-eight days, but the feminine brain runs the gamut from virtually no sex hormones passing through it to a high concentration of two female sex hormones and one male sex hormone irrigating every one of its cells. No wonder many women tend to be moody at certain times of the month. Some have more trouble than others. Beth's reaction to this monthly hormonal merry-go-round is not unusual.

"Doctor, every month I feel like I'm riding a roller coaster. My period started when I was about twelve and it never really affected me until about a year or so ago, when I was twenty-two. It seems to be getting worse every month. The actual period isn't much. I flow for about five days and that's that. But then about twelve or thirteen days after I start, I begin to feel so sexy I think I'm going out of my mind. Now I come from a good family and my mother taught me the difference between right and wrong but half-way through the month it gets very confusing."

"Confusing?"

"I can't describe it but it's like nothing I ever felt before. The only thing in the world that matters is sex. It's much worse in the summertime, especially on those wonderful warm evenings in the mountains or when there's a full moon and pounding surf at the beach. I just can't help it. I know it's not right but those are the times when I've gone all the way on dates. I mean, it's heavenly when I'm doing it but I feel so awfully guilty afterward."

Why does Beth feel that way?

She is the victim of a head-on collision between her mother's idea of "right and wrong" and the compelling necessity to respond to the urgent demands of her surging hormones which never heard the words "right or wrong." As much as she may dislike the idea, on those sultry summer nights, Beth is coming into heat. As a result of millions of years of refinement of the sexual instinct in female mammals, each month just before her egg is ready to be released, Beth has the compelling necessity to make herself available for fertilization. The underlying mechanism is the same as in other female animals. The pineal gland, a tiny structure clinging precariously to the base of the brain, acts as a biological photo-electric cell. In dogs and cats, for example, as the days grow longer in the springtime, the pineal absorbs more light (entering through the eye) and triggers the pituitary gland to act upon the ovaries and other sources of hormone. At that time the family pet becomes restless, then agitated, then overwhelmed with the desire for sex.

Beth's deeply-buried sexual instincts operate another way. She is most receptive sexually each month just before ovulation. However, her sexual feelings intensify dramatically during warm weather since the pineal gland is attuned to the long summer hours of sunlight. No one knows exactly why, but among human beings conception (and incidentally marriage) seems to reach its peak around June twenty-second, the longest day of the year. One possible reason, rooted in man's primitive past, might be that infants

conceived at that time will be born about April first
of the following year. This gives the new child a full
six months to grow strong before the cold weather
sets in. Not very important to babies born in Beverly
Hills, but for a child who saw the light of day in a
cave 50,000 years ago those first few months were
critical.

Do many women react the same way?

The majority of modern women feel the tremendous
pull of hormones each month. The impulses may
never reach the surface in their original form. Some
women simply experience a ravenous appetite for a
few days each month. Others become cross and irrita-
ble just before the onset of menstruation. A few
women experience profound depression before their
period. Many of those who have these non-sexual
symptoms related to menstruation are women who
are unwilling or unable to acknowledge their sexual
feelings. They succeed in suppressing their sexual desires in response to the increased output of hormones,
but the emotional pressure is there and must be released in some form.

Sheri's response was a common one: unbearable
headaches for three days before each period. She is
thirty-one and has been married five years—her relationship with her husband is good but restrained.
She had been brought up to believe that it was not
"respectable" for women to show any interest in sex.
When she was flooded with hormones each month, a
crisis occurred. To comply with her unconscious desires would go against her mother's instructions. To
ignore the internal rumblings was impossible. She decided, unconsciously, to compromise. Bad headaches

solved the problem nicely. To Mother they signified, "See, I don't really care about sex," and to her own inner wishes, "Gee, I'd like to do it, but I feel so sick!" Everything was fine except Mother didn't care about Sheri anymore (if she ever did), Sheri's husband, Bill, did the cooking and cleaning three days a month, and Sheri had terrible headaches. But Sheri was a thoughtful girl and suspected there was something going on behind the mental scenes. She consulted a psychiatrist who had an unusual idea:

"Just as an experiment, Sheri, this coming month why don't you arrange to have intercourse with your husband on each of the four days just before your period starts, that is, starting one day before your headaches begin?"

"But that sounds silly, Doctor. What if Bill and I don't feel like it?"

"This month don't worry about it. Do it as if I had written you a prescription."

"Oh, that sounds silly, Doctor, but if you think it'll work I'll try it. I can't take many more headaches like these."

Three weeks later she returned to report on the experiment.

"Doctor, I just can't believe it. For the first time since before I got married I didn't have a headache before my period, not even a twinge!" With a smile she added, "Say, is that treatment any good for dry skin?"

How do single women handle the problem?

It isn't easy. The monthly surges of hormones with their accompanying sexual symptoms, either disguised or obvious, are hard enough for a married woman to handle, but for a single woman they can be almost unbearable. This is another area where unrealistic "morality" comes face-to-face with biology. There is no denying the fact that sexual organs were designed to be used regularly and frequently. If reproduction were the only goal of sexuality, then the genitalia are vastly over-designed. To meet the needs of preserving the species, flimsy disposable sexual organs would be sufficient. They could be used about once a year for ten years or so and then merely discarded like an aluminum beer can. Fortunately it doesn't happen that way. (Having beer cans strewn over the countryside is bad enough.)

Why is sex so important to a woman?

For a number of reasons. The vagina and clitoris remain in perfect functioning condition for about thirty years *after* the uterus and ovaries have gone to their final rest. It seems obvious that sexual organs and sexuality have a far more important role to play in human destiny than merely replenishing the population. If one looks beyond reproduction, some interesting results of sexual intercourse begin to come into focus. First of all, there is the indescribable feeling of well-being that comes from vigorous copulation. The emotional release, the dissipation of tension, the sense of fulfillment after orgasm have no equivalent in any other human experience. Sexual intercourse is the only remaining activity in which the over-controlled, over-regulated, self-conscious modern woman can completely let herself go and experience the sheer euphoria and animal exuberence that dwells within her.

Secondly, *the key to eternal femininity lies within*

the sexual act. In every group of women there are one or two who stand out. They seem younger, more alert, more vibrant, than those around them. Even in their fifties, they are attractive to men and have a zest for life. Almost without exception, these are the ones who have had a long, active, and still interesting sex life.

Why is that?

It works like this: although the ovaries and adrenal glands work under the influence of the pituitary gland, the mechanism is a two-way street. Impulses are fed back from these sex hormone producers to the master gland, the pituitary. With each copulation, and to a greater extent with each orgasm, nerve impulses from the clitoris and vagina are sent directly to the brain. They act on the posterior pituitary and then on the anterior pituitary, triggering it to stimulate further production of sex hormones by the ovaries and adrenals. In addition, at the time of orgasm, the blood supply of the ovaries increases tremendously and allows substantially more estrogen to flow outward into the bloodstream and into the sexual organs themselves.

The process quickly develops into a beneficial cycle where more sex produces more hormones which produce greater interest and deeper gratification from sexual activity. The big bonus comes from the effect of estrogenic hormone on the female body. Besides developing and maintaining clitoris, vagina, breasts, uterus, ovaries and other sexual structures, sex hormones are the essence of femininity. Firm, wrinkle-free skin, soft hair, attractive curves (due to flattering distribution of subcutaneous body fat), good posture and a supple spine (from adequate calcium and phosphorus deposits in the bones), absence of excessive facial hair, and most important the joy of being an alluring vibrant woman, all depend on estrogens. *The more a woman fulfills her sexual role, the more female she becomes.*

What keeps single women from satisfying their sexual needs?

Nothing except the full force of our society. One of the greatest social injustices of the twentieth century is the denial to the single woman of her womanly birthright. In most parts of the country, a single woman, unmarried, widowed, or divorced, who has sexual relations with a man is technically a criminal. (By a fascinating quirk in the laws of some states, if the woman is a homosexual, her sexual activities are not illegal and apparently have the blessing of society.) Even if she is not prosecuted as a criminal she is made to *feel* like a criminal by all those who sit in judgment of her.

Karen knows how it feels. She is twenty-eight and unmarried. But her ovaries can't tell the difference. Karen is sophisticated and articulate but that doesn't seem to make her life any easier. Let her tell it:

"I'm an interior decorator, Doctor, and I spent six years learning my profession. I'm not ready to get married yet. Just now I'd rather decorate beautiful rooms with beautiful things than decorate some tract house with squalling kids. Maybe that will come someday but not just yet. But what really bothers me is they're driving me out of my mind."

"Who are 'they'?"

"It seems like the whole crazy world is against me!

Whenever I bring one of my boyfriends home for dinner, my landlady peeks through her curtain as if I were some kind of B-girl. I pay my rent every month and I didn't see anything in the lease that says she only rents to virgins. If I have sex twice a week with someone I'm really fond of, everyone considers me cheap. If I do it once a month with a husband I hate, I'm a pillar of society. Somebody's mixed up!"

"Do you plan to get married one day?"

"Of course. But that's not the point." Karen smiled wryly. "You know what that license entitles you to do, Doctor, and for the time being in spite of what everyone thinks, I'm going to drive my body without a license."

Karen has worked out some kind of compromise between her own unsuppressible sexual feelings and the impossible demands society makes on single women. But she pays a stiff price—guilt. Even though what she is doing—using her sexual equipment the way it was intended with the best possible partner she can find—she still feels the impulse to apologize, to explain that what she's doing is really all right.

Why does Karen feel so guilty?

One reason she feels that way about sex, in spite of her intelligence and sophistication, can be illustrated by an interesting social custom of certain African tribes. At the age of thirteen, each girl in the tribe undergoes a terrifying operation. Two fat ladies hold down the screaming child while another lady removes the clitoris and labia minor with a broken piece of glass. After the bleeding stops and the infection heals, the now-mutilated teen-ager is accepted into the tribe as a woman. (Broken glass being what it is, there is always an infection.) She has paid the price of admission to her society—submitting to a sadistic and mutilating operation. The most fascinating part of this quaint ritual is that *the victim never refuses*. In spite of all the pain and suffering, she submits. It is not that she is eager to have part of her genitals hacked off but that she has a desperate need to be accepted as part of the group. She has no way of knowing that girls in New York, Beverly Hills, and a thousand other places celebrate the onset of puberty in a somewhat less flamboyant fashion. Even if she learned that American teenagers are expected to keep everything they started out with it would make no difference because semicastration on entering womanhood is the only way she knows. In her society it has been that way for hundreds of years—for the African Miss, there is no alternative.

Every unmarried American woman is expected to pay her own price for being accepted in her society. That price is to deny and suppress her sexual activity. In our modern world we shudder at the thought of depriving a girl of her clitoris and labia. We allow her to keep her sexual organs intact. We only make it impossible for her to use them, except under carefully delineated and socially-approved circumstances. For some women the effect is the same as not having any genitals at all. Maybe the Africans are a little more honest about it.

Does it really affect American girls that much?

Apparently. Carol's experience is a good example. She is a nurse, thirty-seven years old and divorced. She was brought up in a small town in Nebraska:

"Doctor, I honestly believe I was seventeen before

I knew I *had* sexual organs. My parents and everyone else in town were strictly religious and they followed the Bible literally. No smoking, no drinking, no dancing, no lipstick, and certainly, no sex! Sometimes I wonder how anyone was ever born in our family!" She laughed nervously.

"As far back as I can remember, everyone I respected—my mother, my father, the minister, all my teachers—preached to me about one part of my body being wicked. They called it my "privates" and honestly I really didn't know what they meant until I started to menstruate. I was too scared to ask. I wasn't even supposed to think about it. I remember wondering how anything could be so dangerous and still be part of the body." Carol pulled her skirt down over her knees, then pulled her hands away suddenly.

"You'll have to excuse me, Doctor, even after thirty years it's hard to get rid of the same old habits. 'Pull your skirt down. Keep your legs together. Don't sit in such a shameful way!' It's been ground into me so often I feel suffocated!" She regained her composure in a few moments.

"Would you care to smoke?"

She smiled. "No, thank you. That's one of the few things I'm glad I learned not to do."

"Have you ever been married?"

A deep sigh. "Yes. Yes, Doctor, I've been married. God, was I ever married!" Tears.

When she was twenty-three, Carol was married to a young man selected by her parents and approved by her minister. His ignorance of sex was less than hers but his guilt was much greater. Their wedding night was a tragedy of mutual fumbling. About three A.M. the bridegroom contributed premature ejaculation and the bride responded with complete frigidity. Carol shook her head:

"Actually, looking back on it, it was one of our better nights. At least we tried. From then on we avoided sex as much as possible. After awhile we began to avoid each other and our marriage just petered out. I guess when the divorce came through we were both kind of relieved."

Years of being taught that sex was "nasty" and "wrong" had paved the way for the fiasco that masqueraded as a marriage. For these two, things were reversed. Attempts at sexual intercourse produced anxiety, sexual deprivation provided relief. Ultimately, when Carol was excused (by the divorce court) from the responsibility of performing as a grown woman, she regressed to the level of a nine-year-old whose awareness of sex is limited to keeping her skirt below her knees.

Fortunately, Carol recognized that there must be a better way to live. She began psychiatric treatment, quickly gained insight into her conflict, made rapid progress, and finally accepted sex as an enjoyable part of her daily life. As a matter of fact, she enjoyed it immensely. Toward the end of her treatment she said:

"You know, Doctor, the past few months have been so wonderful for me I almost feel as if *I* invented sex. But I realize that these feelings were inside me all along—you just helped me discover them."

How about older women?

For them the transition may not be quite so easy. Joyce was one of these. Three years ago, when she was forty-seven, her husband was killed in an auto accident. Trim and well-dressed, she supports herself selling real estate. She sounds upset:

"If I understand you correctly, Doctor, what you're saying is impossible! For the past fifty years I've been living a clean decent life and now you say that I should have any kind of sex with anyone I want to! Why that's disgusting!"

"Where did you get the idea that I said that?"

"Didn't you say, 'Sexual activity is natural and everyone has to have it'?"

"Yes, but that's a lot different from your version. It seems to me there are two ingredients to every sexual experience—the mechanical and the emotional. The mechanical part brings the sexual organs into contact with each other—that's the easy part. The emotional aspect makes sex enjoyable, or terrible, depending on the relationship between the people. 'Having any kind of sex with anyone' is a pretty good way to be disappointed. It's not really on my list of recommendations."

"But my husband was a clean man. He never lowered himself when it came to sex."

"But who said that sex was unclean? And except anatomically speaking, there is nothing low about sex. How was your sexual relationship with your husband?"

"None of your business! What kind of question is that?"

"I'm sorry but that's the kind of question I have to ask if I'm going to be able to help you with your problems."

Her face flushed angrily. After a few gulps of coffee she was in control of herself again.

"I'm sorry. I've been lying to myself for so many years it's hard to face the truth. What was sex like with my husband? What would you call thirty sec-

onds every two weeks? The pause that refreshes?
Hardly. I was telling the truth when I said my husband was a clean man when it came to sex. He was
so clean he never even touched me except for that
unavoidable inch or two. I kept telling myself that
my mother was right, that good women didn't enjoy
sex. Well, Doctor, I must have been the best woman
in the entire world because for twenty-five years if I
had a choice between brushing my teeth and going
to bed with my husband, I would've taken the toothbrush every time. At least the toothpaste makes your
mouth tingle."

"Okay, Joyce, you're getting on the right track.
Honesty, even if it hurts, is the only way to deal with
this kind of problem."

"Goodness knows I'm ready. I have an awful lot of
lost years to make up for."

Joyce attacked her sexual problems with the same
energy she devoted to selling real estate. The results
were dramatic in both departments. She soon accepted sex as natural and after three months, experienced her first orgasm. Each sexual experience
was a new revelation for her. On her last visit she told
me:

"Well, I've finally found a way to combine my two
new obsessions in life. There is nothing I enjoy more
than having sex and selling real estate, in that order.
Now I'm going to bring them together. Next week I'm
marrying a most talented man in both fields—my
boss!"

Why are many people so ashamed of sex?

One of the real tragedies of recent times is the attempted corruption of the human body. A small

group of moral crusaders, working with that fevered devotion seen only in the mentally deranged, has been trying to convince every American that the perfectly synchronized, beautifully designed, elegantly planned mechanisms of their bodies are nasty, filthy, and horrid. They nearly succeeded in the case of menstruation. That physiological masterpiece which makes human reproduction unique has been distorted by those who should know better into a curse and a sickness. In reality menstruation signifies perfect health. The ounce or two of blood that is passed each month is the banner of a normal reproductive system. If blood is unclean, imagine what the moral crusaders can make of a nosebleed.

When it comes to sexual intercourse, the guerrilla fighters for purity bring on their big guns. Their favorite word is "dirty"—and they are wrong again. By every test, sexual intercourse is probably the purest and daintiest activity that a man and woman can engage in, aside from being the most enjoyable. The genitals themselves are normally free of harmful bacteria, the secretions are perfectly sterile, and the penis and vagina were obviously designed to be brought together in their own inimitable style. By contrast, the throat of every person, including the anti-sex orators, is crammed with a dozen varieties of lethal bacteria. These include the bugs that cause diphtheria, gonorrhea, strep throat, and rheumatic fever. If they want to start a crusade, it should probably begin in their own noses and mouths.

Actually the sexual reformers are on the wrong track. If they really hope to make men and women afraid of themselves, they might devote their attention to other organ systems. Breathing offers a good opportunity. We take in good clean air and pervert it into bad breath! Only a few cynical mouthwash salesmen have jumped on that one, but there is plenty of room for moral education about how the body ruins God-given oxygen. Sweating is another good area. Fifty thousand years ago human beings used their noses as much as their eyes. They could identify a stranger by his smell and could distinguish approaching animals and men by their specific odors. The need for that talent has diminished somewhat but the human aroma still clings to man. It is now known as "body odor" and must be eliminated at all costs. A human who smells like a human is headed for social and occupational disaster. In order to be accepted by the rest of his race, his breath must reek of carbolic acid, his armpits give off the scent of gardenias, and his skin exude hexachlorophene. A few years ago chlorophyll tablets were developed to expunge once and for all every trace of human smells. (As a tribute to man's sanity, they were tried and quickly discarded by all except fugitives wishing to avoid the bloodhounds.)

Perhaps the last frontier for those reformers who want to protect us against ourselves is the digestive system. If they really concentrated they might be able to spoil the pleasure of eating for a hundred million or so fellow citizens. All they would need to do would be to explain, "When you take that beautiful food, provided for you by Heaven's bounty, and put it into your body, it is attacked by filthy chemicals and changed into a green stinking mass. Do you know what that food finally becomes? Do you know what it is turned into?"

The lecture would have to stop at this point because the devoted moralists couldn't say the word.

Then sex is all right?

Every organ, every secretion, every cell of the human body was put there by nature, by the Creator, for a purpose. The respiratory system, the digestive system, the sweat glands, all have a vital function in the preservation of the body. The sexual organs are no exception. For the past few hundred years, not more than a fleeting moment in the history of mankind, a strange collection of misguided do-gooders and moralizing misfits have tried to make us forget how we all arrived in this world. They miss the point. Ever since the beginning of the human race, sexual intercourse has been the most noble and wholesome of all man's activities. In spite of the shrill protests of those self-appointed moral guardians, nothing is going to change that. Every woman, *married or not,* deserves the freedom to enjoy the ultimate expression of her sexual potential. With knowledge and determination and courage, that achievement is within her grasp.

THE WOMAN
WHO NEVER MARRIED

Why is it that some women never marry?

The answer isn't easy. Among the sweetest words any woman ever hears are, "Will you marry me, darling?" Yet there are more than nine million American women, who have never heard these words at all—or if they have, weren't listening. The vast majority of them are healthy, intelligent, attractive human beings who are directing the course of their lives stubbornly against the tide of society. To do something as dramatic and as difficult as that, they must have some pretty good reasons.

Our American way of life is designed, like Noah's Ark, for those who march two-by-two. Nearly every form of entertainment from sports cars to king-sized beds is designed for the mutual enjoyment of a man and a woman. At parties, at clubs, at bars, at virtually every pleasurable activity in this land of supreme pleasures, a woman alone feels *and is made to feel* out of tune with the rest of the world.

Even more emphatically, the most "successful" women in our culture are constantly in the company of a man. In that great electronic mirror of modern society, television, there is no place for an unescorted woman. From situation comedy to soap commercial, every desirable lady is firmly attached to an eager male. The outstanding exceptions are the forlorn damsels who impulsively snatched the wrong personal product from the drugstore shelf. These foolish girls are punished by being forced to spend an entire evening *alone*. Before the commercial ends, salvation appears in the form of an understanding friend who sympathizes with the victim and explains the virtues of the sponsor's product. Once she convinces the offender—who by that time is so miserable she is willing to try anything—to use the right deodorant or mouthwash, the screen instantly fills with the image of a smiling lass embracing a lusty young man. Even to slow learners the message is clear: if there is a fate worse than death, it is to be alone on Saturday night.

What effect does this have on a single woman?

In this country every woman who is not married by the age of twenty-one is treated as if she were suffering from a progressive disease that makes the bubonic plague seem like a bad cold. Until the age of thirty, the chances of recovery are considered favorable and the victim is allowed to mingle freely with the rest of society. As the years slip by the outlook dims and the period of quarantine begins. Those of her friends who are engaged or going steady, and the natural elite who are already married, slowly withdraw to avoid becoming contaminated.

After the age of thirty she is the topic of hushed conversation. "Did you know that Ellen is *thirty-one* and doesn't even have a steady boyfriend?" This is the equivalent of saying, "I just heard from Ellen's doctor—the poor dear has only a few months to live!"

As the thirty-fifth year comes into view, even Ellen's single girl friends begin to avoid her as if absence of a husband were some crippling malady that might infect them all. Upon celebrating her fortieth birthday, she is officially consigned to emotional limbo from which she is resurrected on certain special occasions. She is dragged out for exciting opportunities such as blind dates with somebody's uncle from Pittsburgh "who has made wonderful progress with his drinking problem," although that progress may not be apparent on the evening she goes out with him. Some other wonderful chances come her way like Billy who is thirty-nine, "dresses with a flair but never really got interested in girls" and Ralphie "who knows how to show a girl a good time." It turns out to be true about Ralphie—if a girl's idea of a good time is spending the evening watching a three-hundred pound man eat.

Is society really that hard on women who don't marry?

It gets worse. In a hypocritical way the unmarried woman is constantly assured that all her problems will be solved if only she will say the right words. In her case the words are supposed to be: "I do." But she doesn't. In spite of all the pressure she resolutely rejects the idea that the solution to everything that confounds her is a massive dose of matrimony. But society (most of it married) persists. Or as one patient put it, "My mother thinks all I need to solve my problems is a name-transplant—performed by a minister." And mothers didn't begin their campaign last week.

When did *they begin?*

About the age of three. Mother and Grandmother begin to bear down on little girls early: "Now when you grow up and get married . . ." It continues as the toddlers start to play house: "You be the Mommy and I'll be the Daddy." The urging intensifies with grammar school and reaches an almost unbearable crescendo in high school, as members of the senior class begin to leave on their honeymoons. The pressure for a single woman to marry is only slightly less than an elephant standing on her chest. From every corner of our existence—movies, magazine ads, television, billboards—the subliminal but urgent message rings out: "If you want to get with it, get married!" All through the day (and most of the night) there is a constant background hum that tells every single girl to become a married girl. It doesn't tell her why or how or who—it just tells her to do it.

How do single girls react to this pressure?

Every girl has her own unique reaction but Jennie's case is typical. She is thirty-one and a fashion designer. Slim and supple, her pale skin and dark eyes give her an intense quality, evident in her opening words:

"Doctor, I have everything in the world except the one thing I want. And no matter how hard I try, I just can't seem to get my hands on it."

"What is it that you want?"

She smiled. "Just what every other girl wants—a man of my own. The worst part is I *have* plenty of men but I can't seem to make any of them stick to me."

"What do you mean?"

"Well, that's why I'm here. I have a wonderful job, I earn a good salary, and I *think* I'm attractive. I really do want to get married and I have plenty of opportunities. I go out a lot—at least three or four times a week—and with really eligible men. Airline pilots, vice-presidents, advertising men—you know, every girl's dream. But for me it's turning into a nightmare!"

Her voice trembled and she bit her lip—hard. Then she went on. "Sometimes I wish I could just buy a husband so I could keep him! *The way it is now, I'm in the rent-a-man business!*"

"*Rent-a-man?*"

"Yes. I get along fine with all the men I go out with. We go skiing and sailing and we even spend great weekends in little mountain cabins, but when Monday morning comes I give back the skis and the cabin and the rented car and I turn in the boyfriend along with them. Then I go home alone to my charming but empty apartment. That makes it twice as bad. It's like seeing a preview of how great marriage could be but never being allowed to stay for the whole movie. I'm getting to the point where I don't even want to go out at all. I'd rather not get my hopes up and then be disappointed."

"You said you get along fine with all of them. What do you mean by that?"

"Well, men seem to be comfortable with me right away. They explain it this way—with other girls they feel a tension in the air, a sort of hunter-and-hunted atmosphere. With me they know there's nothing to worry about. I'm not going to make them worry about getting roped into something."

"Tell me about your parents."

"The less said about them, the better, Doctor. My parents' marriage was an emotional disaster area.

They fought from the first day I can remember until they were divorced when I was nine. After that I lived with my grandmother and never really saw them again. That's the reason I'm so anxious to have a happy marriage of my own."

During the course of the next few visits, a few other facts about Jennie's relationships with men came to the surface. It turned out she was friendly with literally dozens of men. She liked them and they liked her but she firmly resisted any attempts to make the friendship any more serious.

If she really wanted to get married, why did she act that way?

Jennie's explanation went like this:

"It's just that I want to be sure everything is right between us. The last thing in the world I'm looking for is a re-run of that mental boxing match my mother and father carried on for fifteen years. I want to get married but I have to be careful."

As it turned out, Jennie's definition of being "careful" was to keep her relationships with men "just friendly" until she was "sure." Jennie considered each candidate carefully, the months flew by, and long before she came to a decision her boyfriends became impatient and found other girls. Jennie said she was battling desperately to find a husband. Perhaps. But at the same time she was engaged in a more frantic struggle at a deeper level. Her wish to marry was effectively countered by the gnawing fear that her marriage would be a carbon copy of her parents' fiasco. For her there was only one solution—suspended animation. She attracted and repelled men simultaneously. She was eager and willing to get married—up to (but not including) the moment that marriage became a real possibility.

What could she do to solve her problem?

Her only solution was to understand it—not superficially but at the deepest emotional level where the problem existed. Psychiatric treatment helped her to recognize the discrepancy between what she *said* she wanted and what she *really* wanted. By tracing her early reactions to her parents' disastrous marriage and relating them to her current outlook on matrimony, she gradually became aware of how she sabotaged her own chances for happiness. Once things came into focus, she didn't waste any time. Some time after her first visit, she arrived for her appointment wearing a wedding ring.

"It looks like we have a new subject to discuss today, Jennie."

She grinned. "No, Doctor, it's an old subject that Jennie started doing her homework in. Yesterday I got married to Mike. I know it sounds strange, but I've known him since I came to New York about nine years ago. I gave him the same 'I have to be sure' routine I dragged all the other guys through but he was the nicest about it. He finally walked out on me like the rest of the men but at least he said, 'When you're really ready to get married, let me know.'"

"That was four years ago. I woke up at one o'clock the night before last and suddenly all the pieces seemed to fit together simultaneously. I knew it was a crazy thing to do but I got up and sent Mike a telegram."

"What did you say?"

"I really didn't know what to say so I just sent one word: 'READY!' and signed it, 'Jennie.' After I did I felt relaxed all over and went back to bed. I was awakened by a knock on the door about 5:30 in the morning and when I opened it, there was Mike. He had a wedding ring in one hand and a corsage in the other. I got dressed, we jumped into his car, raced to the airport, flew to Virginia, got married, and flew back."

Jennie paused, then went on:

"I'm just lucky he was still available after I spent four years telling myself all those wonderful self-righteous little lies. I am absolutely the happiest woman in the whole world—I want everybody to know it!" Jennie's grin filled the entire room.

"I'm delighted that things are happening the way you wanted them to. There's just one question: Where did Mike get a corsage at that hour?"

"I wondered about that too. It seems that this crazy city has everything—including an all-night florist for people who want to get married in the middle of the night."

"And the wedding ring? Is there an all-night jeweler too?"

"That puzzled me for awhile until I asked Mike about it. He said he was so much in love with me when we were going out before that he bought a wedding ring just in case he should have to use it in an emergency. Well, I guess you could call my telegram an emergency—a kind of delayed-action emergency."

Is it that easy for everyone to get married?

Not by any stretch of the imagination. Jennie was lucky in many ways. Her game was matrimonial brinksmanship. She dated men, brought them to the very edge of marriage, and then drew back at the last moment. An important part of her method was to keep herself as attractive as possible to assure a constant supply of admirers. Her social life was a full one and all her activities were superficially directed toward marriage. Once she gave up her wish to remain single, she only had to change her approach a little and everything worked out according to her new plans. It doesn't always happen that way. Sometimes the unconscious mind chooses techniques that can't be turned off so quickly.

What kinds of techniques are those?

There are many of them, but the one Marge used was typical. She was twenty-seven, had the face of an angel, a keen mind, and a good job—interior decorator for a large motel chain. She dressed well but there was one problem:

"Doctor, I don't know how it happened. I've spent the better part of a year trying to understand it but I can't make any headway. That's why I'm here."

"How much do you weigh?"

"Without my clothes, two-hundred and five. But when I graduated from high school, nine years ago, I weighed one-hundred and thirty, which is about right for five feet seven. I can't help it and I know I'm eating myself into a lonely old age." She paused. "You don't have to tell me—I know what's ahead. When all the other girls have a husband and children, I can look forward to evenings with a good book, a faithful cat, and—a bowl of nice hot spaghetti. I don't want that! I know what you're going to say about that too. If I don't want it why did I bring it on? I don't know. That's why I'm here."

"When did you start putting on weight?"

"As soon as I left high school."

"You mean as soon as you were in danger of getting married?"

Marge's face turned bright red. "I—I never thought of that. But it makes sense. There's one thing that my mother once said that I've never been able to forget. It was just before the last week of high school. She told me: 'As soon as you graduate, Marge, you better start looking around for a husband because I'm certainly not going to support you the rest of your life!' That really must have made an impression on me because that's when I became one of the world's champion eaters. I guess I was so terrified at the prospect of leaving my mother that I was willing to do anything to keep myself at home. Wow, I sure was mixed up! I guess I'm still mixed up. Doctor, do you think you can help me?"

As the story began to unfold, Marge's mother emerged as cold, indifferent, and remote. Her method of controlling her daughter (and incidentally her husband as well) had been to dispense affection in carefully measured doses and withdraw it at the first sign of independence. When it looked as if Marge might be getting ready to go out on her own, her mother made her famous threat—long before her daughter was ready for it. Marge panicked and fought desperately to maintain her dependence on Mother. The weapons she used were her teeth, applied to hamburgers, hot dogs, and her mother's favorite recipe—mashed potatoes. To Marge, the discomfort of weighing over two hundred pounds and the frustration of a lifetime of loneliness were less painful than the thought of losing what little affection her mother had for her. In emotional terms, the greater the fear, the more desperate the defense against it—and Marge had plenty of fear. A month or so after her first visit she explained:

"Since that first day here, Doctor, I've done a lot

of thinking. I realized I was a fugitive from marriage. My idea of running away to keep from finding a husband has been hiding behind an enormous pile of mashed potatoes. I've been hibernating in pounds of blubber and it's time to get out while I still can. You tell me what to do and I'll do it!"

Marge kept her word. In less than a year she made significant progress. She began to understand the real meaning of her obesity and lost sixty pounds. She was still unmarried but as she put it, "It's only a matter of time—all those beautiful men can't hide from me much longer." Some months later there was a long distance phone call from Marge. She had moved to another city.

"It's Marge—remember me, Doc? I was the two-hundred-pound weakling?" She laughed. "Well, I just wanted to tell you since I saw you last I've gained another one-hundred sixty pounds." She laughed again. "His name is Mark and we're getting married next month. And let me tell you, he's more fun than mashed potatoes."

Aren't there some women who just don't want to get married?

Emotionally speaking Jennie and Marge seemed to be miles apart. Jennie was glamorous and sophisticated, Marge was average in looks and without a polished veneer. But they had one vital point in common—a genuine and compelling desire to get married. With that as the starting point, all they needed was insight into their underlying emotional attitudes. Marriage followed as a matter of course. Not every single girl is in that position. Some women reject marriage. They feel most of the reasons advanced by society in justification for marriage just don't make sense. Many

people, both men and women, find the social custom
known as matrimony baffling and frustrating. Sharon
was one of them. She is thirty-nine and assistant to
the head of the chemistry department at a large university. She is pert, efficient, and direct:

"Marriage just doesn't make sense anymore, Doctor
—if it ever did."

"What do you mean?"

"Well, let's take the reasons one by one. First of all,
there's the religious reasons. According to some people, their religion says they have to get married. Most
of them are misinformed. Actually there is no legal
marriage ceremony mentioned in the Bible and in
those days people never got married anyway—at
least not the kind of marriage we think of. They just
found somebody they liked, reached an understanding, and lived together.

"Then there are the moral reasons. You know, get-
ging married is better than living in sin and all that
nonsense. It seems to me that spending thirty years
beating each other's brains out and calling it marriage
is really living in sin." Sharon frowned.

"Then there's the part about making a home for
the children. Again, wouldn't it be better for the children to grow up in a nice friendly orphanage instead
of taking eighteen years of persecution from parents
who never wanted to have them and can't wait to get
rid of them?"

"You've spent a lot of time thinking about this,
haven't you, Sharon?"

"Well, I try to use my brain to make my life easier."
She raised one eyebrow. "May I continue?"

"Certainly."

"Where was I? Oh, yes, I was talking about the
children. There are many different ways to raise children these days and marriage isn't necessarily the
best way. For example in the Israeli kibbutz, children

spend very little time with their parents and don't seem to be any the worse for it. And the most important reason of all is that in this modern world, marriage as a social institution is obsolete." She smiled resolutely.

"Take me for example. I earn my own living, I have a pension fund to take care of my old age, I don't feel emotionally dependent on anyone and I take my sex where I find it. I certainly never feel deprived in *that* area."

"What you've said certainly sounds logical. What about having children?"

Sharon smiled—or almost smiled. "I haven't figured that one out yet. But I'm working on it."

"Well, Sharon, I only have one more question. Do *you* want to get married?"

She spoke slowly, emphasizing each word:

"What do you think I'm doing here? Of course I want to get married! If I could manage it on my own, do you think I'd have to think up a thousand excuses for *not* doing it? Can you help me?"

Sharon's distaste for marriage was really no more than a superficial defense. Discouraged, frustrated, nearing the matrimonial deadline of the fortieth year, her approach was to run away from reality, deny her own fears and shortcomings and put all the blame on marriage. Actually, it was a facade—she welcomed the chance to prepare herself for all the aspects of married life she pretended to scorn.

But aren't there some girls who really don't want to get married at all?

Certainly. Some women absolutely reject the concept of marriage and try to fashion a new way of life for themselves. Lorraine was one of those. At twenty-eight she looked like an advertisement for suntan lotion. Tall, well-proportioned, she had high cheek bones, long blond hair and penetrating blue eyes. She teaches art at a junior college.

"I know how you feel about marriage, Doctor, but I think you're wrong."

"Fine. Let's hear about it."

"This idea of one man and one woman doesn't make sense anymore. For example, in the past ten years I've lived with six different men and enjoyed every one of them. We had complete sexual freedom and yet made no demands on each other. We got what we wanted out of the relationship and then without any obligation, moved on to the next stage in our lives. As far as I'm concerned, marriage is obsolete."

"How long did you live with each man?"

"It varied from six months to two years."

"What kind of arrangement did you have?"

"That varied too. Usually we rented an apartment together. Once we spent a year touring Europe in a camper—it was marvelous."

"Did you ever become pregnant?"

"Yes, three times but I had an abortion each time. Is there anything wrong with that?" She frowned.

"Under the circumstances I think it was an excellent solution."

"What do you mean?"

"Obviously you didn't want to have children and there was no realistic way to care for them. Having an abortion is your privilege in a situation like that."

"I'm glad you feel that way. I was afraid I was going to get a sermon." She smiled.

"You're in the wrong office for that." She smiled again.

"That's why I'm here. My mother is a very religious woman and has been making my life unbearable.

She's had her minister call me at least once a week to try to get me to 'change my ways.' I finally got her to agree to accept your opinion about it. I mean, can't you tell her that things have changed and if a girl decides not to marry, there's nothing wrong with it?"

"Certainly. As far as I'm concerned it's not the psychiatrist's job to pass moral judgment. His goal should be to help patients find the greatest possible happiness in this mortal existence. It would've been all right with me if you'd never gotten married."

Lorraine's eyes widened. "What do you mean, *'if I'd never got married'*? I never have been married!"

"But didn't you tell me that you set up a household with six separate men, cooked and cleaned for them, had sexual intercourse with them, got pregnant by some of them, and conducted yourself like a wife in every other way? The only thing you didn't do was take out a marriage license and as you know that's only a formality."

Lorraine was holding her head with both hands and rocking back and forth.

"Is everything all right?"

"He explodes my entire world and asks if everything is all right!" Suddenly she began to laugh, slowly and softly at first, then faster and louder until she could barely stay in the chair. Tears rolled down her cheek in torrents. Finally the deluge subsided.

"It's the funniest thing I ever heard! You're right! You're right! I thought I was the wave of the future. I thought I was blazing new trails of feminine freedom. And all I accomplished was six short-term marriages and two cases of bigamy that I didn't get to tell you about yet."

It was even worse than Lorraine suspected. After making a list of dates and places it turned out that two of her "non-marriages" had been legally binding.

How can a "non-marriage" be legally binding?

In many parts of the country, if a man and woman set up housekeeping together, whether they plan it that way or not, after a reasonable amount of time (usually six months or more) they have cemented a common-law marriage. According to the law, this relationship is virtually identical in every way to the conventional marriage the parties are trying so hard to avoid. The only thing missing is the marriage certificate. The husband is obligated to support his wife (and of course any children that ensue), the wife has the right to inherit his earthly goods when he goes to a better world, and they are bound by all the dozens of other legal formalities that have become part of marriage over the years. Ironically, in rushing toward "the new sexual freedom," many liberated spirits find themselves living out a carbon copy of the kinds of lives they are so desperately trying to avoid.

During one of the periods when she was rebelling most vigorously against the "enslavement" of marriage, Lorraine's routine went something like this:

After a hard day at the art department, she would stop off at the supermarket on her way home to pick up some things for dinner. Usually Tim, whom she was living with at the time, was already home from work. He had the cocktails mixed and they had a drink together before she fixed dinner. After dinner, he helped her with the dishes and if they weren't too tired, they went out to a movie. Otherwise they watched television until about eleven o'clock and then went to bed. Two or three nights a week they had sexual intercourse before they went to sleep.

What's the difference between that relationship and the usual type of marriage?

There are several. First, there is no wedding picture on top of the dresser. Second, there is no wedding certificate in the safety deposit box. Third, both parties think of themselves as daringly unconventional.

As Lorraine said later on:

"You know, living together is pretty much like having a second-rate marriage—except it has one really big advantage—when you finally break up, you never have to pay for a divorce."

Lorraine was mistaken. Living together (in many states) has no advantage over marriage—second-rate or otherwise. If either party chooses to assert his rights —as many of them have—the relationship can only be legally dissolved by divorce. Unless the partner with an itchy foot is willing to take the risk of bigamy, he (or she) has to terminate the imitation marriage with a genuine divorce. But the biggest problem with living together as a substitute for marriage is the same problem that exists with every substitute— it is a pale imitation of the real article.

What prevents ten percent of all women from even trying to achieve any kind of marriage?

The exact reason is different for every woman—in that sense each human being is unique. But the basic underlying problem is similar for most of those who choose, willingly or unwillingly, to be ones in a world of twos. The brain of *homo sapiens* (male or female version) can only think in terms of what has gone before. For example, when the first automobiles were developed—an entirely new concept—the average person could deal with the idea only in terms of something he already knew. Automobiles were known and accepted as "horseless carriages." In a similar way, every woman has her first emotional experience with her mother (or mother substitute). So much of what happens to her after that depends on that earliest and most vital of all experiences. If the mother is loving and affectionate, reassuring and tender, she produces a girl who is self-confident and optimistic and who is determined to reflect these qualities in any close relationship in adult life.

If the mother is indifferent and remote, if the girl has a childhood that is barren and empty of emotional fulfillment, the unfortunate young lady has no basis on which she can build a rewarding relationship with another human being—least of all a husband.

Then what does she do?

An unbelievable variety of things. Many women in this situation establish profound and lasting relationships with subhuman partners. These are ladies who substitute a cageful of parakeets for a living person. Others develop deep emotional ties which are guaranteed to be temporary by the very nature of the situation. Sometimes a woman like this devotes herself to a cause—to poor children overseas, or to improving understanding between diverse groups around the world. No one will deny that these are worthy endeavors, *but* the worthiest endeavor of all is planning for her own happiness.

What about the girl who has to take care of her parents?

Robin is a good example of that problem. She summarized the conflict well:

"What can I do? My mother is seventy-five now and she's completely senile. All she does is sit in her chair and watch television all day—even when the set isn't turned on. It's pathetic. I'm thirty-four and I have a good job—supervisor with the phone company —but I can't just abandon her."

"What do you think your mother's life expectancy is, Robin?"

"Oh, her doctor says she could live another five years—or she could go tomorrow."

"If she lasts five years you'll be thirty-nine."

Deep furrows appeared in her forehead. "Yes, I know, Doctor, that's why I'm here."

Robin quickly recognized that there was something peculiar in her compulsion to avoid even the thought of marriage until some unknown date in the future. She was engaged in a living lottery—and her unfortunate mother held the losing ticket. As long as Mother lived, Robin was in no danger of marrying. Fortunately it didn't take her long to realize that her attachment was not really so much to her mother as to the "obligation" her mother represented. In effect, she was hiding from marriage (and everything that goes along with it) behind the skirts of a senile woman. Poor Mother probably would have been happier in a quiet rest home than being forced to play the role of living alibi for a terrified daughter. When Robin finally got up the courage to make realistic plans for her mother, both of them were better off.

Are there any other reasons that women avoid marriage?

There is one other underlying motivation that most women who shun marriage have in common. In the deepest sense, marriage means more than just establishing an enduring relationship with another human being and taking on the care and feeding of a brood of children. The marriage ceremony is a formal termination of childhood. At that moment all the rules of the game of life change. Instead of being played for fun, from the moment the minister says, "I now pronounce you . . . ," everything is for keeps. The carefree little girl is instantly transformed into a woman who may have love in her heart but also has a man on her hands. Besides all the genuine joys of a happy marriage there is also breakfast to make every morning, dinner to cook every night, and the laundry in between. No matter how patient a man may be before the wedding bells ring, he expects things to be different after marriage. As a forgotten philosopher once said, "The one thing a woman never gets to the bottom of in marriage is the ironing basket."

Is there anything else that keeps women from getting married?

Yes—many single women have rejected all candidates for marriage simply because they do not live up to the girls' unrealistic expectations. No man in the world can stand comparison with the latest hero of television or movies. The reason should be obvious: the actor is paid big money to do just that—act. If

they behaved naturally on the screen or TV tube,
most male heart-throbs wouldn't be hired for a dog
food commercial. No flesh-and-blood man can begin
to compete with this impossible example. Girls who
are deeply attracted to the current stars of stage and
screen can save themselves a lot of unhappiness and
disappointment when it comes to evaluating a real
man by investing in a long distance telephone call to
their ideal's girl friend (or wife) of the moment. If
the lady is willing—and many of them are eager—in
three minutes of person-to-person comparison, many
single girls will realize that Charlie who works at the
bakery is a much better deal than the chap they see
on TV every Friday night.

But is marriage really so good?

Maybe not. Human beings are basically defective
and marriage, being a human institution, is far from
perfect. Unfortunately, at this stage of evolution of
the human race, there just aren't a lot of alternatives
to choose from. By a margin of nine to one, American
women have voted for marriage—they must have
found something to like.

For the one woman in ten who is convinced that
marriage is not for her, there are ways to be satisfied
though single. But for those who want to join the
other nine, insight and understanding into the basic
feelings of women and their men can help her get
what she wants—from her husband and from her life.

6

THE DIVORCED WOMAN

What is the hardest day in a woman's life?

It's difficult to say. But certainly one of the hardest days in a woman's life is the day after her divorce. Finally the battle is over. The bitter conflicts with her (ex) husband have been decided—usually in her favor. The crushing pressure of the previous months or years has lifted. The unbearable tension of the days leading up to the divorce has been dissipated. The material possessions of the two combatants have been meticulously divided right down to the golf trophies and the dog's leash. The only tangible evidence that a marriage once existed is a divorce certificate (in duplicate) and a stack of dusty papers in the bottom drawer of an old file cabinet in the County Clerk's office. By a flashing stroke of his gavel the judge symbolically severs the bonds of holy matrimony and magically restores the woman to exactly the same condition she was in the day before her marriage.

Exactly the same condition?

Well, there are a few differences. First of all, she is older. The precious months and years she squandered on a marriage that went bankrupt are gone forever. No earthly judge can change that. Secondly, at least for the moment, she is weaker. After hundreds of days of turmoil and bitterness she feels drained, cheated, exploited, disappointed. Most of the youthful enthusiasm and hope she brought to her wedding day have been cancelled along with the original contract.

But the biggest difference is the massive transition every woman has to make when she decides to go it alone—again. Suddenly, from one moment to another, she has traded all her old familiar problems for a whole new set of equally distressing and often totally unfamiliar ones. Some of the new tasks are simply tedious, like sleeping alone in a single bed again or figuring out when to have the oil changed in the car. Others are more annoying, like holding hands with yourself at the movies. For some women finding a new apartment or learning to cook for one person all over again make the first days after a divorce harder. The divorcée with children often has a hard time explaining why Daddy doesn't come home any more. These and hundreds of other tiny nagging nuisances make the period just after a divorce uncomfortable. But it is the big changes that make a difference. By the time she gets around to endorsing her first alimony check, the reality of her new situation begins to register. As a divorcée she has simultaneously and instantly acquired all the disadvantages of a single girl and most of the disadvantages of a married woman. As one patient put it, "Most divorced girls start their new life with the 'big three': children, debts, and regrets."

Is there anything good about divorce?

For one thing it is bold and dramatic. In a sense, the woman performs a do-it-yourself amputation without anesthesia. The husband, the marriage, everything that once constituted a vital emotional relationship, suddenly has its brains blown out like a race horse with a broken leg. It is the ultimate solution. It is emphatically irreversible. (With the questionable exception of those few women who after a divorce, remarry the same man. Usually they end up proving that you *can* have it both ways—for a while. Another divorce follows shortly and the message is clear. They didn't like it *either* way. But for most women, divorcing the same man *once* is enough suffering.)

In a certain way divorce is an ideal solution to a bad marriage. Like a mental hydrogen bomb, it obliterates all traces of the mutually unsuccessful venture. If only the problems that *result* from the divorce could be disposed of so neatly. Most of the time they tend to persist for years, like a radioactive cloud, polluting the emotional atmosphere. Marlene can describe it well:

"It was over a year ago but I remember the feeling as if it were happening right now. When I walked out of that courtroom with the decree in my hand I was drunk with power! I finally gave Carl exactly what was coming to him! I felt like taking on the whole world!"

"How long did that feeling last?"

Marlene put her tea cup down slowly. "You've heard this story before, Doctor?"

"Yes, I think so."

"Well, anyhow by the next morning I wasn't feeling

so tough. As a matter of fact the thought that kept coming to me over and over again was, 'Big deal, now what do I do with my life'?"

A divorce is powerful medicine. It throws out the baby, the bath water, the bathtub and sometimes the whole bathroom. But it doesn't do a single thing to change the emotional make-up of the unhappy woman who stands alone in the court room. One of the great ironies of divorce is that the legal proclamation that liberates a woman may also enslave her. As she is released from the prison of her intolerable marriage she may step into the confinement of a new and perhaps even more damaging situation.

What about the sexual effects of divorce?

Divorce has been described as "instant sexual marooning"—by a patient who went through it. An even better description is *retroactive sexual marooning*. Usually, long before the case comes up on the court calendar the sexual relationship has died. Sexually, the divorce proceedings are usually nothing more than a somewhat delayed funeral. By the time a woman is free to begin over again she has nearly always suffered a critical blow to her sexual happiness. It was that way with Regina. Tall and slender, pale and blonde, she resembled some of the misty water colors she painted in her job as a commercial artist. At twenty-nine, she had been divorced about eight months:

"Doctor, if I didn't know any better I'd say I was suffering from battle fatigue."

"What do you mean?"

"Well, you know I was divorced from Ned last year. We were married three years but for the last year or so our sex life was terrible. Most of the time I never had an orgasm and if it seemed like I was going to he always ejaculated too fast and that finished it. It was really awful. Toward the end—I'd say the last four months—I wouldn't even let him touch me. One of the things I was looking forward to after my divorce was starting to enjoy sex again. Now I can't do it." She shook her head.

"What seems to be the matter?"

"I don't know. That's why I call it battle fatigue. Maybe all those years of fighting and arguing before and after—and sometimes during—sex, just wore me out. I don't have any trouble attracting men but I've tried it at least a dozen times since I left Ned and it's —it's nothing."

"In what way?"

"It's like I'm not even there. I mean, I want to do it but there's no feeling. Sometimes I have a little sensation, like something might happen but it always goes away. I almost feel like sex has been scared out of me."

Regina was closer to the truth than she realized. Sex plus unhappiness, sex plus disappointment, sex plus arguments usually becomes no sex at all. The part of the brain that controls sexual responses just draws back into its shell like a turtle and waits for better opportunities. If those opportunities never come, sexual feelings and orgasms may never return. Sex and anger don't mix. After countless bitter scenes with Ned all that remained was the mechanical part of intercourse. Carol and her husband could put the pieces together but they couldn't make them work. She was sexually marooned before her divorce, and her old problems followed her into her new life. After an interval of treatment she understood the interaction between the brain and the sexual organs much better and made a few changes. First, she stopped choosing men who unconsciously (and sometimes even consciously) reminded her of Ned. Secondly, she threw the image of Ned out of her life and out of her bed. If she had intercourse with a new boyfriend but responded to him as if he were Ned, she was doomed to feel only as much as she had felt with Ned—nothing. Thirdly, she relearned something she had forgotten during the last year of her marriage— sex is an expression of love, not a weapon to wound an enemy. She began selecting men with whom she shared a common emotional bond and to whom she could relate sexually. Sexual feeling returned, rapidly followed by orgasms.

Does divorce cause any other form of emotional damage?

One of the more unpleasant aspects of divorce is the sudden loss of confidence that accompanies the loss of the wedding ring. At that particular moment most women feel an overpowering sense of failure and defeat. They consider themselves unloved, unwanted, and unattractive in the fullest meaning of those powerful words. If they can only remember that these feelings represent a *temporary* emotional reaction to the sudden disruption of their lives, they can avoid a lot of immediate unhappiness. Whenever a human being loses something important to him, he or she responds with what is called a *mourning reaction.* This is expressed by withdrawal, feelings of inadequacy, fear, and depression. It is the inevitable unconscious response to the loss of a parent, a brother, a sister, a cherished pet, or a marriage. The most important characteristic of this emotion is that *it is temporary and clears up by itself within a few weeks.* If every divorced woman can arm herself with the facts ahead of time, her life will be much easier. Ginny wasn't able to and tells what happened to her:

"It happened two and a half years ago but I still can't get it out of my mind. The first week after my decree came through was terrible. I felt so small I could have done a tap dance on the head of a pin." Ginny laughed. "I wish I could have kept my sense of humor then. But I felt as if I'd lost everything. I was sure I was ugly and I just knew no man would ever look at me again. That was when I made my first mistake."

"What was that?"

"I tried to prove it wasn't true. I got dressed up and went out to see if I could still attract the opposite sex—men."

"Could you?"

"I'm sure you know the answer, Doctor. Yes and no. I attracted the opposite sex all right, but men? Not a one."

"What happened?"

"Ohhh, I even hate to think about it. Well, I went to one of these single bars. You know the kind of place—dim lights, red velvet wallpaper, wooden tables and wooden customers. The place I picked even had sawdust on the floor. Looking back on it now, I think most of the sawdust must have trickled out of the fellows there. Anyhow I sat at the bar trying to look glamorous and prove—oh, I don't know what I was trying to prove!

"After a while this fellow came up and started talking. We talked for about an hour and then he invited me up to his place. From then on it was like a puppet show. A couple of drinks, we went to bed, I went home about three in the morning and woke up feeling worse than I had the day before. I should have quit right then!" Ginny paused, then went on.

"Back the next night?"

"You bet! In those days Ginny was a slow learner. It must have been a different guy every night for the next three weeks until—I don't even remember his name—he was some kind of an engineer. A short guy with red hair and freckles. I ended up at his place at the usual hour—about midnight—and he was pouring me a drink. He had the glass half full when all of a sudden it finally hit me—I must have said it out loud: 'What am I doing here?' He jumped about a foot off the ground but I didn't even wait to see whether he came down. I was out the door in a flash and home in my own bed in fifteen minutes. It was as if those three weeks had been a bad dream and all of a sudden I woke up. Here I was having a drink in the apartment of this middle-aged midget whose name I didn't even know and getting ready to go to bed with him. It was a miracle I didn't get pregnant or syphilis or both from that collection of losers I got mixed up with."

Ginny misinterpreted her post-divorce depression. She thought it was a reflection of her inadequacy as a person. Her self-prescribed treatment was to collect sexual scalps to prove how attractive she really was. In her own words:

"All I really proved, Doctor, was that this world is full of men who were trying to use me for the same reason I was trying to use them. Both of us should have known better."

Some women try a different approach. A Caribbean cruise, a trip back home, or a tour to Europe or Mexico, often gets the credit for helping them over a difficult period. The truth is that any activity that uses up three weeks or so allows the mind to get over the period of mental mourning. Twenty-one days of spring cleaning is just as effective (though not as enjoyable) as three weeks on the beach at Waikiki.

Doesn't a divorcée have some advantages over other sexually-marooned women?

She should. Of all the women who are sexually marooned, the divorcée theoretically has the best chance of finding her way back. She has already traveled the road from single girl to wife. She knows the way the land lies and needs only to retrace her steps—a little more carefully this time. Compared to the girl who never married and must start from scratch, or to the widow who usually gets back in the game so much later that she's forgotten most of the rules, things are easy for the divorcée. Easy that is, if she can do one thing.

What's that?

She must face the harsh reality of why her marriage failed. She must honestly and courageously admit where *she* went wrong and ruined her chance for happiness. To prepare herself for a better life, the woman must recognize that divorce is a public declaration of failure—failure times two. It is never a case of villain and victim but rather two not-so-innocent victims. Unfortunately the bizarre and archaic divorce laws of our society are better suited for deciding a prize-fight than untangling an unhappy marriage.

With rare exceptions, divorces are granted on the

basis of the adversary system, a misbegotten legacy from medieval England where most disputes were settled with sword and club. Under those knight-and-damsel regulations a tragi-comedy unfolds. The ideal setting would be the court yard of The Castle; most often a stuffy court room has to do. The wife plays the role of the Maiden Who Has Been Wronged while the husband is cast as The Knave. The judge, of course, is King. Damsel-wife recites her complaints, Knave-husband squeals in protest (nobody believes him anyway), and the King punishes the Knave. Sometimes the punishment can be more than symbolic. Generous alimony, staggering child support, and a whopping property settlement can cripple a man economically. And if he doesn't pay up, the King throws him into the dungeon. (That brings up another interesting point. If a husband does not pay his wife he goes to jail—no trial, no sentence— he just stays there, for years if necessary, until he capitulates.)

No woman can afford the luxury of believing that the collection of legal fairy tales known as divorce represents reality. The official version listing the sins of the husband is fine for society. The unrevised edition that tells it like it really was is the one the woman has to untangle. In the privacy of her own mind or with the help of an understanding and experienced psychiatrist she has to sort out all the little nasty malicious inhuman things *she* did to bring on the mutual catasrophe known as divorce. She has to face her own mistakes and poor judgment which precipitated her into a non-viable marriage.

How could she know her marriage wasn't going to work out?

Often the future failure of a marriage is decided sometime before the second payment on the engagement ring is due. Regrettably, this decision always takes place at the unconscious level where neither the prospective bride nor bridegroom has the slightest idea of what is taking place. Most of the time they are mired up to the neck in the fantasy of romantic love. Unfortunately they have every reason to be since it has been beaten into their mutual heads since they were old enough to read a magazine or stare at television. The story is always the same—and always completely removed from reality. A keen-witted ravishing young beauty, by a charming twist of fate, encounters a muscular genius with unlimited financial resources. Too clever to reveal her true feelings, she rejects him at first but he persists and finally wins her hand. They march off hand-in-hand to face a lifetime together guaranteed to be one long exquisite senior prom.

This fable has some distinctive qualities about it. First, it is always completely sanitary. There are never any dirty dishes, cramped apartments, car payments, or missed opportunities. Secondly, the hero and heroine are somehow gifted with perfect dispositions. Unruffled, serene (probably because nothing much ever happens to them), they drift through life. Never angry, never depressed, never out of sorts, they are always smiling benignly right to the last scene in the film or the mouth wash commercial on TV. Probably the most remarkable quality of this universal fantasy is that so many people actually believe it. Not only believe it, but expect to relive it in their own marriages. They are, of course, doomed to failure—and usually failure of the most disappointing sort. Even more appalling is the way they project the blame for this failure onto each other. The wife actually holds the husband responsible for not fulfilling this impossible dream. (The husband, in turn, responds by attacking his wife for her failure.)

Don't the husband and wife realize this?

Apparently not. A painstaking analysis of complaints leveled by couples during divorce proceedings yields some surprising results. Almost invariably they accuse each other of *failing to live up to the terms of the mutual fantasy*. The wife accuses the husband, not so much of being wicked, but of *being himself* rather than the man she created in her imagination. "You're not the same man I married!" is the complaint. The unpleasant fact (all too often) is that he is *just* the man she married. Unfortunately it has taken her the better part of two years to realize it. And now she feels cheated. The romantic charmer is demoted to plain old human being full of faults and shortcomings. He bites his nails, drinks too much, and maybe even gets mixed up with other women. In twenty-four months he destroys the fantasy that took twenty-four years of watching television to create. No wonder he must be punished.

In ancient times it was the custom of kings to kill the messengers who brought bad news. All too often that custom lingers on in the form of punitive indignant divorce. Rather than face the bad news that her husband is unable to fill the impossible role she has created for him, the woman decides to tear down the stage, kill off the star actor, and begin the quest for a new leading man. She is doomed to failure. At this point, what she needs to do more than anything else is realize that life is *not* a stage and her husband (and herself) are *not* dramatic actors. She has to learn that love is not a combination of mawkish sentiment and adolescent nostalgia that must constantly be reinforced by replaying the first date every two weeks or so. The mutual identification and sharing of every level of existence that constitutes true love is the only assurance of happiness in marriage. That is the kind that never shines through the shadows of light and dark that play on movie or TV screens.

It has been said that love begins with a Prince kissing an Angel and ends with a baldheaded man looking across the table at a fat lady. If a woman believes *that* she might as well not get married in the first place because she is going to spend most of her free time commuting between the lawyer's office and the divorce court. The quest for the ideal mate is doomed to failure—perfection is not a characteristic of the human race. Humans can be attractive, appealing, charming, inspiring, and in a multitude of ways, delightful. They can also be stupid, indifferent, exasperating, and disappointing. The bad qualities come right along with the good ones. If you take one you have to take the other. The man who is handsome and dashing may also be selfish and conceited. The man who is wealthy and worldly often turns out to be short and plump. The first thing a woman needs to learn is that men are not the same as macaroni.

Men are not the same as macaroni?

Yes. One of the great deceptions of modern American culture is the concept of packaging. Years ago, for example, macaroni was from the bin. The housewife told the grocer, "Two pounds of macaroni, please," and he scooped it into a brown paper bag. Later on some unknown genius discovered macaroni sold better rolled up, a pound at a time, in pale blue paper with a fancy label on it. The concept was progressively refined until now macaroni is packaged like rare jade. It comes in layers of multi-colored and multi-textured papers and plastics with a gleaming gold foil outer wrapper. Not by accident, gift-wrapped macaroni costs twice as much as the old kind that came out of the bin. Even more disappointing, since the wrappings are not edible, once the paper is thrown away, all macaroni tastes the same. Over the last twenty years or so, people have been packaged in a similar way. Women are often attracted to the man who says the right things, drives the right car, wears the right clothes, and earns the right money. Sometimes it takes her years of marriage to unwrap a husband and discover what she may have suspected all along—underneath all the glitter is nothing but a pound or two of mental macaroni. Returning pasta to the grocery store is easy—exchanging husbands is expensive, time-consuming, and takes a lot out of a girl. If she can only look beneath the outer layer—beneath the pretense and pseudo-sophistication—and see *before marriage* exactly what kind of package she is buying, the result can be surprising. Sometimes what looks like macaroni on the surface is really pure gold underneath.

Chris found that out—the second time around. At thirty-five she has been divorced for five years. She supports her two children by operating a small nursery school:

"Boy, it sure took me a long time to wake up!"

"What do you mean?"

"Well, my first husband was the answer to all my dreams—I thought. I was brought up in a small town in Illinois and I went to teachers' college in an even smaller town. The only boys I'd known thought a really big evening was a movie, a hamburger, and driving out to the lake to neck. I remember in college a fellow took me out to dinner once—I was so overwhelmed I kept the menu for years. Anyhow, when I moved to Chicago and started meeting more sophisticated men I just didn't know how to handle it. You know, night clubs, parties, weekends skiing, sailing. I felt as if I were the star of a Doris Day movie. And Les acted like the leading man. He was tall, lean, and sophisticated—sort of a blond Rock Hudson. He was in the advertising business and to me he was the most exciting man I had ever imagined.

"About six months after we met, we got married—it was on my twenty-second birthday. The two weeks we spent on our honeymoon were the happiest days of our marriage. It wasn't much of a comparison because they were the only happy days I ever had with him. Les was everything I *thought* I wanted in a husband —good-looking, suave, a good sense of humor, liked by everybody. He was also about two inches deep. He didn't care about money—either making it or spending it. When he made it, he wouldn't spend it and when he didn't make it, he couldn't get rid of it fast enough. But anyhow that's not why I'm here. I got my divorce and the kids and that was that. Or at least I thought so."

"You thought so?"

"Yes. After the shock of the divorce wore off, I started looking for another husband. Looking back on it, it seems so dumb."

Chris stared into space as if she were recalling the past.

"All I could ever find were second editions of Les. The only men I met were tall, blond, handsome, *and shallow*. They were charming, witty, lovable, and— empty. I had a great time for a year or so until I stopped to think. How come I only met this kind of guy? You know, I wasn't exactly getting younger by the minute and my kids still needed a father. Then it dawned on me. I was looking for a re-run of our marriage. Without being *consciously* aware of it I was going to the same places I used to go with Les. To the same cocktail lounges, the same ski lodges, the same sailing parties. Of course there were all kinds of men there but I just happened to get paired off with a carbon copy of my ex-husband. What I want to know is, how come?"

Chris asked a good question. The answer was within her grasp but it took her about three months of treatment to really understand it. Her description of it, later on, was a good one.

"It's frightening, now that I realize what I was trying to do to myself, Doctor. I guess I was willing to try anything to make my daydreams come true. When I saw that Les wasn't going to work out, I started up with someone else. If only I hadn't been so stubborn and admitted it was my mistake in the first place. When my first marriage was a flop, instead of facing reality, I tried to make it work *my* way. What a dope I was! I think I've worked it out better this time. My new boyfriend certainly isn't the movie star type. He's about forty-five now and his hair is even getting a little thin. He has a chain of travel agencies —not quite as glamorous as the advertising business, but it doesn't matter. I know he's the right man for me. I just want to say one more thing before I go, Doctor."

"Certainly, what's that?"

"I'll never forget what you said about some people complaining that love begins with a Prince kissing an Angel and ends with a bald-headed man looking across the table at a fat lady. I just want to say there's such a thing as a bald-headed Prince—and I'm about to marry him!"

How do divorcées feel about getting married again?

It is a well-known fact of human nature that women are more optimistic than men. There is however no category of women more recklessly optimistic than the woman who has just been divorced. It would be a sensible guess that a woman who has just gone through the emotional meat grinder of the typical American divorce would want to put about two continents between herself and marriage. That sensible guess would also be almost completely wrong. More than ninety percent of divorcées remarry within one year of the date their divorce becomes final. To the sociologists, the explanation is elusive. Have they been brainwashed by marriage? Is it simply because they are used to a double bed on cold nights? Perhaps it only takes twelve months for the cloying sentimentality of television and movies to work their magic again?

It doesn't seem that way. Careful analysis of hundreds of divorced women reveals an actual compulsion —an unconscious drive—to re-establish another marriage as soon as possible. Even more fascinating is the phenomenon of multiple marriage (or as one patient called it, "bigamy on the installment plan"). Often the woman with the most failures behind her has the greatest wish to try it again (and again).

What's the reason for it?

The explanation is two-fold. Part of the secret is hidden in the pillowcase of the divorced woman. There are two versions of every divorce—the one that comes out in court, "for the record," and the one that every woman tells her pillow, sometimes night after night as she tries to understand what really happened to her and to her dreams of a happy marriage. One of the most pathetic thoughts, and the one that virtually every woman has at the moment her divorce is granted is: *This is not really the way I planned it.* Few brides take time on their wedding day to plan the details of their forthcoming divorce—at least not consciously. But sometime between the moment the bride says, "I do" and the moment the judge says, "You aren't," all the young girl's wonderful dreams of love and happiness have been trampled on.

Who does the trampling?

Every disappointed ex-bride knows the answer. Her marriage was kicked to death by two pairs of shoes— one pair size 10½ oxfords, the other 6 A with little flat heels and tiny buckles. Deep deep inside, every woman knows the precise details of how she co-conspired (with her ex-spouse) to assassinate whatever tenderness existed between them. For every bitter accusation in the divorce court there is the honest equivalent that was whispered into the secrecy of the pillowcase at two o'clock some lonely morning. Sometimes it goes like this:

To Judge (tearfully): I want a divorce because Frank was always running around with other women.

To Pillow: When Frank came home from work I was always such a grouch, I'm surprised he waited a whole year to find someone else.

To Judge: I can't go on living with a man who won't have anything to do with me sexually.

To Pillow: For all the interest I took in sex, Frank could have gotten more satisfaction out of a pillow like you.

To Judge: My husband wasn't willing to support me.

To Pillow: The way I wanted to spend money, the U. S. Mint wouldn't be willing to support me.

To Judge: My husband never let a day go by without insulting me!

To Pillow: I never let an *hour* go by without insulting him!

Because almost every divorcée knows *unconsciously* what she did to scuttle the ship of matrimony she is anxious, if not eager, to overcome her original failure in her subsequent marriage. Secretly, often without even realizing it, she promises that the next one will work out better. If this inner wish to cancel her original mistake is not enough to speed her back to the local wedding chapel, the irony of the divorce proceedings gives her the final shove. Most of the participants at the divorce hearing are dedicated to proving that the husband is to blame. (Even the husband makes his contribution to this pretense by involuntarily financing the proceedings.) After it is all over the new ex-wife may make the fatal mistake of believing her own publicity. Because she is so vulnerable at that moment she welcomes confirmation of what she knows cannot be true. Because the law usually requires one of the parties to be at fault, she is only too willing to pin the blame on her husband.

As a result of these dual forces she may be propelled like a cannon ball into her next marriage.

Unconsciously she knows that *at least fifty percent of the blame for the disintegration of her marriage belongs to her.* Consciously she is convinced (almost) that it was her husband's fault and all she has to do is change partners to find happiness. The harder she is squeezed by these competing emotions the faster she goes—into another marriage.

Isn't it a good idea for divorced women to remarry?

In a certain sense, a new marriage is a good choice. One of the better solutions to sexual marooning (though by no means the *only* one) is marriage. But the marriage has to be truly a new one—not just a re-run of the old situation tragedy. There are two important steps to achieving that. The first step is to make divorce illegal. The entire process is destructive, wasteful, and basically dishonest. For many years California has had the highest divorce rate in the nation with two out of every five marriages ultimately collapsing. More than 140,000 Californians are divorced each year. But by a bold stroke of the state legislature, the divorce rate for California in 1970 became exactly *zero.* On New Years Day 1970 the state officially abolished divorce, making even the word illegal. It has been replaced by the concept of "dissolution of marriage"—and more than just the name has changed. Under the new law, the marriage can be dissolved by the request of either partner. Only two grounds are recognized—irreconcilable differences or incurable insanity. In a marvel of simplicity, irreconcilable differences are defined by the new law as any difference which constitutes a substantial reason for not continuing the marriage. Not only is it unnecessary for the wife to prove the husband is to blame (or vice versa), it is prohibited. Furthermore, any information obtained by eavesdropping will be rejected by the judge and the eavesdropper prosecuted as a criminal. Provisions are made for alimony in cases of need—not as punishment—and community property is divided fairly. In a blow against bureaucracy the legal forms themselves have been simplified to the point where it is only necessary for the parties to check the appropriate boxes.

What's the advantage of the California law?

Although no one expects this law to solve the underlying problems of defective marriages it does accomplish two things. It makes the ordeal of shattering a marriage mutually less traumatic. And even more important it takes away from the wife (and incidentally the husband) the last remnants of the alibi which keeps her from facing her contribution to the mutual self-destruction. In this sense it should reduce some of the pressure for her to precipitate herself into another catastrophic marriage to prove the first one wasn't her fault after all.

What else can the divorcée do to help herself?

If the first step toward undoing the sexual marooning that results from divorce is passing a new law, the second step might be considered repealing an old law. That's the one that says: "All the bad things in my life are caused by someone else—all the good things come from me." This form of selective retroactive amnesia guarantees a succession of disappointing marriages to the one who believes it. The girl who insists on shifting the blame for her marital mishaps to her latest ex-husband has the same problem as the finicky shopper in the fruit store. She selects a promising tomato and squeezes it—*hard*. Then she discards it because it's too *soft*. Unfortunately the chronic divorcée will run out of prospective husbands long before the demanding shopper runs out of tomatoes.

A woman who has just plowed her marriage under is in an ideal position to do some hard thinking. She knows better than anyone else *at that moment* that human beings are fragile objects. She has seen herself and her now defunct husband transformed over the years from lovers into losers. If she can only nail down that realization, once and for all, the next time around her job will be much easier. If she approaches her next marriage consciously armed with all the knowledge she has gained from her previous failure, she will have the odds overwhelmingly on her side.

There is only one thing worse than getting a divorce—and that is submitting to the devastation of a bad marriage. Once a woman has made the soul-searing decision to strike a blow for her emotional freedom, there is no room for hesitation. She must either plunge boldly ahead or sink forever into bitterness and recriminations. Every divorced woman senses that instinctively. She has felt herself slide into the physical and emotional isolation of sexual marooning. At the most important juncture in her life there is only one way for her to go—*forward*. By using every scrap of insight she can muster by learning from the mistakes of others, and by drawing on that particular brand of tenacity and determination that only females seem to possess, she can have her chance for true happiness and make her second marriage everything her first marriage should have been.

7

IT COULDN'T HAPPEN TO ME

Do single girls have different sexual problems from married girls?

Yes and no. Married or not, all women have the same sexual equipment and the same sexual feelings. Both live under the relentless domination of female sex hormones which are constantly poured into their bloodstreams. Both ride the crest of the menstrual tide every twenty-eight days or so. Married or not, every woman wants to love and be loved.

The married girl has a blank check, written on the day of her wedding, that theoretically entitles her to enjoy her sexuality to the fullest extent of her ability and ingenuity. From the moment the knot is tied, she lives under the protective umbrella of husband, marriage, and a marriage-oriented society. Sexually a married woman can do no wrong—almost. Sexually, a single girl can do *nothing* but wrong.

In what sense?

From the moment a single woman begins to seek sexual satisfaction she is in trouble. First of all she is made to realize quickly that she is in business for herself. Should she venture out into the sexual jungle in search of gratification, there is no one looking out for her. If she gets into trouble, there is no one waiting to bail her out. She must drag herself home and lick her own wounds. Second, in sexual matters she is expected to meet men on equal terms—although the terms can never really be anything like equal.

Third, she must constantly furnish herself with an adequate supply of eligible and interested men—*without ever appearing to do so*. Fourth, she must manifest a vital interest in sex and sexuality while being "every inch a lady." As one patient said, "Couldn't just a few inches of me be unladylike?"

In every sexual encounter a woman is at the disadvantage. What makes her partner happy on the first of July can make her a mother on the eighth of April. The same string of sexual conquests that makes a man a "lover" can tag her with the label "swinger," complete with obscene phone calls at midnight and propositions from shoe-shine boys. A bit of bad luck that infected her partner with gonorrhea can return to haunt her years later when, legally married, she tries to get pregnant and can't.

Women deserve equality with men in every possible area—jobs, voting, property rights, and everything else. The only place where they will never be equal is in the area of sexuality. As one clever young lady put it, "When it comes to sex, women will never be the same as men—we just aren't equipped for it."

What can a single woman do about sexual inequality?

Unfortunately, she can't change the rules of the game. As long as men make women pregnant (instead of vice versa) and as long as the Pilgrims' and Puritans' style of life is imposed on every unmarried girl, a single woman has to utilize every ounce of insight, understanding, and information to survive and find happiness is a world she never made. By emphasizing those uniquely feminine attributes of intuition and sensitivity, she has every chance of enjoying the sexuality that she was born with—married or not.

What is the biggest sexual problem of single women?

Pregnancy. The identical event that brings euphoria (or at least satisfaction) to most married women who choose it strikes terror into the heart of every unmarried girl. Anatomically, a single pregnant girl and a married pregnant girl are *almost* identical. The ovum is the same, the sperm is the same, the uterus is the same—the only structure missing from the body of the single miss is a narrow strip of gold alloy around the fourth left digit.

Instead of two hundred eighty days of pre-natal vitamins, maternity clothes, showers, and long discussions over what to name the baby, for a single girl the months of pregnancy are filled with deception, lies, and dread. Mona went through it herself:

"Well, first of all, Doctor, I didn't believe it. I had been late with my period before and I just put it down to worry. You know, I still have that old mistaken idea deep inside that pregnancy is the *punishment* for sexual intercourse." She sighed, then managed a half-hearted smile. "Now that I mention it, who am I to say? In my case, pregnancy *was* a punishment. Actually the first six weeks were the hardest. That's when I had to face reality. I went to Roger—he was the father—and told him. He admitted it, of course, but then he reminded me he was married. He followed the news flash with a little lecture on how I should think twice about breaking up a happy home —you know, out of consideration for the mother of his children and all that. I reminded him that, thanks to him, *I* was about to be the mother of one of his children, too." Mona sighed again.

"Then I thought about getting an abortion. I was feeling kind of desperate and I started to make all the arrangements but I just couldn't bring myself to do it. Maybe I'm just soft-hearted or maybe I just wanted to have a child, married or not. I mean I was twenty-five and not getting any younger. With my job—I'm a freelance illustrator—I could afford a baby and I could work at home and—well, everything just seemed right. I just moved to a new neighborhood, told everyone my husband had died in an auto accident, and waited for the baby to come. Of course it wasn't as easy as it sounds. For the first time in my life I realized what it was like to be really alone. No friends, no dates, nothing and no one. If it hadn't been for my cat, I really would have gone out of my mind. That, and the thought of my baby who was on the way. Once I got past the fourth month and he started moving at least I felt I had company." Mona looked despondent.

"What's the matter?"

"That's the worst part—I mean, nobody to share it with. I still can't understand why I had to hide out like that—like I was a burglar or something. I actually had to run away from everything just because I was going through a perfectly natural experience."

"Did you really have to run away?"

"Are you kidding? Would you like to explain to my father the police sergeant how his unmarried daughter got pregnant? And my mother who probably still feels guilty because she never told me the first thing about sex? I'm sure they'd be delighted to have me around the house and introduce me to the neighbors. When the lieutenant stops by to pick up Dad in the morning, he could say, 'Lieutenant, I'd like you to meet my only daughter, Mona. Don't pay attention if she's a little chubby—she's pregnant and going to get married someday.' You just don't know how these people think."

"The hospital was another great experience—all those sweet little nurses asking when my husband would be along. *That* was the hardest part. But I finally got through it and now that Kevin's here— that's the baby's name—I'm really glad I did it that way." Mona smiled.

"Of course there are still some problems. I've gone from spinster to widow without getting married and I certainly don't want to raise a whole family this way. I have a new boyfriend and I made sure *he* wasn't married. I hope it's going to work out better this time but I'm sure of one thing—no more offspring until I can do it the right way—I mean, the regular way—I mean—" Mona grinned and shook her head. "*You* know what I mean, Doctor!"

Is Mona's case typical?

Not really. As a practical matter more and more unmarried girls who get pregnant by mistake these days are choosing abortion as a solution. Instead of nine months of agony concluded by the addition of another unwanted human being to the roster of this already crowded planet, they are deciding to undo their mistakes as quickly as possible. Finally the abortion laws which have remained basically intact since the Dark

Ages are beginning to catch up to the needs of modern women. Instead of vesting the control of reproduction in the impersonal state legislature, it has been handed first to the physicians and now, state by state, women are being given something to say about it. One of the greatest ironies of our way of life is that in our country, the freest of all nations, a woman's uterus is *nationalized* from the instant of conception until the moment after delivery. The government exercises absolute control over the female reproductive system and the products of conception and is willing to send the mother (and ironically in some cases the unborn child) to jail to enforce its power. Imagine the outcry if legislatures were to pass laws telling *men* how and where they could ejaculate. (But most legislators are men, so that is unlikely to happen.)

But isn't abortion immoral?

That question should be decided by the pregnant woman—not by a group of middle-aged males in the State House. If you happen to be an eighteen-year-old secretary living away from home, making ninety-seven dollars a week and you suddenly wake up pregnant one morning—and aren't married—the finer points of legislative morality are wasted on you.

Every woman has the right to decide whether or not she wishes to become a mother—*and when*. Sometimes the odds are stacked impossibly against her. During the excitement and abandon of sexual intercourse a woman has the full force of thousands of years as the bearer of children working against her. Every ounce of her being is directed toward fulfilling her sexual role with absolute disregard of everything else around her. To ask her to take the responsi-

bility for family planning during those few supercharged moments is like asking a man to recite his
Social Security number at the precise moment of
orgasm—it just isn't fair.

It is fair to give a woman a second thought about
becoming pregnant, and abortion gives her that
second thought. In a certain way, abortion is retroactive birth control. Every woman is entitled to it.

But isn't abortion dangerous?

That depends. For at least fifty years the same operation used for abortion (dilation and curettage or "D
and C") was performed on women a thousand times
a day by expert surgeons in first-class hospitals
throughout the country to diagnose and treat conditions of the uterus. The only catch was it could rarely
be used where it was needed most—to end a pregnancy. The majority of women who sought an abortion
were thrown into the hands of incompetents, criminals,
and bunglers who charged up to a thousand dollars for
a hundred-dollar operation. In addition most women
had to do without hospital care, antibiotics, and every
advance of modern medicine. The message of society
was clear: "Want an abortion? Try and get one and we
hope it kills ya!" For too many women, the wish came
true. A small fraction of abortions were done by well-
qualified doctors who took big risks (and usually
charged equally big fees). But now things have
changed.

How?

Now abortion is completely legal in several states and
at least one jurisdiction, New York, allows the pro-

cedure with virtually no limitations and no residency requirements. The charge for an average abortion there runs about two hundred dollars and many patients are allowed to go home the same day.

The technique for abortion has also been vastly improved. The D and C required the contents of the uterus to be painstakingly scraped out with a long-handled tool similar to a melon scoop. The operation took about fifteen minutes in skilled hands and always resulted in some bleeding and pain.

Now things are different. By utilizing the suction evacuator, abortions can be done rapidly, safely, *and* economically.

How does it work?

Like a charm. A small suction device is inserted into the cervix, a button is pushed, and the entire contents of the uterus are suddenly sucked out, as if by a painless vacuum cleaner. From start to finish, in skilled hands the whole affair should take under three minutes. Bleeding and pain are almost nonexistent, and physician and hospital charges should be held to a minimum.

How safe is this technique?

Much safer than the old D and C, which was pretty safe to begin with. The vacuum abortion device has been used in Europe and the Middle East for the past ten years with excellent results. In the history of modern medicine, few mechanical devices have ever saved so many people from so much suffering.

Abortions after the sixteenth week of pregnancy require more complex techniques—saline injection, hysterotomy, and things like that. A girl who wants to end her pregnancy should make the decision before the fourth month, if possible. In every abortion, the woman is spared an unwanted child and the embryo is spared a life that begins (and probably ends) unawaited, unwanted, and unloved.

Isn't there a better solution for single girls than abortion?

Certainly. It's called contraception. Finally, after fifty thousand years, human beings are dependably able to separate copulation from conception. The single woman can choose from about a dozen thoroughly tested techniques ranging in effectiveness from exactly one hundred percent to about ten percent and varying in safety from absolutely safe to somewhat more dangerous than flying in an airplane.

The success of any birth control method depends on intercepting and neutralizing the wiggling sperm somewhere between the time they leave the penis and the time they merge with the ripe ovum halfway up the fallopian tube. Working against contraception is the overwhelming number of these tiny squirmers. In each act of intercourse more than four hundred million spermatozoa are launched toward their target; only one of them has to get through to make that evening—and many others to follow—a dismal failure.

What's the best method of birth control?

Unfortunately, every method has its advantages and drawbacks. Probably the most frequently used technique is the simple condom or rubber. This thin latex sheath which fits firmly over the penis theoretically collects all sperm from each ejaculation and prevents them from even entering the vagina. Condoms have the same basic construction as a rubber glove, which, incidentally, is one of their biggest disadvantages. Placing a latex barrier between the opposing surfaces during intercourse seriously interferes with sensation— it is the modern-day version of making love in mittens. To get around this manufacturers have made condoms thinner and thinner so that some of them feel as if there is nothing there at all. That brings up another problem—if they get thin enough, they may tear apart, and at the most important moment there *is* nothing there at all. Condoms also have a tendency to overflow and dribble sperm at just the wrong time. Their best feature is their low cost and ready availability. A unique feature of condoms is their interchangeability. Long before stretch socks became popular, condom makers could boast "One size fits all." They provide about eighty-five percent protection. Another point against using a condom is that it puts control of conception in the hands of the man.

Isn't there something like a condom for women?

Yes. The equivalent approach in women is the diaphragm. It consists of a thin rubber dome (somewhat thicker than a condom) about four inches in diameter with a circular metal spring making up the rim. (Diaphragms come in a wide range of sizes and must be fitted by a doctor.) It is inserted into the vagina and wedged between the pubic bone and the back wall of the vaginal space. The aim is to cover the cervix and protect it from the spray of sperm. As a backstop, a chemical jelly *that hopefully kills sperm* is spread over the edges and the cervical side of the dome.

Diaphragms, being derived from condoms, have some of the same problems. Like a condom, a diaphragm can leak. If it leaks outward, some of the contraceptive jelly drips into the vagina—a bit of tissue takes care of that. If it leaks inward, sperm by the millions can enter the uterus—it takes more than tissue to solve that problem. Even worse, in spite of the sturdy spring holding it in place, under heavy use the diaphragm can slip out. Once it has been kicked to the foot of the bed, even the best diaphragm offers absolutely no protection.

In addition to its original cost, the diaphragm also has the disadvantage of upkeep. It must be washed and powdered after each use and replaced as the user outgrows it.

How does a woman outgrow *a diaphragm?*

With each act of intercourse, the erect penis stretches the vagina a tiny bit. After months or years of sexual activity the vaginal space becomes "ironed out" and permanently stretched beyond its original size. A diaphragm that is not held snugly against the vaginal walls on all sides does not hold sperm back—it guides them to their destination. Women who depend on this method should visit their doctors every six months or so to have the size rechecked—just to be safe.

Are there any other methods of birth control that a woman can use herself?

Yes. There are several chemical approaches to conception control. The basic principle behind all of these is to kill all the sperm before they get out of reach. It isn't as easy as it sounds. Neither of the participants know exactly when the gush of spermatozoa will occur. When it does come, there are four hundred million of them in half an ounce of slippery liquid, all desperately rushing toward an eager uterus. To make matters worse, the pelvic thrusting and pumping motion of the penis and vagina tend to speed them madly on their way. On the positive side, it isn't hard to demolish the sperm themselves. They are very vulnerable to most chemicals—even a strong salt solution will destroy them quickly. (Pickle brine and the juice from olives has saved the day on more than one occasion.) Waxy vaginal suppositories have been tried, creams and jellies were popular for some time, and even little foaming sponges have been used. They all have their problems—sometimes the suppositories don't melt, the creams and jellies melt too much and tend to be messy, and the foaming sponges usually foam too little and too late.

Modern technology has recently saved the day (and a lot of other things at the same time). A harmless chemical that is deadly to sperm is put up in an aerosol foam can. A small amount (about a quarter- to a half-teaspoonful) is placed in the vagina just before intercourse by means of a plastic applicator. Since the amount of foam is so small, neither party is aware of it and it gives a high degree of protection. But it, too, has some dangers.

What are they?

Kathy had a few anxious moments because of it:

"Dick—that's my husband—and I weren't really satisfied with the diaphragm so we decided to use the new foam I saw advertised. I got a can and we tried it for a couple of nights. It seemed okay, but about the second week, one night after we finished having intercourse, Dick turned to me and said, 'They certainly make that stuff smell good!' I was almost asleep so it took a moment or two to hit me. Then I realized one of the things I liked most about the foam was that it didn't have any smell at all! I snatched the container off the night table and my heart almost stopped! For three nights we'd been fending off pregnancy with Dick's shaving cream!"

What about birth control pills?

Theoretically, oral contraception is a great idea. One pill a day for twenty days each month prevents an egg from being released by the ovary, and conception becomes nearly impossible. The pills themselves are a combination of two female sex hormones—estrogen and progesterone—either combined in one pill or offered separately to be taken in sequence. When used according to directions, the pills are nearly one hundred percent effective in preventing pregnancy. But they also prevent a lot of other things, too.

Like what, for example?

According to the manufacturer's warning that accompanies each advertisement for the product in medical journals, birth control pills can also prevent a long and happy life. Although the warnings are directed at physicians and couched in terse medical lingo, there are a few spine-chilling passages:

"Studies . . . estimate there is a seven to tenfold

increase in mortality (*death* rate) and morbidity (sickness rate) due to thromboembolic diseases (blood clots) in women taking oral contraceptives."

Translated into English, this sentence means that women who take the birth control pills are seven to ten times more likely to *die* from conditions caused by blood clots, than women who use other means of contraception. Even the dice tables in Las Vegas give better odds.

The drug manufacturer's warning gets more sinister as it goes on:

"Discontinue medication pending examination if there is sudden partial or complete loss of vision . . ."

The risk of sudden complete blindness seems a high price to pay for the convenience of contraception-by-tablet.

The warning, which takes up a full page, ends with a long list of symptoms occurring in women who take the pills:

"The following adverse reactions are known to occur in patients receiving oral contraceptives: Nausea, vomiting, gastro-intestinal symptoms, breakthrough bleeding, spotting, change in menstrual flow, edema, chloasma (heavy pigment deposits on the face), jaundice, migraine, rash (allergic), mental depression, change in weight (increase or decrease), amenorrhea (total absence of menstruation), breast changes, changes in cervical erosion, suppression of lactation (milk flow), rise in blood pressure."

If the woman is still intrepid enough to take the pill after her doctor gives her the full warning, there is the question of harming her newborn child. The message from the drug maker says:

"A small fraction of the hormonal agents in oral contraceptives has been identified in the milk of mothers receiving these drugs. The long range effect to the nursing infant cannot be determined at this time."

The nursing mother is gently advised that no one knows what she is inflicting on her helpless child by feeding him birth control hormones in his milk. It hardly seems fair.

Does every doctor tell his patients all these things?

Probably not. If he did, no one would take the pill—and there are some women who, for medical or emotional reasons, are better off taking contraceptive tablets. The majority of women who have a choice of birth control methods deserve to know the whole story. Recently the Food and Drug Administration ruled that every package of birth control pills has to include a warning directed at the patient so she will know at least part of the story.

Should the average woman use birth control pills?

This is a decision she has to make herself based on her knowledge of all the facts and her willingness to take the risks involved.

What about the "loop"?

Recently gynecologists and their patients have become interested in the revival of an ancient form of contraceptive device known as the IUD or intra-uterine contraceptive device. Any foreign body placed deep inside the uterus decreases the chances of pregnancy by some still unknown mechanism. Toward the turn of the century gold and platinum wire was placed within the uterine cavity to prevent pregnancy. More recently plastic coils have been used.

What are the results?

Variable. The protection rate varies from less than ninety percent to somewhat better than ninety percent. A small number of women using this technique have severe pain or bleeding and a few reject the plastic by ejecting it spontaneously. In about one woman out of two thousand, the plastic coil drills through the wall of the uterus into the intestinal area and can cause serious trouble. It would be fair to say that the IUD is not perfected yet, although improved versions are constantly being introduced.

How about the rhythm method?

How about it? This approach depends on timing intercourse to avoid the days when an egg is fertilizable. It valiantly tries to apply a predictable pattern of behavior to a totally unpredictable natural phenomenon —ovulation. The only thing dependable about the rhythm method is the ultimate result—pregnancy.

Are there any other means of birth control?

Well, there are always the "before and after" methods. Before ejaculation, the man can withdraw his penis and deposit the spurt of sperm onto the lady's tummy. Aside from ruining everyone's fun, unless he has the reflexes of a purse-snatcher, he may be taken by surprise. His surprise is nothing compared to his partner's when she starts looking for maternity dresses a few months later. The "after" approach is usually an exercise in futility. It is characterized by a mad leap from the bed into the bathroom, and a frenzied douche directed with trembling hands. Since any sperm that are going to do what they were constructed to do are probably well on their way to the fallopian tubes by then, the only benefit of douching is related to the calories burned up during the frantic race to the bathroom.

Is there anything else to prevent pregnancy?

Birth control methods are characterized by extremes. The "crossing" approach ranges from one hundred percent dependable to zero reliability. Both techniques are in common use and there is little to recommend either one for the average woman alone, although in specific cases they may be the method of choice. Complete contraceptive confidence comes from crossing the *legs*. No pregnancy, no intercourse, no nothing. Absolutely no security results from crossing the *fingers*. Once the sperm are deposited in the vagina, wishful thinking will not alter their course. The outcome is in the hands of reproductive biology and the laws of probability.

If a girl was foolish enough to just cross her fingers, isn't there anything she can do?

Until recently, she just had to count the days on her calendar. Now there is another possibility. It is called the "morning-after" pill. If she takes a powerful female sex hormone, diethylstilbesterol (DES for short) within a day or so after having intercourse, there is an excellent chance the pregnancy will not develop. There is one catch, however. The pills must be taken for about five consecutive days and the side effects are sometimes formidable. The worst one is overwhelming vomiting, lasting throughout the treatment. Some women who have taken it call it the "never again" drug. Each morning as the nausea begins to overtake them, the users moan over and over, "Never again—never again . . ."

Are there any really safe and sure methods to prevent pregnancy and still have sex?

Yes. Intercourse with a man who has had an effective vasectomy is probably the only completely safe way to enjoy sexual intercourse without any chance of motherhood.

In this operation, the tubes carrying sperm from the testicles to the penis (and ultimately to the vagina) are carefully cut and tied. If the operation is done right, the chances of pregnancy are almost nonexistent. There is however one pitfall—not every man who says he has had the operation actually saw the surgeon's knife. Every prudent woman will check for herself by identifying the small scar on the scrotum near the point where the testicles join the body. There should be scars on *both sides* because, as some women have found out to their dismay, reproduction is ambidextrous.

In the same way, a woman who has had her tubes tied or ovaries or uterus removed cannot conceive. To be absolutely safe she should check with her doctor, since sperms and eggs tend to be athletic. Many women who leave the operating room with, say, a left tube and a right ovary—and a false sense of security —are back in the same hospital two hundred eighty days later to have the baby they thought would never come. Better safe than half-safe.

For the average woman on her own, what is the best approach to contraception?

There is no single "right" technique for everyone. Each method has its advantages and drawbacks. The birth control pills are probably too dangerous in their present form to be unconditionally recommended. The diaphragm (plus contraceptive cream) is dependable, proved by time, and free from any risks to the user— except for the very small risk of pregnancy. Unfortunately the diaphragm is a little cumbersome and mechanical in use—a reasonable alternative is one of the more effective vaginal aerosol foams. For the woman who wants to be supersafe, the combination of this type of foam and a condom used by the man offers belt-and-suspenders type of protection. Even if the condom breaks or overflows, the foam neutralizes any stray sperm.

What about venereal disease?

For the past thirty years venereal disease was, for the most part, something that happened to someone else. Now things are changing, and the United States is in the grip of a virulent VD epidemic. Syphilis is increasing at the rate of almost ten percent per year with monthly increases of nearly thirty percent.

Gonorrhea has increased sixty percent in the past five years. In addition to all the other problems facing a woman alone, VD has emerged as a real threat to her happiness.

How come?

There are a lot of reasons. First, since World War II our country has been sending servicemen around the world. For many of them, prostitutes are the only means of sexual outlet. Most of the girls are infected with syphilis or gonorrhea or both. When the boys come home, those who have been with prostitutes often involuntarily bring their diseases with them.

Second, our society becomes more mobile and more promiscuous every day. A traveling salesman may have intercourse with a woman in New York on Monday, Chicago on Tuesday, and Houston on Wednesday. If he was infected in Manhattan he has started a chain of infection that may multiply into the hundreds and spread to ten states before he gets back home a month later.

Third, the birth control pill has changed contraceptive habits. The most common form of contraception in the casual sexual encounter used to be the condom, which offers both parties fairly good protection against VD. Pills protect against sperms, not germs.

Fourth, and most important, is complacency. Everyone believes that VD was cleared up after World War II and that was that.

Wasn't it?

Not quite. Because penicillin *used to be* so effective against these infections everyone let their guard down. Now in many cases *penicillin doesn't work*. The Asian form of gonorrhea is especially tough to cure and resists most common types of therapy.

How does this affect the single woman?

Not at all—unless she has sexual intercourse. What it all adds up to is these days every sexual experience (except between husband and wife—and there may even be exceptions in these cases) carries with it a certain risk of venereal infection. To protect herself, a woman has to know how to deal with the problem.

What can she do?

She can select her partners carefully. Aside from the usual emotional disappointments of an ill-chosen sexual relationship, bad judgment can pay off in a dangerous infection. To protect herself against surprises, a blood test for syphilis every six months is good insurance. At the same time she should ask her doctor to take a smear and culture for gonorrhea.

Is all that really necessary?

If she doesn't want unpleasant moments it is. Syphilis and gonorrhea in women are strange diseases. After the original exposure, the conditions can lie dormant for years without any symptoms whatsoever. In many cases, the bacteria are doing their deadly job attacking the brain, the bones, the joints, and the heart. A semi-annual blood test and smear/culture are the cheapest and best protection available. It would have saved Ellen a lot of unhappiness:

"I just can't believe it! I mean it was positively unreal!" Ellen was thirty-four, a striking redhead, expensively dressed, and very upset. "I mean, after all, Doctor, I live in a good neighborhood! It's not as if I was poor or something like that."

"What seems to be the problem?"

She brought out her imported linen handkerchief and began jabbing at her eyes.

"My husband is going to leave me. We've only been married six months and he's going to leave me. And I worked so hard to get married again! I was divorced two years ago and I wanted to have everything right this time. What can I do?"

"Why is he leaving you?"

"You won't believe it when I tell you—he said I gave him gonorrhea. Only he didn't put it that way—he called it 'the clap.' Honestly, Doctor, I don't see how I could have. I haven't had sex with another man for almost two years—and then it was only my ex-husband and one old boyfriend after my marriage broke up."

"Have you been to any other doctor yet?"

"No, Jerry—that's my husband—wanted me to go to his doctor but I came here first."

That afternoon, Ellen was examined by a gynecologist who sent his report a few days later. When she came in again, she was more subdued.

"It still doesn't seem possible. You mean I had those

gonorrhea germs living in my body for nearly two years?"

"That's right. You probably got them from your former husband or maybe the old boyfriend. The germs lived in the cervix without causing you any symptoms—but it didn't take long for you to infect Jerry and make everyone understandably unhappy."

When Jerry saw the medical evidence, he accepted it graciously. Both of them agreed to be treated and he and Ellen gradually settled down again. She described it:

"Things were a little strained during those seven days when we had to take the medicine. We sat at the breakfast table gobbling our pills and staring down into the scrambled eggs. Of course, Jerry had a right to be mad. He gave me a Jaguar for a wedding gift, and I gave him a dose of gonorrhea. It's going to take me a long time to make it up to him."

Then any woman can avoid a problem like Ellen's by having a vaginal exam and a blood test before she gets married?

Not necessarily. The usual premarital test required for a marriage license is simply a blood test for syphilis. For some reason the health department doesn't bother with gonorrhea. Unless the patient specifically asks for "a cervical smear and culture for GC," most doctors will not include it as part of the exam before marriage. But there are other reasons for having periodic vaginal check-ups as well.

Jackie came to her appointment in tears one afternoon. Thin and dark with large expressive eyes, she was obviously upset:

"It couldn't happen to me! I just know my life is ruined! Why did it have to happen?"

"Why did *what* have to happen?"

The answer came out like a moan. "My boyfriend, Jim, gave me syphilis! What am I going to do?"

"What kind of symptoms do you have?"

"Everything! I have this terrible discharge and this itching! Everything down there seems to be on fire!"

"When did it start?"

"About a week ago but it keeps getting worse. I know it's his fault. He's been away for two months, but right after we started sleeping together again I came down with it."

"It doesn't sound right. Maybe things aren't as bad as you think."

A trip to the gynecologist confirmed the suspicion.

Then Jackie didn't have VD?

Yes and no. She had a vaginal infection known as "trichomoniasis" (or "trich" for short). The symptoms resulted from the growth of tiny microscopic organisms within the vagina. She might well have picked it up from Jim, but probably it wasn't all his fault—very likely he got it from her in the first place.

How does that happen?

The tiny organisms can live for months in the male urethra without causing any symptoms in their unsuspecting host. During sexual intercourse, they are propelled into the vagina along with the evening's quota of sperm. The creatures multiply rapidly and itching, discharge, and burning appear promptly. The treatment is simple but tedious. Vaginal medication and the regular use of a condom during intercourse is required to prevent "ping-pong" reinfection—the man gives it to the woman who reinfects the man who returns the "trich" to the lady. In stubborn cases tablets by mouth may be prescribed.

But is trichomoniasis a venereal disease?

It is, in the sense that all infections transmitted by sexual behavior are "venereal"—having to do with Venus, the goddess of love. But it is entirely different from syphilis and gonorrhea since it does not respond to antibiotics and almost never affects the rest of the body.

There is another important aspect to the whole question of VD—venereal diseases are nothing special —they are just another category of malady like tuberculosis or arthritis. They should not be considered punishment for sexual intercourse. Fear, guilt, and anxiety are no more appropriate in a case of syphilis than in a case of typhoid fever. Early detection and treatment are important in both conditions to prevent epidemics and minimize individual suffering.

Are there any other venereal diseases?

Yes. There are three more: chancroid, lymphogranuloma venereum, and granuloma inguinale. So far they are confined mostly to medically underprivileged groups like blacks and homosexuals, but if the nationwide epidemic of VD continues, they will inevitably extend to the white heterosexual population. Research into treatment of these infections has been neglected, but as more infections appear treatment methods should improve.

Are there any other sexual problems that are especially troublesome to single women?

Yes. Any woman is more vulnerable sexually than a man simply because she is a woman. A woman alone is the most vulnerable of all. To a married woman, an obscene phone call is an annoyance. To a single woman it can mean a week of sleepless nights. The risk of a married woman being sexually molested or raped is very small. For many women alone, the possibility of those experiences is always with her. The overwhelming majority of sexual crimes against women involve victims who are single, widowed, or divorced.

What can a woman do to protect herself?

All criminals have serious emotional problems, but sex offenders have a psychological makeup all of their own. By understanding the mental mechanisms of those who commit sexual crimes, any woman can reduce the risk of being personally involved almost to zero.

The most common sexual offense women are exposed to is the obscene caller. These childish, frightened men who try for gratification this way need the victim's cooperation. If she won't talk to them, they can't do anything. As soon as it becomes obvious that the call is sexually directed, all the woman has to do is hang up—hard. Unless the caller gets sexual kicks from a punctured eardrum, he usually won't call back. If he should be persistent, the lady can always fracture the other ear. Shrieking, crying, *listening* are exactly what the poor psychopath is looking for—why give it to him? Besides, there is nothing in the telephone company's regulations that says a woman has to answer her telephone every time it rings.

How about other types of sex crimes?

Like rape? Discounting the lurid accounts in detective story magazines, the real facts are fascinating. Most women who are forced to have intercourse against their will are imposed upon by men whom they know and usually know well. Uncomfortable moments on dark streets do happen, but they are distinctly rare by comparison with awkward situations that can occur in the privacy of one's own home. But an understanding of the mental state of the rapist can enable a woman to avoid most of the risks and effectively deal with the unavoidable ones.

How?

Most unwanted sexual experiences result from a misunderstanding of a woman's wishes by a man and misreading a man's intentions by a woman. If a woman expects to drive out to the lake to look at the moon and maybe trade a few kisses, and her date (the second time they are out together) thinks she's looking for a romantic place to go all the way, potential tragedy is brewing. The first rule is for a woman to let her companion know *exactly* what she expects of him—and how far she is willing to let things go. Before she can do that she has to know herself what the limits of the occasion will be. With old friends, spontaneity in sex is exciting—with new friends, if things get too spontaneous, it is known as "carnal knowledge without consent." It helps to avoid isolated locations, too many drinks, and taking things for granted with new acquaintances. Of course, not every case of rape is rape.

What does that mean?

There is such a thing as retroactive rape. Morning-after regrets, guilt about "going too far," fear of pregnancy, and other types of second thoughts sometimes bring on accusations that don't really correspond to reality. That's not playing fair, and in addition to being the perfect way to ruin a wonderful relationship, it can be embarrassing. The district attorney (who decides whether or not to press charges) isn't exactly a choir boy, and he knows how these things happen. Under these circumstances, discretion is the better part of valor.

What about the other kind of rape?

Most forcible rape can be avoided. Dark alleys, late hours, chance meetings with "nice" strangers all spell trouble, and most women avoid them as a matter of course. But there is always the possibility that in spite of everything a woman finds herself being really raped.

There are two things she should be aware of—one is obscure, the other obvious. First the obscure one. Many criminal rapists are not directed toward penis-vagina intercourse. They force the victim to engage in what police reports refer to as "oral copulation." The psychopath applies his mouth to the vagina and clitoris of his victim or forces his penis into her mouth —or both if he can manage it.

Why do they do that?

Rapists are sick men, emotionally. One aspect of their sickness is their immaturity in every way, including sexually. By *substituting* fellatio and cunnilingus for sexual intercourse (instead of utilizing it as a preliminary), they are manifesting the same symptoms of illness that made them choose rape in the first place.

What's the other fact?

The obvious one is that every act of penis-vagina intercourse requires the active cooperation of the woman (unless she is unconscious or drugged—few rapes take place under these circumstances).

There is the old story of the Royal Guards officer who was being court-martialed on a charge of raping the Colonel's daughter. After the damsel tearfully described her ravishment from the witness stand, the defense attorney stepped forward with the accused officer's sword in his hand. He removed it from the scabbard and handed it to the astonished young lady. He ordered her to put it in the sheath. Just as she was about to replace the tip of the sword he suddenly moved the scabbard a few inches to one side. She tried again and once again he avoided the sword point by averting the sheath ever so slightly. As the alleged victim reddened, the attorney turned to the judge and said, "Your honor, the defense rests." His client was acquitted.

How does this help a woman protect herself against the threat of being sexually molested?

No woman can be raped without a minimum amount of cooperation—willing or forced. Rapists take advantage of this knowledge by terrifying the victim into complying with their wishes. The key lies in the mechanism of rape itself—the offender must expose his own sexual equipment to the victim. The next step is described by a veteran police officer who has investigated thousands of sex crimes:

"Most women don't know it but they can turn off an attacker at least ninety percent of the time with hardly a risk to themselves. All they have to do is appear to cooperate until he exposes himself. If the lady then takes his testicles in her left hand and smashes them as hard as she can with her right fist—once or twice —he will lose all interest in sex. Tell her to leave the scene, call the police, and we will be happy to take the subject to the hospital."

Should a woman really do something as terrible as that?

It's up to her. Being raped can be pretty terrible, too.

Is it fair for a single woman to have to handle all these problems herself?

Probably not. But in spite of the complexity of our civilization, socially and sexually we are exposed to many of the same dangers that threatened our ancestors twenty-five thousand years ago in the jungles and wild forests. They only survived because of their cunning, their ingenuity, and their intense dedication to self-preservation. The woman who happens to be single, widowed, or divorced lives in a modern jungle. If she uses every one of her abilities to the utmost, not only will she survive but she has a chance for real happiness.

BOTTOMLESS PITS OR MEN HAVE THEIR PROBLEMS TOO

What is a bottomless pit?

In the early days of the movies, a standard feature of the Saturday matinée was the serial. Each week the beautiful but somewhat frazzled heroine would be exposed to thundering locomotives, storms at sea, desperate ravishers, and worst of all, the bottomless pit. Usually about episode seventeen—out of twenty —she found herself pitched into a mine shaft, a chasm, or an immense pool of quicksand. The prime feature of this stock episode was her desperate struggle while she slowly disappeared beneath the surface. As every loyal movie-lover knew, episode eighteen would find her bobbing to the surface valiantly prepared for whatever new punishment awaited her.

In real life, it's not quite the same. The girl who becomes emotionally involved with a man who isn't right for her sinks just as surely as her cinema twin. The big difference is she doesn't pop to the surface promptly at two P.M. the following Saturday. Years later she may still be thrashing around, sinking deeper and deeper and deeper.

Selecting a husband is the most urgent and critical

decision a woman will make in her lifetime. Her future happiness is almost completely dependent on the man she chooses. No matter what cruel blows fate may deal her as the years go by, if she has a loyal and loving husband, she can overcome disappointment and tragedy. On the other hand, no matter how fortunate she is in life, a bad man will bring it all tumbling down. No one has to look any further than the headlines to find the evidence.

For example?

For example, many of the world's richest and most beautiful women—heiresses, film stars, former wives of public figures—have destroyed any chance they might have had for happiness by choosing men who were Bottomless Pits. Ironically, when a woman chooses a man who drags her down, often it isn't all her fault.

How come?

By some twist of destiny, the men who are equipped to do a woman the most damage are also the most charming, the most alluring, the most irresistible. As a direct result of their inner emotional defects they project a superficial image that leaves the average nice guy looking like a Chevrolet convertible parked next to a new Rolls-Royce. The Chevy will get you there in comfort and safety, but the Rolls is made of dreams. It is more than a car, it is a way of life. It is a new dimension. It also costs as much as a large house (and lot), is very expensive to maintain, and can be hard to dispose of when the time comes.

The Bottomless Pit who walks into a girl's life wear-

ing a $400 suit and a hand-made silk shirt has about
the same attributes. He can offer her things that no
other man can: glamour, excitement, a whole new
world. (*Offer* is the right word because much of the
time these chaps never deliver.) He can talk her into
abandoning everything she has ever worked for in
exchange for beautiful dreams that have a habit of
fading out right in the middle. It always ends that
way because there is one thing every Bottomless Pit
forgets to tell his latest girl friend.

What's that?

He never gets around to reminding her that about
two inches beneath the surface, he is just the same
as any other man, except maybe a little shallower.
That's one reason why a man like this can only excite
the latest woman in his life. The last conquest is still
furious at him, and the ones before her have recovered sufficiently from his attentions to be totally indifferent to him. The best example of a man who
operates this way happens to be the one that many
single girls are most likely to meet.

Which one is that?

The married man. As far as every woman alone is
concerned, a married man is a contradiction in terms.
He simply cannot be in the market for her products—
love *and* marriage. The husband who is looking for
another woman besides his wife wants to try things
another way—a way that cannot possibly solve the
long-term problems of a woman alone. He usually has
given up on sex that involves another human being.

What he wants now is a computerized doll who will keep him company when there's nothing good on television. As he tells his friends in the locker room at the country club—at least the ones who aren't too sick of him by now to listen—"I'm through with responsibilities. I don't want to get involved. All I'm looking for is a little action and a chance to pull out when I get bored." At the conclusion of his weekly speech, the other country club philosophers sagely nod their heads in agreement, stack up their golf clubs, and drive home to their wives and children.

The same night, when he is out on the town with his girl friend of the moment, his oration has been rewritten slightly. Now it goes something like: "What I really want is a chance to get close to someone. Someone I can really have a meaningful life with. Someone like you." Of course. He invariably leaves out the part about "pulling out" when he "gets bored." As far as single girls are concerned, married men have all the cards.

In what way?

It's usually two against one. Unwittingly the man's wife is her husband's staunchest ally against the other woman. She provides him with a home, security, clean shirts, and self-confidence—all the weapons he needs to succeed in his campaign to "make it with the chicks." If he had to attend to all those little details himself, he wouldn't be half as debonair and half as snappy. As a matter of fact, most married heartbreakers, if they had to fend for themselves, would look distinctly seedy before the end of the week. The irony of it all is: *it should be so obvious.*

What should be so obvious?

If a man can't maintain an honest relationship with
one woman, he's unlikely to conduct himself decently
with another one. But every woman alone likes to
think of herself as "the exception." She then becomes
particularly vulnerable to the most common variety of
married parasite.

He's the one who insists: "The mess I'm making of
my life isn't my fault. All I need is someone who
understands me. Like you, and you, and you . . ." His
current date has the dubious distinction of being
elected "Living Alibi of the Month." When she is no
longer willing—or able—to agree constantly that her
married friend's problems are all the fault of his wife,
she gets traded in for someone who will. In a sense
this kind of fellow is less damaging than the other
varieties because he moves quickly from one girl to
another—they all seem to suffer from inability to see
things his way for long. Somewhat more sinister is the
next married charmer—the one whose wife *is* understanding.

How can a wife understand a man like that?

It isn't easy. However, some women instinctively com-
prehend the immaturity of their spouses and treat
them with a grudging tolerance. They think it's better
to forgive and forget than break up the family, spend
a couple of years in the divorce courts, and mess up
two lives.

Wives who feel this way keep their husbands on
long leashes. After he's had his fun with a woman

who doesn't have a man of her own, his wife blows the whistle on him. She keeps careful track of just what's happening and when she decides he's gotten it out of his system, she has a little talk with him, he has a little talk with his girl friend, and he's back with his wife again. He solemnly promises never to stray again—until the next time.

One of the most dangerous types of married man to team up with is the one who uses his girl as a weapon against his wife. These chaps tend to be over forty, well-off financially, and possessed of a cold-blooded outlook that is anything but reassuring. When they feel rejected by their spouses, they carefully select a girl who is her opposite. For example, if the wife is a Radcliffe graduate from a socially prominent family, tall, thin, and brunette, her husband's choice of weapon is likely to be a chunky girl who bleaches her hair, worked hard to get through business school, and is naive enough to believe that her boss really is interested in her. Actually, his only interest is in finding a guided missile to launch at Mrs. Boss. Once his wife gets the message, "You asked for it. You treated me badly and now look who I'm throwing myself away on!" the girl friend becomes disposable. Unless a girl enjoys playing the role of a living telegram, this game is not for her. Ironically, the most cynical married man of all is the one who is the most fun.

Which one is that?

He's the fellow who's delighted with things the way they are—that is, almost. He loves his wife, he's attached to his children, he enjoys his job—in fact, the only thing he misses is a little excitement. His sexual relationship with his wife has become routine, as sometimes tends to happen after ten years or so, and he's looking for thrills. One thing that makes him particularly disarming is his willingness to absorb all the costs of an extramarital affair. He eagerly promises a girl anything—because he has no intention of paying off. He spends money freely—the best restaurants, expensive gifts, nice trips, because he is determined to share the enjoyment and feels he is spending the money primarily on himself. In a sense this fellow is like the twenty-year-old college boy who lives at home with his mother and whoops it up with the cheerleaders on weekends. He's a barrel of fun mostly because there's nothing worrying him. He knows he will settle down someday—and not with one of his baby dolls. The married man who is ninety-nine percent satisfied at home has a serene mind, too. He knows that when the fun is over, he can pick up right where he intended to all the time, with his wife, his children, and his cocker spaniel. There is no place in his future for his girl friend. Which of course is the basic problem.

In what way?

Relationships with married men are like piecrusts, made to be broken. All the usual ingredients—the thrill of the forbidden, the excitement of secret meetings, the sharing of a conspiracy—are made even more acute by the unconscious awareness that one day it will all come crashing down.

For the woman who insists on trying to beat the odds against finding happiness with married men, a short memory is a real asset. She must be able to forget instantly that the money her lover boy spends to take her to dinner and the theater could be put to better uses. Like paying the dentist to straighten his little girl's teeth so she can attract her own boyfriend when she grows up—and hopefully one who's not already married. It also helps if she can overlook other annoying little details, including the fact that for every compliment he pays her he has to tell a lie to another woman (his wife) who not too many years ago was hearing exactly the same compliments. (Sometimes at the same table at the same restaurant.) Even if a woman can overcome all these emotional hurdles, the biggest one of all has to catch up with her in the end.

What's that?

The immutable fact that human beings are repetitive machines who are unconsciously compelled to go through life repeating the same mistakes over and over again. (Except for the rare ones who suddenly wake up and realize what they are doing to themselves.) Sooner or later the man who betrays his wife will do exactly the same thing to the woman he has chosen to replace her. Tina's story is typical:

"The big question I want to ask, Doctor, is why do we all tend to think that we are the exception to the rule? The slogan of the human race could almost be, 'It can't happen to me!' Believe me, I know what I'm saying."

"What happened to make you feel this way?"

"It's still painful—even after three years. I was assistant to the vice president of a chain of department stores out West—it was about ten years ago and it was my first job. I was—let's see—twenty-four at the time. Harold—my boss—wasn't happy at home and we started going out together. Then he set me up in an apartment and things got even cozier. Even now I don't understand how he fooled his wife for so long, but I still don't think she ever suspected what was going on. Anyway, after two years of sneaking around, I told him one day, 'Harold, we're getting married or I'm going to get a new apartment where I pay the rent and you don't have a key.' He tried to wiggle out of it, but I had him where I wanted him— or I thought I did." Tina shook her head.

"Anyway, I twisted his arm—and some other parts of his body—to get him to divorce his wife and I became Mrs. Stelzer, or, as he used to introduce me, 'The second Mrs. Stelzer.' Ugh! Everything was fine —at least, I think it was—for the first two years. I quit my job and stayed home. Then came Christmas of the third year. I took our son—he was two and a half—to Harold's mother for two weeks. Harold had to stay behind for a few days after Christmas to supervise the big sale. Then his mother got sick, I couldn't reach him on the phone, and I drove back home. It was only about seventy-five miles and I took little Rickie with me. I walked in the house about 3:30 in the afternoon and there was Harold still in bed—with his new assistant. Ohhh, what a disaster! There I was in the doorway of the bedroom, holding my two-year-old by the hand and my half-crocked husband was sitting up in bed next to this little blonde. Apparently when she took over my job she wanted to do it in a big way. She filled my shoes, my nightgown, and one or two other things as well. That was the last time I ever saw my husband outside of court. Let me tell you, Doctor, any girl who goes out with a married man is just keeping the bed warm for the girl who's going to take over from her. I know—I still have the scars."

But what if a girl is really in love with a married man?

Then maybe she should wait until he's unmarried. There's an old law of physics that has an imposing title: *The law of Impenetrability of Matter.* All it really recites is the obvious: "No two objects can occupy the same space at the same time." There is a more profound law of the unconscious that states: "Two deep emotional relationships cannot exist simultaneously." A man can't do justice to another woman while he is still emotionally involved with his wife. Even in the final stages of a decaying marriage—where the primary emotion is mutual hatred—there is not enough unconscious energy to support an enduring bond with the next woman in his life. These days a legal divorce is possible in six weeks to six months in many states. It's better to wait until the emotional dust settles than to spend the next year or so trying to untangle a hasty decision.

Can't an affair with a married man ever turn out well?

Of course it can. And a girl can win the Irish Sweepstakes or become the first lady astronaut or break the bank at Monte Carlo. That's the real problem. Theoretically almost any type of relationship can turn out well—but with a limited amount of time (there are about twenty years between voting age and the menopause) a girl has to plan objectively and select the situation that has the best possible chance of providing both her and her husband with the happiness they deserve.

What about single men who don't want to marry?

Of all the Bottomless Pits a girl may encounter, the dedicated lifetime bachelor is probably the most frustrating. They are always charming, always engaging, but regrettably never charmed and never engaged. Their lives are devoted to fluttering from flower to flower, savoring the sweetest nectar from each petal. That may be fine for the man, but like a flower, a girl can get very faded from having her nectar constantly savored. There are two big problems with professional bachelors—and neither one becomes obvious until much later in the game.

First, they are so terribly attractive. They dress well, they know all the right places to eat, the right wines to drink, and the right shows to see. They drive wonderful cars and never have trouble getting reservations at the best restaurants in town. Everything about them is exciting, flashy, and marvelously "in." The exhilaration of going around with one of these chaps is unmatched by any other experience—at least, for a while. It is as if there were no limits, nothing to interfere with nonstop pleasure. That, of course, is the problem. These dedicated solo fliers never have to think about the future because for them there isn't any—at least, in the usual sense. There is never the prospect of a wife, no worry about children, no mortgage on a three-bedroom house, no saving to put children through college. Incidentally, there is also no room in their future plans for the girl they are currently dating—a fact they usually do their best to conceal.

There is another problem besides. These lads are emotional freeloaders. They sop up affection and understanding like a fifty-cent sponge—no woman on earth can ever give enough to satisfy them. Not only do they specialize in savoring nectar, but they can quickly drain a girl dry, which gets down to the second problem.

Probably the most valuable asset of a woman alone is *time*. And the world's most accomplished time-waster is the perpetual bachelor. His low-pressure schedule is never upset by that distant appointment with the Justice of the Peace. In fact, squeezing the last luscious moment out of each affair is one of his favorite labor-saving devices. The longer he can stretch out each romance, the less looking around he has to do. Every day a woman devotes to a man who is dedicated to avoiding marriage is one day less than she can devote to making her life the way she wants it to be.

How can a girl tell a professional bachelor from an eligible man?

It isn't easy. A dedicated bachelor and the man who is going to make an ideal husband sometimes have a lot in common—at least, on the surface. The difference is often very subtle. With the confirmed bachelor everything is perfect—too perfect. Things happen too fast and too smoothly. Because he has no intention of forming permanent relationships, there are hardly any obstacles to overcome. Every conflict can be quickly put aside or postponed indefinitely. The man who doesn't have marriage in his future can eagerly agree to anything, secure in the knowledge that he will never have to deliver.

Another characteristic of the fellow who plans to go
it alone is all the other girls he knows—or who know
him. He is the darling of the hatcheck girls at the
clubs, every waitress greets him by his first name, and
his telephone keeps ringing on those quiet evenings
alone at his place. The average girl on her own may
not insist on marrying the world's oldest living virgin,
but the Playboy of the Year is not the man for her
either.

By contrast, the path of true love is never a super-
highway. A man who really intends to spend the rest
of his life with a woman will be attacked by doubts
many times along the way. His plans for the future
will come into conflict with other unconscious feelings
and he may from time to time become moody and
hesitant. Sometimes he even needs his woman's help
to work through periods of mixed emotions and
ambivalence. Reassurance and encouragement from
the ones he loves usually enable him to overcome
these momentary problems. But the professional bachelor never has any doubts. He knows right from the
start that *he* isn't going to get married, and he never
has to give it another thought.

Can a girl change a dedicated bachelor?

Maybe. If she sacrifices enough, she can get one to
marry her, but that doesn't mean she can change him.
Even after marriage these men cling to the old way
of doing things. They are used to living on an emotional one-way street—everything coming in and
nothing going out. Their world is like a telephone
booth—comfortable for one person and unbearable for
two. It is almost as if each of them planned unconsciously to end up the way they usually do—living

alone with buttons off their shirts watching old movies on television. It's a shame, but that's the way they arrange it. Alcoholics arrive at the same point, but by a different route.

Is alcoholism a serious problem?

No. Alcoholism is just a joke—if your only contact with it is the funny drunks on television. To the girl who marries one, it can be the blackest tragedy of her life. The facts are hard to face, but every woman needs to face them. Of all the mind-altering drugs known to man—including marijuana, heroin, cocaine, hashish, and LSD—*alcohol is the most common source of mental and physical damage and death*. There are, according to the U.S. Bureau of Narcotics, about 100,000 narcotics addicts in the United States. There are at least nine million alcoholics. Alcoholism costs the country about two billion dollars a year; the bill for crimes related to narcotics runs about a sixth of that. As any expert on drugs will testify, a man who is addicted to narcotics, so long as he obtains his daily supply at a reasonable cost (such as the fifty cents' worth the government provides free to many addicts in the methadone program), will live his normal life expectancy, keep his job, raise a family, and remain a model citizen in every way, if he has no personality traits that interfere. Many thousands who are furnished drugs at public expense are doing just that. If he is addicted to alcohol, he will ultimately lose his job, turn his back on his family, and, penniless, meet a premature death. Temperance lecturers miss the point; alcoholism is not a moral problem, it is a desperate problem of addiction to a legal drug. The evidence can be seen in any large city any afternoon in the living purgatory known as "Skid Row." The men and women who agonize there are not dope fiends—they are all former social drinkers who for one reason or another lost control.

What does this have to do with selecting a husband?

Just this: for the girl who loves Russian roulette or doing ninety on the expressway with her eyes closed, marriage to an alcoholic will be the biggest thrill of her life. To other kinds of girls, it can be nothing but trouble.

How can a girl tell if a man is an alcoholic?

Sometimes it's easy and sometimes it isn't. Not everyone who takes a drink at Christmas is a drunk. But a man who takes more than ten drinks a day—every day —and is addicted to alcohol—is clearly an alcoholic.

The future addict is harder to spot. An important warning is given by the fellow who can't skip a drink. The test is easy. Simply say, the next time the occassion comes up, "Let's just have a Coke this time, okay?" If he can do it with ease, things aren't too bad. If he can't, give him another chance in a week or so, under different circumstances. If he still *has* to drink, watch out. He is displaying the emotional dependence on that clear liquid, ethyl alcohol, that marks the beginning of addiction.

Another danger sign is the chap who is at his best after a couple of drinks. Often he is manifesting an early sign of making liquor an essential part of his life.

There are eight fairly reliable psychological clues to the potential alcoholic that any girl can keep track of:

1. Sexual failure due to alcohol. If he drinks enough to interfere with more important things like sex, everyone is in for trouble.

2. He insists on one specific brand and won't drink anything else no matter how much inconvenience results. This is a measure of the control that drinking exerts on his life.

3. He will drink *any* brand of *anything*. This is sometimes the next step after step number two and is *not* an improvement.

4. He has been in trouble because of alcohol. If a man has ever lost his job, been arrested in connection with drinking or otherwise let it damage his life, it will probably happen that way again.

5. He has been convicted of drunken driving. The grim truth is that the man who drinks and drives risks his girl's life as much as his own.

6. He can't wait to drink. The man who stays at his girl's place overnight and then races out at 7 A.M. when the liquor stores open is telling his girl what is most important to him—she had better listen.

7. He denies the very existence of the problem. The chap who becomes indignant when the subject comes up and angry if it persists is confessing by his very denial.

8. He increases his consumption when the going gets tough. If there is any doubt in her mind, it is sensible for a woman to introduce a little conflict into the relationship. If her man really starts drinking at that stage, she might want to avoid the biggest conflict of all and make her departure then and there.

Is any drinking at all acceptable?

When the human race becomes perfect, the consumption of alcohol will suddenly fall to zero. Until that moment, it probably has its place as a natural tranquillizer, soothing the rough edges of life and acting as a chemical shock absorber to cushion fate's most jarring blows. As a form of emotional lubrication, drinking in moderation may be relatively harmless. When the man takes a drink, little damage is done. When the drink takes the man, any chance of happiness ends right there.

Can a girl help her man to overcome alcoholism?

Probably not. Unless she wants to play double or nothing, signing on as the wife of an admitted alcoholic is guaranteed to be a losing proposition. Treating a man who is addicted to alcohol is the most challenging job ever faced by a psychiatrist, by Alcoholics Anonymous, or by any minister. The success rate of the best methods rarely exceeds fifty percent. In the hands of amateurs—like a wife—the odds are about a thousand to one the wrong way. There are too many other good men available to justify taking the risk. Of course, alcohol isn't the only dangerous drug around.

What kinds of problems do the other drugs cause?

That's the worst part. The only advantage of excessive drinking is that scientists know how bad the effects are—and they *are* bad. When it comes to the other mind drugs, LSD for example, no one can really say what the long-range damage will amount to. Ignoring the usual moralistic horror stories, there is a real chance that LSD damages chromosomes, can cause birth defects, and sometimes turns on a psychosis that won't turn off. Heroin and other opium derivatives cause a true physical addiction—much like alcohol—but have the further disadvantage of being illegal and therefore very expensive. The usual addict's supply costs from fifty to a hundred dollars a day, which is a heavy addition to the budget of most young married couples.

Amphetamines—"speed"—are nothing more than the familiar diet pills gone out of control. The fat ladies who take three a day under their doctor's supervision may benefit significantly without side effects. The chap who takes twenty, fifty, or even a hundred a day is asking for big trouble. Agitation, hyperactivity, words and ideas that come tumbling out wildly, are the symptoms of a "speed freak."

At the other end of the drug rainbow is the man who uses barbiturates. Instead of a lonesome little Seconal tab at bedtime, he may take eight, ten, or a dozen during the day. It makes him relaxed and easy to get along with, but it also makes him dependent on the drug and apathetic to the world around him— not to mention indifferent toward women.

Actually, men who use LSD, heroin, speed, and barbiturates rarely are a serious problem for the girl who seeks a husband methodically. Most of them will be quickly screened out and discarded early in the game. When it comes to marijuana, things get a lot more complicated.

In what way?

Because there are two sharply divided schools of
opinion about marijuana. On one side most ministers,
law enforcement officers (at least publicly), law-
makers, and professional moralists insist that marijuana is a dangerous habit-forming drug that leads to
physical and moral decay and ultimately to narcotics
addiction. On the opposing team there are most adults
under thirty, and at least ninety percent of scientific
experts on drugs, including physicians, pharmacolo-
gists, toxicologists, and psychiatrists. They point out
that, medically speaking, *marijuana is less harmful
than any other commonly used social drug, including
alcohol and tobacco*. At a recent meeting of the
American Psychiatric Association, a well-known professor of psychiatry at Harvard Medical School expressed this medical opinion about marijuana:

1. Marijuana is not an addicting drug.
2. There is no such thing as a marijuana psychosis.
3. Long-term use of marijuana does not lead to character change.
4. Marijuana is not associated with criminal behavior.
5. Marijuana does not lead to sexual excess, but can
   actually increase sexual enjoyment.
6. Marijuana may have some very important medical
   benefits.

Then it's all right to use marijuana?

Certainly. If you want to risk spending one to ten
years in the penitentiary after conviction for sale,

use, or even possession of the dried weed. Most law-makers have chosen to ignore the scientific evidence; as a result, the hapless user of marijuana gets the same treatment before the law as a burglar, bank robber, or unpremeditated murderer. (Child molesters are treated somewhat more leniently.)

Every single girl has to make up her own mind concerning the use of marijuana by a potential husband. Once she knows the objective facts—uncolored by the shrill cries of the moral redeemers on one hand or the professional pot-heads on the other—she can come to a reasonable decision. In the same way, knowledge and understanding can avoid endless suffering in relating to homosexuals.

Is that really a big problem for women alone?

Yes, indeed. Some of the world's most attractive men happen to be homosexuals—or to put it more precisely, some homosexuals are superficially the most attractive men in the world. They are friendly, charming, suave, and sophisticated. Often they know more about what pleases a woman than many women themselves. It is no accident that some of the most successful women's clothing designers and hair stylists are dedicated homosexuals (although this is far from being the rule).

Men who are not attracted *sexually* to women may still identify with them in many ways. The homosexual man often has a particularly seductive and appealing manner with his female friends. He remembers a girl's birthday, her favorite drink, the kind of flowers she likes best, and even her choice in lipstick. All those little things that the average heterosexual male is indifferent to or too busy to think of, the homosexual may be keenly aware of.

Just as important, many homosexual men devote a lot of time to the tiny details of grooming that make for smashing good looks. Their hair is impeccably styled; their clothes are cut perfectly, fit divinely, and often anticipate next year's fashions. (It is no coincidence that a few of the most stunningly attractive male film stars are also tuned in to homosex rather than heterosex.)

The combination of these qualities in certain homosexuals can have a devastating effect on a girl. When a man like that comes into her life, she thinks she has finally found someone who is sensitive, understanding, and who really loves her to the exclusion of all others. She may be right about the first two of these suppositions.

But why is she wrong about the third?

One of the primary necessities in a happy marriage—mutual sexual happiness—is an impossibility for the homosexual. Instead of finding his sexual satisfaction only with his wife, his source of gratification is mutual masturbation, oral sex, or anal intercourse with other men. It doesn't take much imagination for a girl to recognize how she would feel if she knew that, after marriage, a night out with the boys means her husband gets out of her bed and into bed with another man. The homosexual may be the perfect date, but he is a terrible husband.

How does a girl identify a homosexual?

It isn't always easy. Some homosexuals make no effort to hide. But the clandestine homosexual often proceeds through the early stages of courtship smoothly—sometimes with higher marks than his heterosexual counterparts.

The first clue often appears when he fails to make any sexual advances at all. At the start some girls consider it a welcome change from the usual wrestling bouts that mark the "getting-acquainted" phase of most new relationships. Then, as more time passes and nothing begins to stir, relief gives way to concern, eventually followed by anxiety, culminating in shocked awareness as the full realization hits a girl. Some women are repelled and disgusted, but their guilt and revulsion are not really appropriate. Homosexuality is a specific sexual problem—there is no room for moral judgments. On the other hand, there is no room for continuing the relationship—if a girl really wants to get happily married.

Are there other kinds of homosexuals?

Yes. The condition exists in many forms. The one which is most dangerous to women alone is the type of homosexual who can respond fairly well to the limited sexual demands of courtship. He makes some sexual advances, obtains erections during the preliminaries, and can sometimes complete intercourse with satisfactory or even impressive potency. Then the girl has to look for less obvious clues.

If her boyfriend has a lot of homosexual friends or

a collection of homosexual books or magazines or seems to identify with homosexuality, it's worth probing deeper. If her man is a homosexual, she's going to find out sooner or later, and the sooner before marriage the better. The man who has unusual relationships with other men—a "cousin" who really isn't a cousin, or another man who is more like a brother than a pal—requires close scrutiny. Any adult male who has been legally adopted by another adult or who adopts another man owes a full explanation to his future wife—particularly if she gets a ready-made father or an instant grown-up son as one of her wedding presents. It pays for a girl to examine very carefully the background of any potential husband she even suspects of homosexuality.

Why?

For two reasons. First, not every effeminate man is a homosexual, and it's not really fair to her or to her man if she discards him on the basis of a hunch or a little malicious gossip.

Second, the man who applies for the position of "husband" is trying to land the most important job in *her* life. The chap who wants to put rivets in the wings at the aircraft factory has to submit to a thorough investigation. The one who wants to play the leading role in her life for the next fifty years deserves to be selected with at least the same discretion.

One simple way to find out if her man is a homosexual is to ask him. The majority of homosexuals are honest, like everyone else, and will tell the truth. That is usually that.

Can't an understanding woman help a homosexual?

No. She can't help someone whose problem she doesn't understand and who may not want to be helped. One of the characteristics of homosexuality is that most homosexuals are resigned to their way of life. The ones who really want to change have a reasonable chance to do so via psychiatric treatment. Marriage is not a cure for any sexual problem—much less one as deep and pervasive as homosexuality.

Are there any other types of men a girl has to be cautious about?

Yes. Although not as numerous as homosexuals, hustlers can be every bit as charming. These are the men who take a woman alone by surprise. Most girls are alert for the man who is interested in exploiting her sexually, which makes them even more vulnerable to those who want to take advantage of them financially. Fortunately, most single girls have a natural immunity to the professional hustler. On what a secretary or administrative assistant earns in a month, the average hustler can't get along for a weekend. But when it comes to a well-off widow or a prosperous divorcée, things are different. Just as the way to a man's heart may be his stomach, the average con man is looking for the shortest route to a lady's bank book. To make matters worse, the days of the gigolo with plastered-down hair and a pencil-thin mustache are gone forever; his modern counterpart plies his trade on the beach and at the country club, drives a sports car, and looks as clean-cut as the lads in the cigarette ads.

The other category of financial parasite wears the costume of the substantial middle-aged business man. His approach is romantic, his intentions are "serious," and all he needs is "a little loan to put over a big business deal." The "big deal" usually consists of arranging a nice trip to Florida for his *real* girl friend who is probably working the same routine on another middle-aged gentleman. A good response to approaches like this is a simple explanation: "People should do what they do best." Bankers negotiate loans and single women negotiate partnerships—*marriage*.

Some of the more enthusiastic and enterprising hustlers even advertise in the want ads: "Charming man seeks attractive woman of means. . . ." The translation goes: "Swindler seeks woman with money and no experience. Will take money and supply [unforgettable] experience."

How can a woman protect herself against hustlers?

Sometimes it helps to be a little suspicious. Even in the later stages of the relationship as the wedding date approaches there is really no reason for money to change hands. One of the non-negotiable requirements for a suitable man is his ability to support himself and his wife—at least at subsistence levels. If he can't manage it without dipping into her savings account, it might be a good idea to keep looking until she finds a man who can. If the woman is widowed or divorced and her boyfriend is significantly younger than she is, she may feel flattered. After all, how many ladies in their forties can attract a fellow twenty-nine years old? Tedious as it may be, she must consider the possibility that the major attraction may be her investments rather than her endowments. The man who is eager to keep his appointment at the wedding but keeps reminding her of *his* plans for *her* money after the marriage must come under suspicion. She wants a man who talks about *his* plans for *her*—money has a way of taking care of itself.

Any woman who has a substantial amount of money or property needs a date with a lawyer and a banker long before she makes that date with the Justice of the Peace. They will be happy to discuss suitable ways for her to put it out of anyone's reach except her own. Later on, after she and her husband are better acquainted, she can make her own decisions and arrange the appropriate changes.

She can also take this opportunity to ask about premarital contracts and the property laws of her state as they apply to women who remarry.

What are they?

Briefly stated, many states have laws specifying that any property acquired by a married couple after the wedding—no matter who earns it—is the joint property of man and wife. Other states give the husband an immediate interest in any worldly goods his new wife may possess. If the marriage fails even after ten days, a woman can stand to lose a lot of what little she may have. In most parts of the country, a woman's will becomes invalid on the day of her marriage, and no matter what she specifies in her new will, a big share of her estate may go to her new husband.

If she has children from a former marriage, it can be a real hardship on them. Sometimes this provision can be nullified by an agreement signed before marriage. The whole idea is full of complications, which makes sound legal advice essential. A woman should go to a lawyer experienced in this area, pay his fee, and listen to every word. Getting the inside story from the milkman's brother, who once sent away for some law books, may save twenty-five dollars, but it's really not the same.

Another means of protection against the professional hustler is to tell him exactly what defensive measures have been taken. Loretta did it this way:

"At first I felt rather embarrassed about it, Doctor, but it had to be done. I'm only forty-eight, and I want to get married again. My husband left me nearly $55,000 in stocks when he died two years ago. I don't really know how to handle investments—especially that much. I went to my banker and he suggested we set up a trust with the bank and me as, he called it, co-trustees. It actually means we have to do everything together, and I can't really take out any of the money without his permission. I wouldn't do it ordinarily, but my husband banked there for forty years and the officers are just like part of the family. I know I can depend on them.

"Well, I've been going with Walter this past six months. He's fifty-one and he knew my husband before he died. We were engaged two months ago and last week I thought I should tell him about the trust arrangement." Loretta shook her head in amazement. "He didn't show up for our date the next night, he hasn't telephoned me since, and he won't even answer my calls. Do you think he's trying to tell me something?" She laughed.

"I'm looking for someone who's interested in a long-term relationship. From now on, I think I'll give them the financial news right away. It'll give me a chance to separate the speculators from the investors!"

The other kind of hustler is more annoying than dangerous.

Which kind is that?

The amateur. This is the overgrown little boy who is always borrowing small sums of money from his girl "until payday." Sometimes he just wants to borrow her car while his is in the garage, or stay in her apartment while she's on vacation. His demands never really amount to much, but he has a tendency to "five-dollar her to death." The real objection to amateur hustlers is that they are such a waste of time. Unless a girl enjoys giving lifetime scholarships to dead beats, she is better off to send them on their way.

What about men who gamble?

The first thing a girl learns when she gets involved with a gambler is that there's no such thing. "Gambling" means taking a chance when there is a reasonable mathematical chance of winning. When there are twelve horses in a race, the man who bets on one has the odds stacked eleven to one against him. The man who accepts odds of that sort isn't taking any chances —he is virtually guaranteed to lose.

In general the same problems exist with roulette, dice games, blackjack, and slot machines. They didn't build those fancy casinos at Las Vegas with all the money the customers *won*.

One of the real drawbacks of being married to a gambler is that on rare occasions they win. Most of them interpret this as a signal to really raise the stakes. As the excitement intensifies they go for the savings account, the lunch money, then the rent money, and finally the TV set makes the trip to the pawnshop. For women who like to gamble—that is

like to *lose*—a gambler makes the ideal husband.
There are, however, two exceptions.

What are they?

First, the man who plays poker or pinochle with
friends for tiny stakes. Everybody takes turns winning,
and it's really a social occasion. The same thing applies to an occasional trip to the race track and a
vacation in Las Vegas. The big objection to gambling
is not the moral one—everyone has to make up his
own mind about that. The real problem is that it's
simply a bad investment. The old saying, "Horse
players die broke," neglects to add that horse players'
wives end up the same way—usually without even
getting the fresh air that goes with the long afternoons
spent at the track.

The second exception is the professional gambler.
He is really a businessman. The man who knows the
rules and plays the insider's game can make a good
living by profiting from the ignorance of others. If a
girl doesn't have any personal objections to the idea,
being married to an occupational gambler can be interesting. She should, however, be prepared for visits
from swarthy men in black silk suits at 2 A.M. and
occasional business calls from the FBI.

For the girl who wants to check deeper into other
aspects of a prospective husband's character, the process is a simple one.

What does she do?

If she wants to, she can uncover most of the pertinent
information about her man in a week or so. Credit

bureaus in every major city provide, at nominal cost, the kind of information she needs. In general they will reveal a man's employment history, whether or not he pays his bills, how much he earns, and how much he has saved. They sometimes provide other fascinating little tidbits like whether he has been married before and mention it if he has bothered to get a divorce.

The girl who wants to know more can use what are called "reporting agencies." These are extensively used by businessmen to check on customers or suppliers and give more detailed and revealing information. They may consist of a chronological history from grammar school on, list all previous residences and employment, military service, any arrests, and even names of associates and friends who have had pertinent legal or emotional problems. An attorney or banker can help arrange either service—the charge runs from five dollars and up for the credit check to as much as one hundred fifty dollars or more for a comprehensive report by ex-FBI agents. If a man has been divorced, it sometimes pays to check the transcript of his divorce proceedings. A detailed account of the charges and countercharges is often available from the county clerk in the place where the divorce was granted. Hearing what his ex-wife said about him may make interesting reading to the woman who is going to take over where she left off.

But isn't it wrong to spy on a man?

That's a decision every girl has to make for herself. However, in Spanish there is a proverb that says, "Look at a suitor with a magnifying glass—observe a husband with half an eye." If there are any terrible secrets to be revealed, thirty seconds before the wed-

ding is plenty of time. Thirty seconds afterwards is too
late.

How about the older bachelor?

The woman who understands male psychology realizes
that she will be taking on the role of a good mother to
her husband—but she doesn't want to overdo it. If a
man has reached the age of thirty-three or so and has
never been married, there is a chance that he may be
unwilling to let anyone come between him and the
original Mother. Unless puberty has been unusually
delayed, by his early thirties he will have had many
chances to think about marriage. If he has resisted
them all, there is usually a good reason for it. That
good reason may be sixty years old, talk to him on the
telephone every night, and wear size 16 navy-blue
rayon dresses with tiny polka dots.

There is another type of mama's boy who is a little
harder to spot. This is the man who was attached to
Mother, broke away long enough to get married, and
divorced, and now is back with his mom again. He
may be using every chance he gets to try and make a
break for it, but as each year goes by his chances get
slimmer and slimmer. Sometimes these fellows can be
pretty hard to identify until too late. Tracy had that
experience:

"I was going with Neil for almost a year—actually,
we met on my twenty-fourth birthday. He was thirty-
four then and had been married and divorced. Things
went fine for a while, except his mother always
seemed to be around. Half the time when we went for
a drive she rode in the back of the car. Neil always
said, 'I hope you don't mind, but I hate to leave
Mumsy all alone. She worries so much.' Now I know

what she was worrying about—she was afraid Neil might realize he could live without her for four hours in a row. Anyway, I kept telling myself, 'He's been married before—he'll probably make the adjustment when the time comes.' I was right about that, but he made the wrong adjustment—he decided to stay with Mumsy. It all came into focus about Christmas time. He sent me a card and it said, 'Merry Christmas and a Happy New Year from Mrs. Anna Walton & Son.'

"It was printed that way! They sent that card to hundreds of people! I'm only surprised that they didn't send one of those cards with a picture on the front— maybe a shot of Neil sitting on Mumsy's lap? That was when I realized I just couldn't compete, so I dropped out. I could just see next year's card: 'Merry Christmas from Mrs. Anna Walton & Son & Tracy,' with 'Tracy' penciled in so they could erase it and use the same cards next year when I wasn't around any more. No, that was one romance I wasn't about to break up."

Sometimes the signs aren't so obvious.

What does a girl do then?

She tries to put the clues together piece by piece. The danger signals begin with the man who still lives with his mother, shares the other half of a duplex with Mom, or lives across the street. The red flag should go up if a fellow demands participation in regular ritual pilgrimages to partake of Mother's burnt offerings known as *Sunday Dinner with MOM*. A man should be good to his mother, but there are limits. A swimming pool, a luxurious vacation, a monthly allowance, are all fine if the gent is a retired millionaire, but if a girl is thinking of marriage, she has to remember that these little trifles will come out of her housekeeping money. No matter how much a woman may think she's in love, if she and her husband spend their vacation at Coney Island while Mother-in-law basks in Bermuda, something has gone wrong somewhere.

How does a man become a mama's boy?

He doesn't. All men start out that way at the age of one day. During the most critical part of their lives, from the age of zero to five they are almost exclusively attached to their mothers. From the age of five to twelve, they are substantially dependent on her. Under the right circumstances, it's a good arrangement and it usually provides a firm foundation for a close relationship with Mother's successor, the wife-to-be. If for some reason the man is unwilling or unable to transfer his emotional attachment to the next woman in his life, things can turn out very badly for her. Sonny and Mommy at least have each other—wife is left out in the cold. Remember, the wedding ceremony says, ". . . forsake all others," and there is no special exception for mothers. Unless she is going to be the most important person in his life, most girls don't want to get involved with a man. As one disillusioned girl put it, "Once I found out he was so involved with his mother, I just faded away. After all, I didn't want to break up such a beautiful friendship."

Then there's the man who tried to be a mama's boy and couldn't make it.

Which one is he?

He's often the fat one. When they were small, these men turned to Mother for love—and she turned away.

So they turned to ice cream, cookies, chocolate cake, and anything else that they could stuff into their mouths instead, to shut off their desperate longing for affection. The worst part was, it worked. They quickly learned to substitute calories for cuddles and began a vicious cycle. Twenty years later, when a really over-weight man like this wants love, instead of reaching out to another human being, a woman, he has gotten into the habit of reaching out to a frozen pizza. Most of his attention has become centered on the digestive system rather than the reproductive system.

For the girl who wants to spend most of her time in the kitchen instead of the bedroom, marriage to a fat man is fine. But a marriage where she has to compete with food for her husband's attention is not the kind she really wants. There is one bright note in the whole picture, however. Obesity is one of the few conditions where a woman has a reasonable chance to help a man overcome his problem before marriage.

How does she do that?

It isn't easy. If she is willing to make the sacrifice, sometimes her man can be encouraged to substitute love and sex for calories. The world's most effective reducing prescription *can* be true love. Under the in-fluence of the one woman who really cares about him, a man who suffers from true obesity occasionally can be encouraged to think, and therefore eat, as most people do. But there are some real risks involved. As any seriously overweight man will testify, obesity isn't a joke. It is a serious, embarrassing, life-threatening symptom of an underlying emotional problem. The chance of helping an overweight man recover is di-rectly related to his degree of overweight. If a fellow weighs more than 250 pounds (assuming he is under six feet tall), his chances of shedding the weight are lessened. If he tips the scales at 300 or over, it is almost a hopeless task.

Should a girl even try to help an obese man solve his problem?

It depends. If the chap is desirable in every other way, if the couple's personalities match perfectly, if the only thing standing between them is fifty pounds of adipose tissue, it may be worth the risk. On the positive side, overweight men are very close to making the final transfer. If they can switch from love of food to human love, they can turn out to be excellent husbands. On the other hand, after marriage, if the going gets rough, they have a tendency to revert to their old ways and put on extra pounds in minutes. Many women have succeeded in helping fat men, but hardly one woman in a hundred thousand has the talents needed to deal with the hypochondriac.

What talents are those?

Four years of medical school. The man who has constant minor or imaginary illnesses is the most frustrating and disappointing candidate a girl will ever meet. The few who slip by the preliminary screening process can never resist the temptation to eventually flaunt their symptoms. The underlying conflict is complex. Instead of settling for Mother's love and subsequently being willing to transfer their affection to a woman, they engage in a constant clinical love affair with themselves. The man who is always taking his own temperature, scanning his plate for violations of his allergy diet, taking shots, and washing his hands twenty times a day, is lavishing the love and attention on himself that he never got as an infant. Unfortunately, no mere woman will ever be allowed to intrude—except if she happens to be a doctor and is prepared to restrict her entire practice to one patient.

The only hazard in dealing with a hypochondriac is the temptation to sympathize. Compassionate girls occasionally feel that if he just gets to the right doctor, a hypochondriac will make a dramatic recovery. They are correct, but the *right* doctor is a psychiatrist, and the pseudo-sufferer's condition requires that he deny all illness except the physical. If he is accidentally cured of one symptom by a well-meaning practitioner, two more diseases spring up to take their place. The harsh facts of reality are these: a basic inflexible requirement for a husband is glowing good health. Aside from the money that is wasted on doctors and medicines—which could be used for nicer things like a washing machine or a new car—there is another risk. Hypochondriacs have a tendency after marriage to suddenly declare themselves totally and permanently disabled and retire, say at the age of 39. What does a wife do then? Sometimes it's back to the typing pool or the department store to support a husband who enjoys ill health.

What about a man with a sexual problem?

That is the most difficult and sensitive area of all. Most of the fellows with obvious problems such as peeping, exhibitionism, transvestism, and similar difficulties are disqualified early. The man with a potency problem is different. Because of the nature of his condition, it may not be obvious until shortly before the wedding, and simply discovering it isn't the end of the story.

Because of the intense emotional pressure on a man during courtship, occasional sexual malfunctions are inevitable. During premarital intercourse he may lose his erection because of anxiety, or he may ejaculate prematurely because of the build-up of intense sexual excitement. There are three possible resolutions of impotence before marriage—it can get better, it can get worse, or it can stay the same. If it gets better, nobody has any reason to worry. But if it doesn't, both partners suffer intensely. The girl's real interest is to distinguish *as soon as possible* between the impairments that will clear spontaneously and the ones that won't. It's hard, but there are some guideposts.

First she can ask, sympathetically, if her man has had the problem before. If he has, it is *not* a good sign. Recurrence of impotence with several successive partners points toward a chronic condition that can take time and treatment to overcome.

The second indicator is the frequency. If a man suffers from copulatory impotence or total impotence (or complete lack of erection) or loss of erection three times during a three-month period, it is a warning that the problem is not just a superficial one. If he has premature ejaculation (that is, if he ejaculates in less than three minutes in a new relationship) three times in three months, both parties may be in for trouble after marriage. The fellow who experiences retarded ejaculation—no ejaculation after forty-five minutes or more of intercourse—even once—usually needs professional help. The next part of the situation is the most difficult.

What's that?

Deciding whether or not to terminate the relationship because of the man's impotence. If he is outstanding in every other way, if he is willing to undergo psychiatric treatment to deal directly with his potency defect, and if the girl is willing to wait until he shows objective improvement, there is a chance for a happy marriage. At the same time there is the risk that, even if they clear up, without warning the sexual symptoms may spontaneously reappear and inflict misery on everyone. Like all critical decisions, this one isn't easy to make. Realistically, if there is any doubt whatsoever in her mind, a girl probably does best to move on to the next man who meets her requirements.

Are there any other problems relating to Bottomless Pits?

There is one more. Sometimes a girl will come across a man who has no obvious character problem—he may not be a homosexual, a mama's boy, a professional bachelor—but for some reason he just isn't equipped (or willing) to make it in this world. His trials and tribulations and desperate struggles to succeed would make an excellent movie. In the film version, all it takes is a devoted woman to press the right button and he snatches victory from defeat in the last eleven minutes of the final reel.

In real life, it doesn't always work that way. Too many of these fellows are born losers who insist on making the same mistake over and over again. For their own reasons they never really want to win. Life with them is inspiring, exciting, challenging, and ultimately disappointing. Men like this just don't wear well, and there is the constant problem of trying to explain to the kids why Daddy is always coming in last.

If a woman becomes involved with a Bottomless Pit, what can she do about it?

Get uninvolved, as quickly as she can. It's like falling into quicksand—those who struggle only sink deeper and deeper. A few words on the doorstep can do the trick:

"Arthur, it just isn't going to work out. After tonight, let's not see each other any more."

The next morning Arthur gets all his belongings back—the pictures, the ski jacket he left behind, and if it's got to that point, his toothbrush. No phone calls, no letters, no tearful reconciliations. Arthur doesn't become "just a good friend"—once he has suffered through a rejection, down deep he isn't going to feel friendly.

Then a woman alone needs an immediate replacement for the man she has passed over. This is when she must be single-minded and plunge back into the selection process without hesitation. As far as she knows, each woman has only one life to live, and it is sensible to make the best of it. If she chooses the man in her life carefully and well, she will have taken a giant step in the right direction.

9

PICKING A MAN

What's the most important thing a girl has to do if she's going to find the right man?

Face reality. In this modern world things change fast and if she's going to get what she wants, a girl has to change right along with them. The first thing she has to realize is that the Frontier is no more. The western town with a hundred and fifty eager cowboys lusting after two dance hall girls lingers on only in TV reruns. The statistical turning point came in 1950 when women officially began to outnumber men in the critical twenty to sixty-four year old age groups. For two hundred years women and sex were in short supply and it was, in every way, a sellers' market. There were a whole bunch of "nice" girls who wouldn't have sex and a few of the "other kind" who would. Now the "new sexual freedom" is here and the landscape is overflowing with "nice" girls who are eager to have sex on any reasonable (and often unreasonable) terms. The social tide has turned against the woman alone who wants to find a man and keep him for her own. But the inner obstacles can be even more formidable.

What are the inner obstacles?

They take the form of negative emotional attitudes that can seriously interfere with selecting the best possible man. Most of them have been lying dormant ever since Mother put them there with the best of intentions years ago. It all started with the whispered —or shouted—warning: "Never talk to strangers!" On the way to school, on the way to the store, going to the park, going to the beach, the message was always the same: "Beware of strangers!" Mother never spelled out the precise reasons but the idea came across. Strangers did horrid things to little girls somewhere between the belly button and the knees. Sometimes it made a girl shiver just to think about it.

Actually it was good advice to give a six-year-old when a man in a parked car offered her candy. It is very bad advice when the girl is twenty years old and one afternoon a charming young man tries to strike up an acquaintance.

There is another "no-no" hidden deep in the unconscious which can filter to the surface to make trouble later on. It is the quaint and courtly idea that a girl never talks to a man unless they have been formally introduced. The rule is appropriate for southern belles greeting gentlemen callers in gracious mansions before the Civil War. It also makes sense for the daughters of kings traveling incognito—or in old movies on television depicting the same events. But for a woman who wants to find a man, the idea is pure poison. Every male in the world is a stranger to every young lady *until* she meets him. Or as they say out West, "A stranger is just a friend you haven't met yet." The girl who is held back by these archaic and unrealistic concepts makes life much harder for herself right at the start. These days men and women usually meet each other by accident. Present day society is too much on the move, too flexible, for a woman to find a reasonable selection of men from among her friends and acquaintances. Insisting on a formal, drawing room introduction is only a guarantee of a lonely old age.

But how does a girl protect herself from bad situations?

Most of the time simply by using common sense. Bad situations can range all the way from an evening with a sex fiend to a date with an alcoholic Mama's boy—sometimes it's difficult to tell which is worse.

Realistically, almost every girl who has ever spent an evening of boredom, awkwardness, or downright terror, can look back on it and say, "I should have known. If only I'd followed my first impulse and never said yes." When things are going to go wrong, they usually start going wrong right away and never stop.

Almost every girl who plunges impulsively into a questionable relationship remembers conversations with herself the next morning like these:

"When I saw those toys in the back seat of his car, I should have realized he was married."

"When he stopped off at four bars in a row, didn't you suspect he might have a drinking problem?"

"When he started talking about whips on the way to his apartment—that was the time to get a headache, not after it was all over."

"What kind of evening could I expect when it started out with dinner at a cafeteria?"

After fifty thousand years of struggling for survival

the human race has developed an instinct for survival which enables every person to instantly and correctly evaluate new friends within the first minute of the first meeting. (The family dog still tells "good people" from "bad people" without thinking about it.) Every woman has the same ability if only she will learn to develop it. Identifying obviously unsuitable men is relatively easy—the technique is covered in detail in chapter 8, *Bottomless Pits*. Selecting the best man from a field of desirable men is a somewhat more complex task.

Where does a girl begin?

Before the first meeting. Probably the most common single complaint of single men is: "It's so hard to meet an eligible girl. I see them all the time but how do I start? Do I just walk up and say, 'Hello'?" The girl who is going to be successful in her search has to make it easy for *the right kind of man* to walk up and say "Hello." It isn't an easy technique to learn. As one young lady said, "You sort of push 'em away with one hand and haul 'em in with the other until you really know whom you're dealing with." The real key to success is "instant qualifying."

What's "instant qualifying"?

Simply an adaptation of the method every psychiatrist and psychologist uses constantly with every patient —and incidentally the method every top-notch salesman uses with every customer and smart detectives use with suspects. In psychiatry it goes by the elegant name of "projective personality evaluation" and this is how it works:

Every human being is constantly revealing his innermost secrets in a hundred different ways. Every word, every gesture, every article of clothing, every reaction, speaks volumes about the characteristics and the intentions of an individual. After spending fifteen minutes with a patient an experienced and perceptive psychiatrist can know as much about him as his own mother—usually more. By applying the same methods in a simplified way, any woman can perform an accurate first evaluation of any man within a minute or so. That gives her a chance to decide whether to encourage him to say "Hello" or to eliminate him as a possibility once and for all. "Instant qualifying" has another advantage. It is most effective in screening out bad risks and almost never disqualifies a man with desirable qualities.

The whole concept is based on rapid evaluation of individual gestures and physical characteristics. Just as words are read as representations of ideas, superficial features of a man's appearance can be read as indications of his internal functioning. These indicators are not selected casually but are based on the accumulated experience of psychiatrists and other experienced observers over many years.

There are two categories of signs—eliminators and cautions. Generally speaking, eliminators are serious warning signs that justify stopping the relationship before it starts. (There may be exceptions but they are exceedingly rare.) Cautions are signs that suggest a high degree of suspicion is worthwhile. Several cautions in the same individual mark the fellow as a significantly bad risk.

How is the method applied?

It rates three groups of three characteristics and introduces an overriding modifier at the end. The nine qualities are these:

PHYSICAL FEATURES: hair—eyes—mouth
CLOTHING: pants—shoes—harmony
BODY IMAGE: gait—stance—hands

The over-riding modifier is: BIZARRE.

A practical example might work like this:

While standing in line at the supermarket check-out counter, a woman notices a man in line behind her. What should she do? Become intensely interested in the box of cake mix in her shopping cart? Smile at him? Do nothing?

In the parking lot after work one evening her car won't start. A nice fellow comes over and finds the loose wire. He starts to talk. Should a girl clam up? Be friendly? Accept his invitation for a drink?

Every day at lunch the same man comes into the coffee shop. He's charming, reserved, and—what should a girl do? By applying the rating technique in each case, the question answers itself. Let's take them one by one:

Hair: The key point is *appropriate*. Long hair or short hair doesn't matter as much as "right" hair. It must be clean, neat, and consistent with the rest of his appearance. Eliminating features are grotesquely bleached hair, dyed hair in a man under forty, and artificially curled hair. Cautions are shaved heads, over-styled hair, and center parts.

Eyes: The main eliminator is that favorite of mystery story writers, "shifty eyes." The man who can't look you in the eye is telling you something about himself—you had better listen. Cautions are plucked eye brows, and nearsighted eyes whose owners don't wear glasses or contact lenses.

Mouth: This is the most revealing of all the features. Eliminators are inappropriate smiles (smiling when there is no obvious reason for smiling), talking out of the corner of the mouth, and of course the mouth with a twitch. Cautions are bad teeth, biting the lip, chronic mouth-breathing, and frequent pursing of the lips.

The clothing group is next in reliability. There are so many possibilities within the framework of fashion that evaluation in this area can be confusing although there are three elements which remain dependable:

Shoes: Eliminators are worn-out shoes and any style that might be reasonably worn by a woman. Cautions are elevator shoes, obviously inappropriate footgear (tennis shoes with a business suit) and super-extreme styles.

Pants: Eliminators are extra-tight pants especially in the crotch or seat, and baggy pants. (Obviously trousers worn for a day at the beach or to go duck-hunting have to be considered with that in mind.) A caution is pants with zippers that don't close all the way.

Harmony of Clothing: More important than any specific mode of dress is the overall harmony of a man's wardrobe. In these days when informality is the rule, a fellow's clothes should fit in with his surroundings and activities. Eliminators are such things as deliberate attempts to disrupt an occasion—for example, wearing a T shirt to a staid wedding reception. Cautions might be clothes worn for shock value and nothing more. An electric blue jump suit with red patent leather imitation alligator loafers and a bright green felt fedora might conceal the ideal man, but the chances of that happening are mighty slim.

The final group is potentially the most revealing but ironically the most difficult to evaluate. Like the others, body image has three important categories:

Gait: The way a man walks through the door tells something about the way he walks through life. Eliminators are anything approaching femininity in a stride. Mincing, hip-swinging, shoulders that alternately rise and fall, spell big trouble. Cautions are shuffling feet and the "tough-guy" stride.

Stance: This is another telling characteristic because men are rarely aware of exactly how they are standing. Hand-on-hip tells a girl to head-for-the-hills along with hands-in-the-pockets. Head hung down and the round-shouldered stance are also eliminators. Cautions are both-hands-on-hips as well as chronic slouches.

Hands: In spite of the fact that Mother told us never to talk with our hands every man still does—if a girl will only listen. Picking at nails, wringing hands, clenching and unclenching fists, rubbing hands together, and hands that exhibit a tremor are eliminating signs. Hands that don't know where to go—lapels, pockets, down at the side, back to the pockets, are cautionary signs along with hands that hang down limply with palms facing backward or worse, forward.

In addition to all these revealing signals, there is the overriding modifier which is the most vital clue of all. If any man during the qualifying process reveals a trait which is *bizarre,* a woman who wants to save herself a lot of trouble rings down the curtain right there. A bizarre characteristic is some element which is discordant, unexplainable, far-out, or in the kids' language, "freaky." For example, a man who wears gloves in the summertime had better have a very good explanation to avoid qualifying as bizarre. The fellow who shaves his head or takes half a dozen showers a day or always dresses in black may have a very good reason for all of it but the girl who gets involved with him is taking an avoidable risk.

But isn't this business of qualifying men carrying things too far?

It depends on your point of view. The average woman alone has to face the world on her own. Her future happiness—or misery—depends on making the best choices she possibly can. Worst of all, time usually works against her. The years silently speed away and she loses some of her advantage with each passing month. If she can improve her chances of finding the man who will bring her contentment by utilizing the principles of modern psychiatry, the choice should be left up to her. Certainly no method is infallible—as no human being is infallible—but if she exercises the same critical method in selecting a man as she uses in selecting a pot roast, she can only help herself.

But is this method of qualifying men valid?

Yes, in the sense that every human gesture and characteristic expresses the underlying personality. When a girl sharpens her senses to the point where she can perform the nine point instant inventory she gets another advantage in the bargain—the psychiatric word is "gestalt." The basic concept is that the whole is greater than the sum of the parts. For example, the seven notes of the scale are simply musical tones until they are played in sequence to form a tune. The individual characteristics of a man across a room take on an entirely new significance when they are strung together to form a total impression. After a few months of using this method, most women, like experienced psychiatrists, will be able to form rapid impressions without being consciously aware of the individual components.

Once a girl decides a man qualifies, what next?

Next, she makes it easy for the man to take the first step by taking it herself. She looks at him directly. No winks, no coy smiles, just a clear calm look. As they say on Madison Avenue, the ball is now in his court. Unless he makes the next move, he has ultimately disqualified himself by lack of enterprise. The woman has done all she can and it's time to move on to the next opportunity. If he comes over and starts a conversation, she is ready for phase four.

What's phase four?

Establishing exactly what the relationship is going to be about. Is it going to be friendship without sex; friendship with sex; sex—no friendship; or, the big one —friendship, sex, *and* love? The sooner a man and woman can settle this question between them, the sooner they can get down to the business of enjoying each other. First the woman has to decide what she expects from that particular man (or from *any* man, for that matter); then she has to find out what he's seeking. If they are both on the same track, things get much simpler right away. If they're not looking for the same things, both of them will save a lot of time by knowing promptly.

By far the easiest way for a woman to find out what a man wants is to ask him. It is like the tourist lost in the wilds of Scotland who walked for hours without seeing another living thing. Finally he came upon a craggy old Scotsman sitting on a rock. He rushed up to the man and shouted, 'Thank goodness I found you! I thought I was lost!" The Scotsman drew back and asked, "Is there a reward out for you?" "I don't think so," answered the traveler. "Then," said the Scot, as he got up and walked away, "ye're still lost."

If a girl is looking for love and the man is interested in sex and *maybe* friendship, it is only a matter of time before he gets up, puts on his clothes, walks away, and assures her that she is still lost.

How does a girl ask something like that?

It's not so easy but it can be done. The best method is the quaint social custom known as the "date." Superficially, a date seems like a nice way to spend an evening, maybe take in a movie, have something to eat and then face the daily routine the next morning. Nothing could be farther from the truth. Every date from the most casual to the most critical is a marriage —or more precisely, a mini-marriage. Every component of the husband-wife relationship is present in every date either literally or in symbolic form. There is usually feeding, advertising the relationship to the outside world, mutual cooperation in some form, sex (either explicit or implied) and some agreement about the future. Misused, the dating experience can feed a girl into a disastrous marriage as surely as round steak is fed into a meat grinder—and with about the same results. On the other hand, if she uses every date to her fullest advantage, she can have a reliable preview of what the next thirty years with that particular man will be like. Anne described her experience:

"Well, I tried it and like you predicted, it told me plenty."

"What happened?"

"You know, having been married and well, being thirty-two, isn't exactly a teen-ager; I've been out on a lot of dates. But last week with Tim was the first time I ever kept my eyes—and my mind—open every minute. I mean, except when he was kissing me good-night." Anne grinned. "But actually this was the first time I ever thought of a date as a kind of trial marriage. Tim came over—it was the second time I went out with him—and he brought me some flowers. It was just a bunch of violets but it was a good beginning. Then he took me to dinner, to a movie, we had a couple of drinks afterward, then back home. I gave him some coffee, we sat around and—you know—made out for a while, then he left. I had a great time."

"When are you going out with him again?"

Anne looked surprised. "Again? Never. I'd never go out with him again."

"But didn't you say you had a good time?"

"Oh, sure, but it was exactly the same good time we had the time before. Actually the first time he brought me daisies and we went to an Italian restaurant instead of the Chinese place but otherwise it was a carbon copy of the first date—same kind of movie, same jokes, same script. You know, one of those package tours—twenty-two cities in twenty-one days? I can just see him after we're married: coming home from work, throwing the paper on the couch, kissing me mechanically, turning on the TV, lighting his pipe, and then looking around to see if he walked into the right house. No thanks. My idea of marriage isn't a thousand weeks of some television situation comedy. Doctor, I'm still looking."

Anne had a great deal of insight that came from

experience which gave her confidence in her own judgment. But she is not unique. Any woman can swiftly arrive at the point where she literally can predict the future from her first few dates with a man.

How is it done?

By adapting the technique of projective personality testing to a longer term relationship. That cynical genius, Sigmund Freud, pointed the way when he observed, "Human beings ooze self-betrayal." Any man, given a reasonable opportunity, will reveal nearly every detail of his future relationship with a woman during his first few encounters with her. All the girl has to do is encourage him to express himself without restraint, sit back, and watch the future unfold. If she likes what she sees, she can sign up for more. If she's looking for something else, she can politely disengage and keep looking. One of the best places for her to start her projective testing is across the dinner table.

Why is that?

There are two functions of human beings which are only partially under conscious control—eating and sex. No matter how much he tries, the average man cannot disguise his defects (and his virtues) either at the dinner table or the bed-side table. Put another way, a man imprints his true character on the table cloth and the bed-sheets. As evidence of how little men (and women) control their eating behavior, a few minutes of observation in the nearest restaurant is worthwhile. Watch those who are in a hurry and eating alone. They bend over the food, spoon it into their mouths, and *every five to fifteen seconds involuntarily raise their heads and scan the horizon!* Ironically few people are even aware that this behavior exists and most deny it when it is called to their attention. Not even behavioral scientists understand the reason for this activity although it is common in animals and may be a remnant of less-settled times when primitive man had to be alert for enemies while feeding.

To accurately evaluate a man, get him to take you to dinner. An evening of keen observation at a restaurant is worth months of holding hands in the darkness of the movies.

Once the couple are settled at the dinner table, the real work begins. Ask him what he thinks you should have to eat and listen carefully: Here are some possible answers with possible translations:

"Anything at all. Whatever attracts your eyes." *"I want you to be happy no matter what it takes."*

"Why don't you have the filet mignon or the steak and lobster?" *"You mean more than money."*

"Gee, I don't know. Let's ask the girl." *"Listen, little kids like me don't know anything. Let's ask Mother."*

"I hear the chicken à la King is good here." *"I hear the chicken à la King is cheap here."*

"I'm just having an omelette and a salad." *"I'm just taking you here to show off. Don't try to eat."*

"What should you have to eat? Oh, I was just going to ask you what you would suggest to me." *"Listen, I don't know what I'm doing. I'm just hoping someone will adopt me before it's too late."*

As the meal progresses, the intelligent girl keeps her eyes and ears open. Watch what he orders and how he orders it:

"I want sardines but only if they're skinless and boneless. I'm allergic to the skins and bones."

Imagine a lifetime of stripping the skins and bones

from sardines while your husband stands around tapping his foot impatiently.

The whole question of food preferences is an important one. Without any question, the best candidate is the man who isn't picky about his food. That doesn't mean the poor soul who thrives on instant mashed potatoes or frozen Chinese dinners makes the best husband—he has problems of his own. But the man who approaches eating in a common sense, matter-of-fact way displays a significant degree of mental health. Even more important, a wholesome attitude toward food usually means a wholesome attitude toward sex.

How is that?

Since eating and sex are basically primitive drives, the man who deals with his nutritional needs rationally will probably deal with his sexual feelings the same way. A fellow who insists on Malaysian mushrooms stuffed with snails at suppertime may have similar exotic preferences at bedtime. The chap whose idea of heaven is canned spaghetti probably doesn't care what he—or anyone else—feels when it comes to sex. A man who insists that the wine be at fifty-seven degrees and the soup at one hundred nine degrees may spend most of the night running around opening and closing windows instead of accomplishing what he is there to accomplish.

But isn't that carrying things a bit too far?

No. Mothers, teachers, nurses, and psychiatrists have known for years that those who are easiest to please and most realistic at the dinner table are the most easy-going and pleasant to be with in every other way.

Another thing to consider is table manners—going too far in either direction is bad news and the girl who doesn't tune in now will have to listen three times a day after she gets married. Wiping the silverware on the tablecloth, eating with his mouth wide open, and picking his teeth at the table are warnings of worse things to come. At the same time, dabbing at his mouth after each bite, hiding the olive pits under the celery, and dissecting the food into microscopic slivers before consuming it can be hard to take meal after meal after meal.

Is there anything else?

The end of the meal is an important time. Watch the desserts. The slightly overweight man who consumes two helpings of strawberry shortcake may be buyng his clothes at the fat man's store before the third wedding anniversary. Someone who "never eats dessert" may have forgotten to tell you something about himself—like about his diabetes.

The moment of truth is when the check arrives. If your host looks it over carefully, don't worry. It's his money and it's a good sign if he manages it carefully. On the other hand, the man who frets over each item —"What do they mean by charging extra for a shrimp cocktail?" may have his problems. The prices are on the menu, he ordered from it, and paying the bill is just part of the game. The last, and perhaps most revealing item is the tip. Anything between ten and twenty per cent isn't worth a second glance but the man who tips less than one-tenth of the bill will be hard to approach when the children need a new winter coat. The fellow who leaves the waitress a five dollar tip on a ten dollar check will be popular with bell-boys and cab drivers too. He will probably be unpopular with bill collectors, people who try to cash his checks, and the men who come to re-possess his furniture.

But how can a girl really be sure about all these things?

She can't. Every characteristic a man displays when dining out is only one more piece in the big jig-saw puzzle. Each clue can be observed, indexed, and considered as part of the entire picture. But the information that a woman ignores is what comes back to haunt her long after the last wedding present has stopped making toast or opening cans. Once in a while, a girl goes all the way, like Glenda:

"I thought a lot about what you told me, Doctor. You know, how important food and eating was in choosing a man. So I decided to do it once and for all. At first it didn't seem fair—sort of playing dirty. But then I decided that getting stuck with the wrong man wasn't fair either. Last Wednesday, right after we finished here, I had Dan take me to dinner. I purposely picked a place where they have waitresses because I remembered what you told me: 'If you're thinking about marrying a man always watch how he treats the waitress because if you marry him, for the next thirty years *you're* going to be the waitress!' Then I went one step further and made him take me to the King's Castle, that old English style place. It's not that I like their food but my friend Dottie is a waitress there. Before I married Dan I wanted to go all out to give

him the best test I could. I got together with Dottie
the day before and we planned everything."

"What happened?"

"I never would have believed it, but your method
really worked! I learned more about Dan in two hours
than I'd found out in the three months that I'd known
him.

"After we sat down, he picked up the menu and
said, 'Why don't we have the *Special Steak for Two?*
You get free wine with that.' I didn't think that was a
good opening move because he doesn't usually drink
wine, and he should know that nothing is really free.
I remembered something else you said: 'If he seems
to show a weak point, give him a fair chance by testing the same area again.' Well, he sounded like he
wanted to cut corners so I ordered lobster, the most
expensive item they had. He sort of winced, but he
didn't say anything.

"Then I said, 'Why don't you have a shrimp cocktail?'

"He said, 'But it's extra!' Then he must have remembered where he was and whom he was with because he grinned and said, 'Let's make it two?' At that
point we both started feeling better. Then Dottie
came to take the order and she was marvelous! She
made him repeat everything at least three times, and
the funny thing was that he didn't get upset at all.
Then she brought the meal and gave him my lobster
and me his roast beef. He just sat there, and after she
left, he switched the plates. I wasn't happy about that.
Then I offered him a taste of my lobster and he
looked kind of shocked. 'I never do that!' he said.

"I asked him, 'How come?'

"He looked puzzled and said, 'Gee, I don't know.
Isn't it sort of unsanitary? I mean, it's bad manners
too, isn't it?'

"Well, I tell you, Doctor, that old computer was clicking away a mile a minute. We hadn't even started the main course and a lot of things had happened: cutting corners for free wine, hesitating on the shrimp cocktail, not asking the waitress to give us each the dinner we ordered, and being shocked at tasting my food. Not so good. If he wouldn't even eat off my plate, what was going to happen later on when we got down to more serious business? On the plus side, he did go along with the lobster and the shrimp cocktail and he was good-natured about everything so far.

"I noticed he had a funny expression on his face. Then I saw what it was. He'd ordered his roast beef well-done and Dottie brought it as rare as I've ever seen meat cooked. So I said to him, 'Why don't you send it back?'

"He just shrugged and replied, 'Oh, I guess it's okay this time.' Then he tried to chew the same piece he had been working on for the past five minutes. I called Dottie and explained the problem to her and she had the meat back in five minutes, cooked just right. He must have thanked me about ten times. I wasn't happy about it, though.

"After that we forgot about the dinner and started talking about where we were going that night and what we were going to do on the weekend and that sort of thing. I wasn't really keeping track until we were finished. He ate everything on his plate except his vegetables—he had peas and carrots. I asked him why he didn't eat those and he said, 'That's funny —my mother always used to ask me that. I hate vegetables, that's all.' Click-click—it all registered. I wasn't going to waste a minute of the precious time. Then he took out the pill box. I'd never seen *that* before.

He popped a couple of pills—without water. That was bad news."

"Why do you say 'bad news'?"

"I guess I'm learning from you, Doctor. It's hard enough for me to swallow a pill *with* water so I assume that somebody who takes pills without water must have had a lot of practice. So I asked him about it."

"What did he say?"

"He said, 'Oh, I always take these after dinner because I have a nervous stomach.' Then he offered me one! I didn't know what to do so I gave him one point for offering to share the pills and took away a point for taking them in the first place!

"By that time we were ready for dessert and I was ready for a nap—my head was really whirling. I don't see how you psychiatrists do it all day. But I hung in there. I asked him what he wanted for dessert, but he just smiled and called Dottie and whispered something in her ear. She went back to the kitchen and brought out two little baked Alaskas in miniature flower pots with a daisy stuck in each one of them. That was his surprise. Then I felt guilty for setting everything up to test him and the tears came to my eyes. He reached over and kissed me right in front of all the people in the restaurant and I just gave up. I don't even remember how he paid the check or if he even paid it." Glenda smiled.

"Do you think it was worth all that trouble?"

"You bet it was! I found out a lot of things about Dan I never even suspected—good things and bad things. I didn't like the way he fretted about the cost of each item on the menu and the way he let the waitress push him around and his prissiness about taking some of my food and not eating the vegetables and taking those pills. But I was impressed by his good-natured approach to everything, by the way he kind of snapped back when he had a chance to think some things over. Most of all I liked his consideration in surprising me with the dessert and his tenderness in reassuring me when I started crying. That made up for everything. I think I still want to marry him. But I want to know a lot more about him first and there are a few things that maybe I can help him overcome. I mean, I don't want him to eat out of my hand, but at least we can share the same plate."

How else does a man tell the real truth about himself?

By his automobile. The make and model doesn't mean as much as the way it looks and—most revealing—the way he drives it. A dilapidated, broken down, untidy car suggests a dilapidated, broken down, untidy personality—deep inside. Worn tires and death-defying brakes point to recklessness in other important areas too. But the real key is the way a man drives. Most human beings never have as much power under their control as they do when propelling a four thousand pound vehicle at sixty miles an hour down a crowded highway. The way they use (or misuse) this tremendous force is an indication of how they will use force in their relationship with their future wives. The man who conducts non-stop one-way arguments with other drivers is only giving a girl a preview of coming attractions if she marries him. The speeder and the reckless driver apparently don't have enough unhappiness in their daily lives—they need to supplement it with the daily risk of death and injury. The man who keeps his car super-clean, who lavishes unlimited attention on it, who buys it little presents every week (new wheel covers, chrome air cleaner, custom ash tray) is worshipping at a different shrine. A mere woman doesn't stand a chance against a four hundred cubic-inch engine and a four-barrel carburetor.

A drunken driver, or a collector of traffic tickets is playing a childish game. Seventy-five miles an hour on a date may be thrilling with a boyfriend—going down to the jail at midnight to bail out your husband isn't so much fun.

What are good signs to look for?

A car is *not* truth, beauty, or justice. A car is *not* a space ship. It is *not* a weapon. It is *not* a fortress against the cruel outside world. It is simply a box on wheels designed to transport people around faster than they can walk—and hopefully just as safely. Best marks go to the man who understands this and handles his car as a useful tool—not as a ticket to the next world. If a fellow shows up with a clean comfortable auto in good mechanical condition and drives it with reasonable restraint, a girl shouldn't have too much to worry about in this area.

There's one final point about cars. Next to a house, it's the largest single investment most men make. In that sense it provides some idea of how a man manages his money. Maybe the fellow who is assistant manager of a branch bank and drives a Cadillac convertible can really afford it. Maybe he can just manage the payments. Maybe he can't even manage those. It isn't hard to find out.

How?

In most states regulations require that the vehicle registration be kept in the car—wrapped around the steering wheel, snapped to the sun visor, or in the glove compartment. Usually there is a space on the form for "registered owner" (or something similar) followed by a space for "owner of record." If the "registered owner" isn't the same as the fellow who's driving, it isn't his car. Maybe it belongs to his cousin —or his daddy. If the "owner of record" is United Finance Company, the car belongs to them. Of course there's nothing wrong with that—but most girls like to know who really owns what right from the beginning.

Is money that important?

Yes and no. One of the greatest sources of unhappiness in marriage (and in life generally) is the lack of enough money to do everything everyone wants to do all at once. Future success in marriage depends less on the exact number of dollars a couple has than on how they manage them. If the husband is going to make the money for the family after marriage he should have a little practice at it before the wedding day. A woman who marries a man who can't hold a job is walking into a lifetime career—supporting a husband. The man who has had eight jobs in seven months and just can't seem to find himself will be found by his wife after marriage—in front of the television set every afternoon when she comes home from work. But these cues are obvious—there are some others, equally sinister, that need to be dug out.

For example, the man who borrows money from his date—or who forgets his wallet when they go out for dinner. Just two dollars here and five dollars there but maybe he needs a banker instead of a wife. One of the hardest situations for a girl to see through is the man who is extravagantly generous with her and stingy with everyone else. Ginny tells her experience:

"Ted was really a great guy! He took me places I'd only read about before and he just couldn't do enough for me. I mean some of the things embarrassed me. Like he sent me a dozen orchids on my birthday—not to my house but to the office. My boss is a big spender—he's in advertising—but even he was amazed! Then there was the watch—eighteen carat gold—and the two lovebirds. The birds actually came in a gilded cage! I just couldn't believe it; I was overwhelmed. But there was something else that bothered me. It was his secretary."

"What about her?"

"Ted was complaining about how his secretary always wanted a raise and why did she sneak home at five minutes to five instead of giving a 'full day's work for a full day's pay' and how she was angry because he docked her pay when she was ten minutes late in the morning. It sure didn't sound like the guy who was sending me orchids by the armload.

"Well, about then I remembered what you told me: 'In the long run, expect a man to treat you only as well as the least important person in his life.' I couldn't ever imagine being treated like his secretary but as it turned out I never had to."

"Never had to what?"

"Imagine it. About two weeks later, I got the 'secretary treatment' myself. He told me about one of his customers who sent back a bunch of bathroom scales that wouldn't work right. Anyhow he laughed and told me the scales had never been any good to begin with. A month later, guess what he brought me as a gift?" Ginny sighed.

"You guessed it—a bathroom scale. Even worse, he didn't remember telling me about it. If a man is going to be stingy, at least he should have a good memory—or a well-paid secretary to remind him. From that point on it was downhill. I started to get sweaters with the labels cut off, the finish on my eighteen carat gold watch wore down to about three and a half carats and the brass underneath turned green. The final blow was last weekend. He took me out for dinner at a fair place—nothing special—and when we finished he pulled a little book and peeled off a coupon. It was one of those two-for-one deals! You know, you buy a book for four ninety-five and then it's 'Pay for one dinner and get the next one free— good only Thursdays and Sundays after 9 P.M.' Come to think of it, I wondered why we were eating so late that night. Well, I learned one thing from it: Beware of strangers bearing gold-*plated* watches and broken bathroom scales."

If a man passes all these hurdles, then does he qualify?

Not yet. There's one more test and it's probably the most critical of all. The name of that test is: Mother. Whether she realizes it or not, virtually every girl who marries a man gets another personality in the bargain—although some women don't *consider* it a bargain. Etched deep into the unconscious mind of every man—no matter how tough or masculine he may be—is the image of his all-powerful mother. The girl who marries him also marries that mother—or at least the part of Mother who lives within her husband. If there is any way to manage it, every woman should make the symbolic pilgrimage to visit with her prospective mother-in-law. Every woman is smart enough not to order a husband sight unseen; why pick the next most important person in her life that way?

Regrettably most women are at a disadvantage when dealing with Mother. The senior partner in a man's emotional development has the trump cards. She knows all about her little boy, she's already been married (at least once), and she knows how to handle kids—like her son's girl friend, for instance. This is where unconscious radar is most important. All the clues that were so useful in qualifying a man are almost useless in evaluating his mother.

Why is Mother so important?

Because each individual carries the indelible stamp of each one of his ancestors. Geat-grandmother molded Grandmother, Grandmother molded Mother, and Mother molded son. No matter how careless a woman is in qualifying her prospective husband or how careful he is in concealing his past, present, or future, the underlying theme begins and ends with his Mommy.

If her presumptive mother-in-law is genuinely warm and loving, if a feeling of openness and mutual trust flows between them, a woman can confirm her judgment about her prospective husband. But if there is a discordant note, if Mother doesn't exactly ring true, it's time to take a good hard look at the whole situation. It cost Penny four thousand dollars to find out:

"Personally, I think it was worth it. I'm thirty-eight and I've been married twice. My first husband was killed in Korea—after the war—and I had to divorce my second husband. To be honest it was a fifty-fifty deal: half his drinking and half my complaining. I never should have remarried so fast. But that's another story. I wanted to do it right the third time so I followed your advice and Jim seemed just perfect. So after we'd gone together six months I went to see his mother. We drove in my new station wagon— she lived about five hundred miles away in a small town. Actually she didn't look bad for the first few days—always smiling, always cheerful, always ready to joke. I found out why later when the joke was on me." Penny winced.

"After about four days we got to be pretty good chums and one day while Jim was visiting some friends of his from college, she needed to do some shopping and asked if she could use my car. I offered to take her but she just chuckled and said she didn't want to bother me. As I handed her the keys, I complimented myself on being smart enough to pick the right man—*and* the right mother-in-law. What a laugh! Well, I stayed there watching TV—there really wasn't much else to do in that town—and about an hour later, the door bell rang. I went to see who it was and you could have knocked me over with a feather! It was a pair of state troopers, mad as they could be! They pushed their way into the house and started grilling me: 'Do you have a green Dodge station wagon?' 'Did you give Mrs. Watson permission to drive it today?' 'Can we see the registration?' 'Is it insured?'

"You can imagine, Doctor, those questions aren't exactly designed to make a girl's lunch digest smoothly. It took about half an hour to piece it together and it was a mess. Old Mother Watson was the town's most dedicated drinker. *That* was the reason she was so jolly. She was bombed out of her mind half the time. Jim never mentioned it—for obvious reasons. How do you tell your fiancée your mother's a lush? She got hold of my car—her license had been lifted three years before—and laid waste to most of Main Street. My poor little station wagon was totaled out and the insurance company wouldn't give me a cent for it. Fortunately they did pay for the damage she did— after reminding me a dozen times that they weren't really legally obligated. It cost them $12,500, it cost me $4000, and I got off easy. I started asking around in the town and there was quite a local controversy —no one could agree who was the bigger drinker, Jim or his mother. It seems he had been on the wagon six months and ten days—he quit getting drunk the week before he met me.

"As I said, it cost me a lot of money but look what I saved: Imagine being married to Jimmy and Mommy Watson for the next twenty years."

How can a girl protect herself?

By applying the principles of projective personality evaluation to the man's mother as well.

The first encounter with a future mother-in-law is probably the most revealing. At that stage she is still planning her approach toward her future daughter-in-law and her defenses, relatively speaking, are not yet in place. There are two vital aspects to the first meeting—the reception and the first statement about her son.

If Mother greets the young lady graciously and warmly—as she would greet the friend of an old friend—everything is off to a good start. If the welcome wouldn't do justice to a vacuum cleaner sales-man, things don't look so good. When a man's mother looks a girl over as if she were the pork roast on sale this week for ninety-nine cents, everyone is in for a rough evening.

Another important clue comes at refreshment time. Since food directly reflects a person's outlook on life, Mother's choice of beverages may unconsciously an-nounce her choice of values as well as the values she has selected for—and drilled into—her son.

The mother who offers home-made cookies and lemonade served from a pitcher on the porch swing can't be all bad. Unfortunately few girls are that lucky these days. More likely she will offer Coke or coffee. These drinks present no problems and also offer no information.

It was the ancient Romans who said, "In vino, veritas."—"In wine, there is truth." When it comes to alcoholic beverages, the unconscious mind speaks more eloquently. The presumptive mother-in-law who offers a young lady a beer right out of the pop-top can is saying something about her opinion of herself and her son's escort—and her son. The mother who offers a champagne cocktail also puts herself in a specific social-emotional category. The difference be-tween a beer mother-in-law and a champagne mother-in-law may not be important as long as a girl rec-ognizes exactly what she is dealing with. Expecting one and getting the other is what causes problems later on.

There are two kinds of refreshment situations that should flash a red light. The mother-in-law who ob-viously has had a few drinks before the party begins may be trying to tell everyone something. Perhaps she can't stand the thought of losing her little boy or maybe she goes through the strain of meeting *the* girl every six weeks or so. In any event, the mother-in-law who can't wait requires a daughter-in-law who can.

The other problem is when Mother offers the bride-to-be one kind of drink and takes another for herself. For example if Mother offers a girl a bottle of Budweiser while she sips Sherry, the message may be: "The fancy brands are for grown-ups. Sonny and his friends drink fizzy stuff." Another bad sign is the mother who begins by throwing open the liquor cabinet to reveal seventy-one famous brands lined up on mirrored shelves. "Now what would you like?" she chirps. No matter how hard the day has been, no matter how good a nice martini would taste, that's the moment to choose a neutral cup of coffee. When mother-in-law starts to psyche out daughter-in-law, all bets are off.

What about her remarks about her son?

That usually comes a little later. After everyone is settled down with their drinks and the weather has been analyzed, air pollution has been discussed, and other essentials dealt with, there will be a short moment of silence while Mother shifts mental gears. Then she will lean over and say the sentence or two that make the whole evening worthwhile.

If she turns to her son and says something like:

"Well, well, well. Is this the little girl I've been hearing so much about?" it's time to get a headache (if the "little girl" doesn't have one already) and leave the scene. Nothing good for anyone will come from a woman who adopts a condescending attitude toward her son's fiancée. More than likely she has played Mother Superior to her son all these years and is anticipating an expansion of her audience. If it isn't fun the first time, imagine how it will be the nine thousandth time.

The mother who gangs up on her boy often begins like this:

"Now, Gloria, there are some things you ought to know if you're going to put up with William. I should know; I'm his mother and I've had to put up with so much over the years!" The girl who is tempted to sympathize should remember that it is only a matter of time before Mother is telling someone else: "You wouldn't believe what I've had to put up with from my daughter-in-law!" Enough said.

The other side of the coin is the mother who sides with her son against the new member of the little family. It can start something like this:

"Now if you're going to marry my boy, you'll have to realize that he has very special kinds of needs. He's much more sensitive than other boys . . ." That's about the time to tune out and wait impatiently for a chance to sneak home. The only introduction more ominous than that one is the gangland approach: "You should understand this from the beginning. We're a very close family and if we like someone, there's nothing we wouldn't do for them. But they have to earn it."

How? By driving the getaway car?

What about the prospective father-in-law?

Certainly he is worth meeting and talking to although his value in predicting future events is somewhat limited. If a man's father is self-confident, contented, and secure, it means good marks for his prospective wife. If the husband is a submissive robot that stumbles around emptying ash trays and compulsively taking out the garbage, apparently the son has less than an ideal male figure to identify with. The personality of a man's father is less decisive in the selection process than his mother's influence.

Above all, in dealing with presumptive mothers-in-law, first impressions are vital. Once a mother senses that she is making a bad impression on her son's girl, she can change her style in the blink of an eye. In the initial interview, the first five minutes count. Anything after that can be considered purely social conversation.

How does a girl evaluate what she learns from a man's mother?

Carefully. There are two major types of information that can be gleaned from the first fateful meeting. First, a woman can get some idea of the attitude of mother-in-law toward daughter-in-law. This enables her to formulate a more or less clear idea of what she will have to face if and when she marries the man. Most of the time this is *useful* but not *critical* information since there are always ways to defend against and counteract the influence of any mother-in-law. Second, and most important, is the way Mother has molded son and how she still controls him. If she has imbued him with just enough self-confidence to allow him to make it to the office and back every day (provided he recharges his batteries by calling her on the phone during lunch), the girl who was thinking of marrying him needs to know. If Mother has brain-washed junior into believing that other women are all right for sex but when you want real affection come home to Mother and a good chicken dinner, a girl needs to know that too. On the other hand, if the relationship between them is based on the recognition that both have fulfilled their responsibilities toward one another and now it's time for them to seek their separate lives, the news couldn't be better. The job of Mother is to pave the way for her successor—wife—and in a way that makes life happier for everyone. There is just one other little obstacle that a girl has to cross.

What's that?

A man's attitude toward his mother is not necessarily transferable to his future wife. The fellow who thinks of his mother as a saint may wish to have his wife become a true believer. The man who considers his Mom a pal probably expects his wife to spend every Saturday night at Mom's pulling taffy or popping popcorn. The fellow who doesn't trust his mother may never be willing to trust his wife.

Is it really necessary for a woman to go to the trouble of evaluating her future husband?

No, it isn't necessary. She will find out all about him sooner or later anyway. On the other hand, if she wants to know *before* marriage she can use the techniques of modern psychiatry to help herself *and* her future husband. If she has a good idea of exactly the kind of person she wants to marry and if she uses common sense plus her knowledge of the human mind to make sure she picks that kind of man, the chances for happiness for two people are increased immensely.

10

THE NEXT STEP

Is it hard to get happily married?

Not necessarily. All a girl has to do is show up on her wedding day and she will find a handsome, prosperous, intelligent young fellow waiting there to live happily ever after with her. Those annoying little details like finding a man, getting to know him, falling in love with him, and finally getting him to propose just take care of themselves. All the blushing bride has to do is get to the church on time wearing her prettiest dress, smiling her prettiest smile, and looking forward to a lifetime of uninterrupted bliss.

Where do marriages like this take place?

On television soap operas. Inevitably they are followed by a toothpaste commercial. (Commercials showing washday misery or kids messing up the kitchen floor are barred from this sacred sequence.) For the girl who doesn't believe the shake-and-bake wedding scenes portrayed on TV, getting married can be a little more complicated. First there are a lot of soul-searching questions to be asked and answered. For example, "Do I really *want* to get married?"

Doesn't every girl want to get married?

It isn't quite that simple. Almost every woman, from the time she is a little girl, thinks in terms of getting married "someday." But when that "someday" becomes "tomorrow," a lot of things can happen, as in the case of Laurene. She is twenty-five, works as a receptionist in a talent agency, and—let her describe it:

"Looking back on it, it's hard to believe. There I was on the night before my wedding, surrounded by all my girl friends, my clothes laid out, the rehearsals all over, the dishes and glasses from the caterers stacked all over the place, and I just didn't feel right. This was what I'd been leading up to all my life. This was every girl's dream come true. Tomorrow the wedding, then the honeymoon, then a new life with Rick. The more I thought about it, the sadder I got. All of a sudden I started crying. My Aunt Helen rushed over and said, 'I know how it is, all this excitement is just too much for you.' Doctor, that wasn't it at all. I'd just realized that I didn't know what I was doing. It was only a few hours until my wedding ceremony and I didn't even know why I was getting married!"

"What did you do?"

"Nothing, thank goodness. I just went into my room, threw myself down on the bed and cried my heart out. Then I started thinking. Ever since I was small the idea of getting married was there like some wonderful milestone in my life—it was something every girl did if she was normal. Sort of a combination First Communion and Senior Prom with a touch of Snow White. But I didn't know why I was getting married and I wasn't sure if I wanted to. Then Rick came over."

"To your house?"

"Yes, I know the bridegroom isn't supposed to see the bride just before the wedding but now I understand why—he might suddenly wake up and face reality. When Rick burst in the door, I saw it written all over his face. He didn't want to get married either! We fell into each other's arms and honestly we were laughing and crying all at the same time. Then all my relatives came in and we told them: 'Don't worry —everything's okay! We're not getting married!' Well, I guess they didn't understand that! But we did and that's all that mattered. We called the whole thing off and it was really a relief."

"What happened next?"

"Nothing. And nothing will happen until Rick and I are sure that we really want to get married. I'm not going to be one of those perfect little plastic brides on top of a perfect little wedding cake."

Laurene was smart—and lucky. A lot of other girls don't make out so well.

Too many girls do what seems to be right—get married—for the wrong reason.

In what way?

The wrong reason is using marriage as a solution to all of life's problems. For twenty years or so most girls are told that sex without marriage is a fate worse than death. When they begin to feel the first strong sexual stirrings, they have their future mapped out for them—instant marriage or overwhelming guilt. The result? A whole new industry based on those little ads in the classified column: "Marry in two hours. No waiting. No publicity. Call 996-1877."

When the dynamite of guilt is ignited by the flames

of sex, the resulting explosion takes the form of instant marriage. (It is no coincidence that "instant" marriage centers such as those in Tijuana and Juarez that advertise "Marry In One Hour," also offer the convenience of "Divorce In Two Hours." Same customers a few months later?)

Another wrong reason is the subtle (and not-so-subtle) pressure from parents and relatives. If they didn't even know what you wanted for your birthday fifteen years ago, how can they know that Chester is just right for you today?

Boredom with the daily routine can drive a girl into a reckless decision to marry. Far too many girls who are tired of going to the office would find a vacation in Bermuda a better solution than a hasty honeymoon.

Instead of marrying the kind of man they really want to marry, some women end up with the man who just happens to be around. Convenience is an important concept in modern American life but marrying someone from your own neighborhood just to avoid the drive downtown is carrying things a bit too far. Yet the majority of American women end up marrying a man who lives within eight blocks of their home. As one patient put it, "I guess my biggest mistake was marrying the boy next door. Now if I'd only gone two houses over . . ."

Most marriages are accidental and most divorces are deliberate. There would be a lot less unhappiness if things could be the other way around.

Is there anything a girl can do specifically to get married to the right man?

Yes, there are a lot of things. The first and most important is understanding why men and women get married in the first place. If a woman can see the whole picture right from the beginning it is just a matter of time and tactics before she gets married to the right man in the right way.

Why do people get married?

Finding the answer isn't so easy. Each year five million Americans pay their money, stand up before the minister or Justice of the Peace and take their solemn vows. If someone stopped them on their way to the parking lot and asked them why, they might come up with five million separate reasons: "To make a home . . . To have children . . . Because we are in love . . . Because it's expected of me . . . Because I'm pregnant . . . To live in a better neighborhood . . . It seemed the right thing to do," and so on for 4,999,993 more reasons. Most explanations for getting married are like a bikini—what they reveal is interesting but what they conceal is vital.

What do they conceal?

The real basic underlying reason. From the time the world began, in every civilization, on every continent, in every country, men and women have chosen marriage as their way of life. The teenage Ubangi in Africa, the bell-bottomed charmer in Beverly Hills, and their pink-cheeked Eskimo sister in the frozen North, all have the same goal: a man and a home (or igloo) of their own. Etched into the unconscious mind of every woman on earth is the compelling desire to find a man whom she loves and who loves her.

It all starts in the maternity ward. From the first

moment she looks up and sees her mother looking down at her, the tiny female infant (and her male counterpart as well) begins her apprenticeship for marriage. For the next five yaars—at least—she is emotionally dependent on a single human being—Mother. (Or whoever takes Mother's place.) They eat together, live together, sleep together, fight and make up together, and are alternately bored and delighted with one another. They are forced by reality to make the best of their involuntary relationship. As one charming girl observed: "You can always get rid of a husband but nobody ever divorced their mother."

From the time of infancy every relationship is an instant replay of the original one. Teacher-and-pupil, employer-employee, hostess-guest, boy friend-girl friend are all watered-down versions of mother and child. Unfortunately none of these substitutes ever have the original satisfaction, the original intoxication, the original gratification, of the first relationship. Until one day, when all the signals are in place, the right man at the right time comes along and every girl sees (unconsciously) her chance to have everything she has always wanted—the perfect happiness and perfect harmony, she had—*or wished she had* —with her mother. To a woman, the closer her husband approaches the role of "ideal mother," the happier her marriage will be. And for a man the closer his wife comes to being *his* "ideal mother," the happier he will be.

But isn't a marriage between two adults?

Oh yes, that's what it says on the marriage certificate. But if we judge by what actually happens, the picture is somewhat different. In the average good marriage it goes something like this:

The wife prepares the food and feeds her husband —just like Mother. The wife washes his clothes and makes his bed—just like Mother. The wife cheers him up when he is sad, rewards him when he succeeds, and scolds him when he has been naughty—just like Mother. Like Mother a wife knows all the things no man ever tells another man—his deepest hopes, fears, and aspirations. Some men go one step further and even call their wives by the name of their predecessors: "Mother." For better or for worse, a wife takes over right where Mother left off.

But then how is a husband like a mother?

The husband (ideally) takes care of his wife—like Mother takes care of her children. He guides her and protects her, sends her to the doctor when she is sick, buys her presents, supplies her with food, shelter, and the material necessities of life. He (ideally) holds her in his arms, cuddles her, kisses her, and tells her what a good girl she is and how much bettter he likes her than all the other little girls he sees every day. However, there is one important difference.

The husband's role is never as direct and emotionally powerful as the wife's. He may give her the money to buy groceries but she is more likely to put food she has prepared with her own hands on the plate for him to eat. She actually washes his clothes and puts them out for him to wear in the morning.

Why is that so important?

Because the closer a woman comes to reproducing the ideal relationship between a man and the first woman he ever knew—his mother—the closer she comes to getting exactly what she wants (and incidentally, giving the man exactly what *he* wants) from the relationship between them. Understanding this becomes especially important once the girl is really on her way to getting married. In fact the emotional foundation for most successful marriages is based on both partners deliberately plotting to make each other happy. If a girl does this sort of thing *before* marriage not only is it good practice, but it also sets a good example for her future husband.

How does a girl actually get started getting married?

There is a famous recipe for the delicious Rumanian dish called "Gypsy Chicken." The instructions begin: "First, steal a chicken . . ." For the girl who wants to get married, the instructions begin, "First, find a man . . ."

It isn't as easy as it sounds. In spite of the fact that half the people in this world are men, finding the right one at the right time is a difficult, time-consuming, often frustrating task. In the words of the old song, "A good man is hard to find—you always get the *other* kind . . ."

Most girls rely on the "modified billiard-ball technique" of selecting a husband. Like an ivory sphere on the pool table they wait more or less patiently as the men in their lives come and go—bouncing gently from one chance acquaintance to another until one day they bump into the man who seems right for them. An attractive young lady who had been divorced twice listened intently to the comparison and noted, shaking her head: "That's me—except I always ended up with the eight-balls."

Most mothers encourage this passive sort of approach toward marriage by assuring their daughters, "Be patient. Someday the right man for you will come along." There *is* a possibility that Prince Charming will one day ride up to the door and saunter into a girl's outstretched arms. But all the laws of probability are against it. Even Cinderella had to work at it. There *is* a remote chance that the young lady who drifts around like a billiard ball may find the man she hopes to meet. But in the meantime she will take a lot of bouncing around and bump into plenty of eight-balls on the way. There are better techniques.

Like what for example?

For example, carefully examining exactly what she is trying to accomplish and then deciding the best way to go about it. When it comes to getting married, twelve minutes of *creative* thinking are worth twelve months of *wishful* thinking. Instead of musing, "Gee, I sure wish something would happen . . ." it is feasible to *make* things happen.

At first the project of selecting just the right man out of one-hundred million males seems like an overwhelming task—almost as overwhelming as shooting three tiny human beings 293,000 miles to the moon and bringing them back to earth. But a girl can simplify her own problem by using the same technique that space scientists (and most other scientists) use when confronted with a monumental task. It is called *systems analysis*. Basically it consists of lining up the problem and the ingredients necessary for the solution, assembling them in the proper order, and letting the system flow together. By monitoring the project as it functions and constantly correcting any errors that show up, maximum efficiency is assured.

But isn't that a kind of cold and mechanical approach to finding a husband?

Maybe. In the same sense that sex education is a kind of cold and mechanical approach to understanding sex. Trial and error is so much warmer—and more disastrous. On the other hand, being a spinster or married to the wrong man can be pretty cold and mechanical too.

How does systems analysis apply to selecting a husband?

The first step is listing the tasks. Simply stated they are:

1. Finding a man.
2. Making him like you.
3. Motivating him to marry you.

The process itself is a fascinating one and even in the early stages can be full of pleasant surprises.

Becky plunged into the technique as soon as it was explained to her—let her tell what happened:

"To be honest, Doctor, when you went through it with me the first time, it really made me feel uncomfortable. I thought, 'Here you are, Becky, 28 years old, never been married—although you played house a lot—and a psychiatrist has to give you lessons in finding a man.' It struck me as a sort of Matrimonial Monopoly—you know, every time you pass Go, you get a little card good for another boyfriend. Then all of a sudden it hit me! Finding a husband is the most important thing I'm ever going to do in my life. Actually most of what happens to me from now on depends on finding the best man I can and hanging on to him as hard as I can and that realization was nothing compared to the next one! As I was going through your method I began to recognize that no one had ever prepared me for husband-hunting. I learned to type, to water ski, to apply makeup, to speak French, all in a careful methodical way. Golly, if I cooked dinner as clumsily as I've been looking for a lifelong companion, I'd have starved to death long ago. And if I had to I could get by with TV dinners. As far as I know, modern science hasn't come up with frozen husbands all curled up on little aluminum beds—just heat and serve."

Becky sighed and shook her head. "When I took your ideas home and started working on them, I really had a revelation. First I wrote down all the qualities I wanted in a husband—every little detail, just like I was supposed to.

Here's the list:

AGE: 32 to 34

HEIGHT: 6 feet minimum

WEIGHT: 180-195

FEATURES & ATTRIBUTES: Blond, blue eyes, muscular and athletic; dresses well—mod style.

EDUCATION: Masters degree at least, engineering or architecture from a good school.

ECONOMIC SITUATION: Must be in business
for himself and earn at least $25,000 a year with
prospects for much more."

She laughed. "You have to admit, I have impec-
cable taste!

"Then I did the next step. There are about 500,000
people living within twenty-five miles of my apartment. Like you said, about half are women, leaving
250,000 men. I eliminated ninety percent as being
kids, old men, married, uninteresting, or unsuitable
in some way. That left me with 25,000 men to choose
from. Again following instructions, I crossed off ninety
percent of those as being—hard to admit—uninterested in me. Now my pool of prospects was down to
2500 men. It didn't seem nearly as encouraging as
25,000 but you're right, I only need *one*. Then I began
to understand why you made me go through all the
calculations. My 'perfect husband,' the blond, blue-
eyed engineer with $25,000 and muscles, had ten
times the chance of being in the 22,500 I had to discard that he had of showing up in the 2500 that
were really eligible. I know the figures are only ap-
proximate but when the message finally penetrated
I felt like banging my dumb head against the desk!
I kept thinking of all the guys I snubbed because
they didn't live up to my 'ideal.' Talk about being
stupid!" Becky's knuckles were white from clenching
her fists.

"So again, like you suggested, I tore up my list and
made out another one. Instead of a male model from
an old MGM musical, the new description added up
to a man:

AGE: 28 to 38 (give or take a couple of years in
special cases)

WEIGHT: Like the airlines say, 'proportional to height'

HEIGHT: At least five-feet four-inches (my height). Actually an inch less is okay—for the right man I would go through life in flats.

FEATURES & ATTRIBUTES: Honest, devoted, hardworking, and in love with me.

EDUCATION: Actually I couldn't care less. As long as he is intelligent and tuned-in to the world around him we can learn as we go along—both of us.

ECONOMIC SITUATION: Able to support a wife or preparing himself to do so. Ability and ambition is more important than position; jobs can come and go but talent is what counts.

It's hard for me to admit it but my first list added up to just the kind of man my mother would want me to marry. Ugh! A perfect prig! It took a week of hard thinking to put list number two together, and I have to admit I learned a lot about myself in the process."

"Like what, for example?"

"Like maybe I really hadn't really been so eager to get married. Well, that's another story. To be honest, with the second list in front of me, I suddenly felt better. I knew I had a real chance to find a man like that and I knew I was becoming grown-up enough to appreciate him. I was ready to go."

Within a week Becky had expanded her chances of getting married—happily married—tremendously. By lifting the unrealistic restrictions on the qualifications of her future husband she had immeasurably increased the probability of bumping into the right billiard ball. Now she was ready for the next step.

What's the next *step?*

Testing the validity of the theory by matching it
against the men she met during her daily routine.
Becky was a receptionist-secretary for a medium-sized
insurance company. In many ways it was the perfect
job for trying out some of her new techniques.

"How many men do you meet a day?"

"Men? Doctor, I don't meet any, that's the problem!
That's why I'm here!"

"I mean how many men do you talk to at work?"

"Oh, that. I'd say about twenty or so but they're
not men—they're customers or salesmen or people who
work for the company."

"Are they all married?"

"How should I know? I guess some of them are
single; most of the salesmen are single."

Like many girls, Becky made a careful distinction
between the males she met at work and "men." By
doing it that way she eliminated about fifty possibilities a week from her preliminary screening process.

What's a "preliminary screening process"?

The Preliminary Screening Process (or PSP for short)
is the next step. *Every* man who crosses the path of
a single girl must be matched against the list of qualifications and evaluated as a prospective husband.
Becky was automatically eliminating customers and
employees as possibilities—they were actually her
greatest source of eligible men. She spoke to more
men at work in one day than she met on her own

time in a month. She estimated twenty men a day
at the office—actually it was closer to thirty. At her
next visit she brought a detailed list:

"Well, Doctor, I must say I'm feeling very scientific about this whole business. I have a desk full of
lists and questions and names—my apartment is beginning to look like a detective agency."

"But isn't that what you're trying to do—track down
a husband?"

"Yes. But why can't I just let it happen?" She
wrinkled her brow. "Wait—I'll answer that one myself. I've been trying to find a good man for more
than eight years now and it hasn't 'just happened.'
There's nothing wrong with using what wits I have
to make it happen. I have to remember that. All right,
here's the list:

> Average day at work:
> Talked to nine salesmen in person, six unmarried (four
> bachelors, two divorced). Greeted eleven visitors to
> the office: four women, seven men. Took dictation
> from four executives: two married, two not. Spoke to
> seventeen men on the telephone: three sounded ter-
> rific. Admitted telephone man, adding machine repair-
> man, three painters, boy from drugstore with coffee,
> and sent away three men who came to the wrong
> office (one was really attractive). Total people: fifty!
>   Net possibilities: twenty-two. (Including two of the
> painters and telephone man. Coffee boy is fifteen, add-
> ing machine man weighs 250 pounds and chews to-
> bacco.)

I did what you told me with that list too. I eliminated
ninety percent as potentially unsuitable. That still
means at least two good hot prospects a day. What
a snob I've been! All these available men rushing
around me and I didn't want to get 'involved at work.'
I have the feeling I could do the rest of it myself but

the whole concept is so fascinating I want to carry it right through to the end."

Does every girl have the same chances to meet men at work that Becky had?

It depends on how you look at it. Actually until she began using PSP, her chances of meeting a man at work weren't as good. Her decision not to "get involved" on the job sprang from a false concept of loyalty. She put it like this:

"I figured that as long as they were paying me a salary it wasn't fair to try to solve my own problems on their time. Then I used one of the ideas I learned from you—I analyzed the time I spent on the job. When I realized I was spending half my waking hours, five days a week, at the insurance company I decided that a little preliminary screening between taking telephone calls—and sometimes *during* telephone calls—was all right. I'm not going to let another eight years go by all alone with my memories—the few that I have."

There are some girls who just don't have the opportunity to meet men where they work. A girl who works in the typing pool or in a ladies clothing store is seriously handicapped when it comes to male contacts on the job. By the law of probability it should take her twice as long to find a suitable man—and a lot of girls just don't have that much time to wait. For them it makes sense to consider another job. The girl who sells ladies' clothes might switch to the necktie section of a department store or perhaps the tobacco counter. Immediately she tips the odds in her favor. The typist can look for a job in an employment agency or personnel department—not only will she meet men but right at the start she will have the full rundown on their backgrounds and qualifications.

What if a girl can't meet men on the job and doesn't want to find another job?

There's always another way to go about it. Natalie had that problem. As a hospital lab technician she didn't have much flexibility in finding a new career. Thin and angular, with straw blonde hair and gray eyes, she spoke in a low voice:

"I heard about your method from a girl friend, Doctor, and I tried to do it on my own. I made the lists and got ready for the preliminary screening but I can't go any farther—I just don't meet any men on my job. There are three other girls in my section and the only males I ever come across are amoeba looking back at me through the wrong end of a microscope. When *they* start looking good, I'll know I'm in trouble!" She laughed.

"I even thought of getting a part-time job as a waitress but I have to work nights sometimes and I just couldn't manage it. Can you help me?"

Natalie had the right idea. Sometimes a part-time job is the answer. Not just for the money but as a chance to meet a better cross section of men. More than one girl with a masters degree in chemistry has found the man she was looking for by filling glasses in a cozy supper club instead of filling beakers in the chemistry lab. But that wouldn't work for Natalie so she had to go on to Phase Two.

What's Phase Two?

Phase Two depends on applying a pair of vitally important scientific principles that most women follow meticulously when buying tomatoes but totally neglect when searching for the men in their lives. Phase Two is the most valuable tool of every mathematician, aerospace engineer, dairy farmer, and woman alone. It works like this:

If the supermarket gets its tomatoes on Thursday, the woman who shops for the red fruit on Wednesday depends on the principle of *adverse selection*. The freshest tomato she can hope to find will be at least six days old . . . if not twelve days beyond its peak. The lady who gets there Friday morning practices *prime selection*—she has the choice of the freshest fruits before they are plucked off the stand by those competing with her. The shopper who arrives any day of the week—whenever she happens to be in the neighborhood—practices *random selection* and takes what she can get. But the smartest one of all gets to the produce counter late Thursday evening and plucks the finest fruit as it comes off the truck. She is the shopping genius who has discovered *enhanced prime selection*.

How does this apply to finding a man?

One of the ironies of life is that most women get a better deal in tomatoes than they do in husbands. *Prime selection* is the order of the day at the grocery store and the rare exception in the game of life. Most single girls deal in terms of *random selection*—that's

the way they were brought up. They wait patiently
(more or less) until a man "discovers them," takes
the initiative, and asks them for a date. Depending
on chance factors they get a good man, a bad man,
or no man at all. Most divorcées and widows practice
adverse selection. They look for men at times and
places which tend to increase the odds against them.
The brightest single girls stumble on the idea of *prime
selection* by themselves and marry early and happily.

When this was explained to Natalie, she grinned
and said: "I get it. The girl who just waits around for
a man to ask her is like the lady who shops for tomatoes on Tuesday—she takes what she can get. No,
wait a minute! She's more like the tomato—she just
sits there while different men come around and pinch
and poke her until after a while she gets overripe and
nobody wants her anymore. That's not the way this
tomato wants to end up!"

But exactly how does prime selection *apply to finding a man?*

The mechanics are relatively simple. All a girl has
to do is consult her list of qualifications, figure out
where men who qualify spend their time, and inject
herself into those situations. It's like looking for a lost
key:

After half an hour of looking in all the drawers
and underneath the furniture for a bunch of keys that
aren't where they should be, the exhausted key-search-
er collapses in an armchair and starts to think: "Now
where would I go if I were a bunch of keys?" Then
the answers start to come: "From the front door to the
end table then out to the garage then back to the top

of the television set, then . . . then . . . then to the big glass ashtray on top of the piano! That's it!" A fast dash to the piano and the keys are found!

Natalie did it like this:

"The first thing I did was think. If there's one thing I learned here it's to use my brain before I go running off in all directions: 'Where would I go if I were the kind of man I wanted?' No, that's for later. The first question was: 'Where would I live?' There's a whole bunch of new apartments down by the beach—modern, with swimming pools and patios— the kind of places a bright with-it guy would choose. I wrote that down. Then I got out the telephone book and looked in the yellow pages under, "Clubs," "Associations," "Organizations," and every other similar listing I could think of. I wrote down each one that seemed anywhere within reason and then broke it down to the twenty-five most likely possibilities. Was that a learning experience!"

"What do you mean?"

"Well, first of all I never knew there were so many groups. I must have gone through at least two hundred and fifty of them. Second, I never realized that there were so many great opportunities to have so many men all to myself.

"My final working list included organizations like: Young Businessmen for City Improvement, The University Civic Club, The Homewood Tennis Club, and even Friends of the Forests. Oh yes, as an afterthought I threw in the Young Democrats and the Young Republicans.

"Then I got on the telephone. At first I spoke to the secretaries but it didn't seem to work out—the first few were obviously single girls looking for a chance to get ahead and they weren't very helpful. From then on I just acted very businesslike and asked

for the membership chairman or the vice-president
and called him directly. Did I make some discoveries!
Doctor, there are thousands of *super* men out there
just waiting to be discovered! These men were all
so nice—even the clubs I wasn't eligible to join invited me to their meetings and it worked out fine."

"What clubs wouldn't accept you?"

"Oh, The Midnight Sun Club, for example. The
name sounded so romantic that I just *had* to call them.
It turned out to be an organization for Scandinavian
engineers—*but* they invited me to their meetings."
Natalie smiled.

"In case you're interested, here's the box score: I
scanned 261 groups in a twenty-five-mile radius of
my apartment. I picked about ten percent of those
because they sounded promising—actually twenty-
three groups. Six were all women or for married couples, four just didn't work out—The Cherry Blossom
Society was for Japanese war veterans. They were
very polite but a little shook-up at a call from a red-
blooded American girl. That left me with thirteen.
That also left me with absolutely no time to worry
about finding the right man. I had every evening during the week filled with meetings and activities except for Friday, Saturday, and Sunday."

"What about those nights?"

Natalie's eyebrows arched in mock amazement.
"Doctor! A girl needs some social life! That's when
I go out on dates with the men I meet from the
clubs."

"You said something earlier about the new apartments down by the beach."

"Oh, yes. Well, I have to shop somewhere so I decided to do my grocery shopping—and every other
kind of shopping I can manage—down there. It adds
an extra fifteen minutes driving time but it's worth it.

I get to the supermarket about six PM just when the bachelors are doing *their* shopping. It works out fine."

Will the technique that Natalie used work for every girl?

It certainly can't do any harm. Naturally the specific approach has to be tailored to the area, the girl's life situation, and the qualifications she desires in a man. For Rhoda, things were a little different. She was forty-one and had been married and divorced once already. With two boys, age nine and ten, and a job as assistant cashier at the bank, the shotgun approach that suited Natalie wasn't for her. *Prime selection* was a good idea but she needed *enhanced prime selection* to solve her special problems.

What kind of special problems did she have?

Unfortunately there are a relatively limited number of men who are looking for a forty-one-year-old divorcée with two pre-teenage boys. But somewhere they do exist and the problem facing Rhoda was finding them—and finding them in a special way. As she explained it:

"I meet a suitable man every once in a while, Doctor. Say, every month or six weeks someone comes into the bank who is interested in me and we go out on a date or two but that's not the way I want it. I just know that somewhere there must be more men who are looking for a woman like me—and my two sons. How do I find them faster than twelve a year?"

During the discussion that followed Rhoda took

careful notes. A week later she was back with a smile:

"I am happy to present, for the first time anywhere, the RIPE technique."

"Sounds interesting. Let's hear it."

Rhoda laughed. "Actually it's *Rhoda's Imaginative Personal Expansion* plan, and it goes like this. Briefly I figured the type of man most likely to be interested in what I have to offer is a middle-aged chap who has just lost his own family—usually by divorce. So I checked over the men who were divorced in the past six months in my county. I found that in the newspaper files. Then I looked them up in the city directory and listed the ones who had children about the same age as my boys. Then I cheated. I have access to the bank's computer so I fed in the names I selected to see which ones were customers of the main branch—that's where I work. I put in 187 names and I got back forty-four customers. I told our chief teller to notify me when each of them come in on business so that I could go over their accounts with them and see if they were satisfied. We're supposed to do that anyhow, periodically, but maybe I can satisfy two people at the same time. But I don't stop there. If they want to continue the discussion over dinner I never discourage them."

Rhoda had a unique advantage over most women and she took advantage of it. On the other hand *every* woman has some specific talent or access to information that she can utilize to further enhance the magic of *prime selection*. Rhoda went one step further.

"My former husband used to be an avid fisherman. I remember how I used to complain about the weekends he spent off by himself with a rod-and-reel. He would ask me to come along but I couldn't have cared less about that sort of thing—*then*. But last weekend

I called the Rod and Fin Club and talked to the president. I told him about my two sons without a Daddy—I didn't tell him about me without a husband—that part comes later—and how they loved to go fishing. To make a long story short, he took it very seriously and called up half a dozen of their members so they could take turns fishing with the boys. The first one called yesterday and the four of us are going trolling this weekend." Rhoda beamed as if she had already landed the big one.

Prime selection and especially *enhanced prime selection* have some little-known fringe benefits.

What are they?

Any woman who spends a big part of her time away from the attentions of men gradually begins to lose confidence in herself as a woman. Vague feelings of doubt and inferiority creep into her life. Slowly, almost imperceptibly, the glow of optimism and the warmth that are the very essence of feminine attractiveness begin to fade. Unless something happens quickly she may become one of the millions of lonely women who are resigned to their fates, plodding through life oblivious to the lost opportunities that pass their way a dozen times a day.

But once a woman—any woman—begins to take control of her own existence everything changes. The constant emotional stimulation of daily encounters with men, the good-natured kidding, the unexpected compliments, all contribute to her new life. Maxine experienced it dramatically:

"I was fifty-four when I began all over again. My husband died the year before and when I got over the shock—and let's be honest, the self-pity—I was in pretty bad shape. I was fat, depressed, and not exactly overwhelmed with self-confidence. Frankly I didn't believe the things you talked about could work. Besides, where could a fifty-four year old grandmother fit in? I was wrapping up some coffee grounds to throw in the trash one afternoon when I saw an item in the paper. The Kiwanis Club in our town sells pancakes every three months to raise money and they were looking for volunteers to help out. Well, I was feeling so bad that day that I was ready to jump into the trash can along with the coffee grounds so I figured—'I can't feel any worse and at least I know how to make pancakes.' I went down to the park the next morning and pitched right in. Pretty soon this old fellow—well, he was only sixty-eight—came over and started talking to me. He complimented me on my hairdo—that was about the only thing I still took pride in—and I suddenly felt as if the sun was coming out. You never saw anyone whip up pancakes the way I did that morning! I was still traveling on the momentum from that conversation when I signed up for the typing course at night school. From then on it was coasting all the way. I met a nice fellow in the class, a few months later I got a part-time job typing at a mail-order company and things are starting to change. I haven't met the man of my dreams yet, but I talk to a dozen men every day, I take care of myself, and I do what I haven't done in thirty-one years—I go out on dates. Even if I don't get married, I'm part of the human race again."

What about adverse selection?

That's the easy part. Like the old song, "You have to have a million dollars to be a millionaire but you can be poor without a cent." Most of the solutions offered by society to women alone are in this category. Computerized dating is a good example. In spite of adroit advertising and smooth selling, "computer-matched dating" is buying last Thursday's tomatoes this Wednesday. Dating bureaus in general are magnets for those who are socially paralyzed. The man who is too passive to interact with the one-hundred million females around him feeds his mind and body into the computer. Women who seek a man by this route find that the wonders of the electronic age have assembled a large proportion of cultural rejects to confound and amaze them. The man who hides behind the IBM card is likely to be as full of emotional holes as the piece of cardboard that represents him.

The basic fallacy of dating bureaus, computerized or otherwise, is the assumption that someone else can choose the right man for a girl better than she can. If the salesman at the shoe store doesn't know even her right size half the time, how can the gentleman at "Electronic Romances, Inc." be expected to fit her with the perfect living breathing human being?

Other striking examples of *adverse selection* are the plaintive pleadings in the "Personal" columns:

"Attractive man, early thirties, 6 ft. seeks sincere woman 25-50 with means. Object matrimony. Box 236."

If the gentleman is so attractive how has he been able to conceal his charms, lo, these many years? Why the box number? Is it so his wife won't know where he is really spending those evenings when he doesn't come home from work? Is "6 ft." his height or is it the closest he's ever gotten to a girl? And "object matrimony"? Does that mean he eventually plans to get married when enough women "with means"

have answered his ad and helped finance a honeymoon with his old high school sweetheart? Women
who habitually bet the long shots at Hialeah, enjoy
the Irish Sweepstakes, and cross the street against
the light will do well to answer newspaper ads. They
will be provided with the thrills they enjoy so much.
For those who want to get married there are better
ways.

Are there any other forms of adverse selection?

There are two more that are fraught with danger. Recommendations from friends heads the list. When another single girl offers an introduction to a single man,
the obvious question is, "Why is she doing this for
me?" Sometimes the answer isn't so obvious. Occasionally a woman breaks off her relationship with a man
by switching him to her best friend. Passing title this
way can be fine for everyone—it keeps everything
in the family, so to speak. On the other hand it's
always good to know just what went wrong between
them before you follow in someone else's footsteps.
If the benefactor is unwilling to tell the whole story
of her punctured romance, maybe it's better to see
what comes up in your own net. Once in a while a
little help from friends helps them instead of you. It
happened to Patty:

"I've known Rhonda for almost two years now. We
work in the same office—her desk is kitty-corner from
mine, or I should say catty-corner, after what happened. She introduced me to Ken; she used to go
out with his older brother and she really built him
up. Well, I knew her, she knew Ken, and I imagined
that she would know what was good for both of us.

What she actually knew was what was good for Rhonda."

"What happened?"

"Just what she wanted to happen—nothing! I was following your plan and it was working—too well to suit her, I suppose! All the men in the office were beginning to notice me and ignore her, so she fixed me up with Kenny. We got along great for the first two months until he got up the nerve to tell me what Rhonda had known all along—he was just about to go into the Army for four years and he wanted to know if I would wait for him. Rhonda had just put me out of circulation for two months and now she was trying for four years. I just chalked it up to experience and started looking all over again—on my own."

Even more hazardous are the recommendations of relatives. Most of them still remember you when you were six years old and still liked lollipops. Even the best of them can't really imagine little Margaret being interested in anything like *sex*. The boys your aunts and uncles are likely to fix you up with are guaranteed to be their choices, not yours. If you are wild for a combination of freckles, Hawaiian shirts, obesity, and receding hair—and a sense of values to match—go right ahead.

The last big pitfall is the hodgepodge known as "singles activities." Like computer dating, it looks good on paper. All you have to do is fill a dance floor or a vacation hotel or a cruise ship with 500 unmarried men and women and each one will find exactly what they want. And like computer dating most singles affairs operate as *adverse selection*. They tend to attract a specific category of men—especially those who find safety in numbers. Many of them don't really know why they are there. Some are lonely, some don't want to "get involved," others just want every-one to *think* they are interested in girls. Even more discouraging, the same faces (with bodies attached) tend to turn up week after week and place after place. Gradually they form tight little groups-within-groups and clubs-within-clubs. Sometimes it goes like this:

Tall, thin chap about forty, wearing a brown cor-duroy suit, somewhat wrinkled, calls across the room:

"Hey, Morrie, what were ya doin' with that blonde at the Single-Tonians Get-Acquainted picnic last month?"

(Correct answer: "I was doin' nothing with that blonde at the picnic—as usual. I just wanted some-body to see me with a girl.")

Tired-looking middle-aged man in bright green tweed sports jacket sitting alone at a table is asked by one of his friends who dances by with a very fat girl in a sequined cocktail dress:

"What's the matter, Hank, can't you get a girl to dance with you?"

(Correct answer: "No, I can't get a girl to dance with me. That's why I keep coming here and wasting my time with losers like you.")

The whole business can get pretty dreary and de-moralizing. There are exceptions, of course, but that goes back to *random selection* again and the endless months of sifting through the social dross in the hope of finding gold. To the woman who is aware of the scientific methods of finding men, the entire world is one big singles club just waiting for her to select the choicest members for herself.

After a girl creates the opportunity to meet men, what next?

Next, she tries to select the one man who is best for her. The goal at this stage is: CHOICE—NOT CHANCE. By utilizing a combination of sound scientific principles plus common sense, she shifts the odds overwhelmingly in her favor.

Success depends on understanding how men actually think, and learning the vital difference between what a man *says* he wants and what he *really* wants. One of the most important aspects of this unique selection process is the amount of time it saves. Instead of wasting valuable months or even years "getting to know" a prospective husband, with proper preparation a girl can eliminate losers early in the game. As soon as she develops confidence in her judgment and narrows the field to a few reasonable choices, she can go on to the next step.

What's that?

Making her choice choose her. By this time she should have assembled all the important elements: a charming attractive woman, an interested and desirable man, and a social relationship between them. Her task is to convert these components into a durable and mutually satisfying emotional bond. As one patient put it: "The last, and most important step, is *setting the glue.*" If done right, the emotional glue will last fifty years or so and hold man and woman firmly and delightfully together for the rest of their natural lives. This is the time when every young lady can take a hint from those masters of practical psychology, the advertising men, who cheerfully remind themselves: "Our job is to create a basic human need —and then offer to fill it."

When it comes to cementing a lifetime relationship with a man, the task is "Understand the basic needs of the man you want—then fill them as no other woman can."

Where can a girl begin to find out about these things?

On the next page.

11

GETTING MARRIED

When a girl finds the right man, what's the next step?

Assuming that she wants to get married, the next part of the project is getting her future husband to marry her. As almost every modern girl has discovered, much to her dismay, not every man wants to get married. Or at least they don't *think* they want to get married, which from the girls' point of view adds up to the same thing. Her major task consists of telling him by word or deed that he can't possibly exist without her—and then proving it. Unfortunately, the job is a lot harder than it was forty years ago.

How come?

In the old days most bachelors lived in rooming houses, carried their shirts to Chinese laundries, and spent their evenings during the week reading the sports page or listening to the radio—if they had a radio. For them marriage meant a real improvement in their standard of living—there was a powerful incentive to find a nice girl and "settle down." Things have changed a lot since then.

The modern bachelor may live in a singles apartment with sauna, swimming pool, and two-and-a-half girls for every man. His clothes are mostly wash-and-wear, the quality of TV dinners improves every month, and his evenings are divided between color television, riding around in his new Mustang, swimming in the pool, and listening to his multiplex stereo. These are some of the *little* things a girl has to compete with. The big ones are even worse.

What are the big ones?

They come in three varieties—blondes, brunettes, and redheads. It may be hard to admit, but there are many young ladies who are willing to "play house"— provide all the usual advantages of marriage without the usual disadvantages. This usually boils down to sex on demand. One of the most powerful incentives that ever motivated a man to pop the question is drowned out three to five times a week by a flood of competing womanhood. Realistically, a fellow who finds adequate sexual gratification with little difficulty is less inclined to marry. He keeps asking himself— and with good reason, "What more could I get from marriage?" Larry describes it accurately:

"Well, I'm thirty now and I guess I don't have anything to complain about. I'm a junior partner in the law firm where I work—I even get to use the company plane when nobody else wants it—usually after midnight or when it's snowing. I have a nice apartment, a new Jaguar, nice clothes, and plenty of time off to enjoy myself. And girls. Doctor, when it comes to girls, I just don't have enough time to keep them all happy. Between airline stewardesses, girls I meet on skiing weekends, and the ones that live in my apartment complex, I could have a different one every night for a month and still not get through the list. I have everything any young bachelor could ever want! Except . . ." Larry frowned.

"Except what?"

"That's it. I don't really know. Most of the time everything's fine, but once in a while I just get tired of what I'm doing and wish I could—I don't know. I just wish it were different somehow. Should I get married or something? I mean, is it better?" Larry shrugged his shoulders.

In that shrug lies the key to inducing a man to give up his plush and sensual bachelor existence and trade it for a (hopefully) plush and sensual marriage.

How does it work?

Deep in the heart of the most confirmed bachelor pulsates the nagging doubt that he may be missing something by not marrying. The more intent a man is on sowing his wild oats—the more frantic his pursuit of new thrills, new games, and new girls—the more vulnerable he is to this inner uncertainty.

Why?

The compulsion to look for new forms of distraction and entertainment is a manifestation of an inner fear that he may be missing out on something big. A man who tries first one type of girl, then another, then another, is looking for the ultimate **in** sexual gratification. The chap who sky-dives, water-skis, scuba-dives, hunts with bow and arrow—everything except shooting Niagara Falls in a barrel—is the type who wants to try everything to make sure he isn't left out. Marriage is the only experience he can't have on a thirty-day-home-trial-double-your-money-back-if-not-satisfied basis. For that reason, if a girl plays it right, the man she selects will be inwardly compelled to marry her—on her own terms and bowing to forces beyond his control. More important, when it comes to conscious pleasures—material things—no woman can compete with what every bachelor has at his fingertips. When it comes to unconscious *emotional* gratification, if she understands the rules, she is in charge every step of the way.

Does that apply to older women—divorcées and widows, for example?

Even more emphatically. For most men, the joys of bachelorhood are like a pair of nine-dollar shoes—with every step they wear thinner and thinner. Ironically, those men who have been married before—even unhappily—tend to remember the best parts of their marriages and mercifully allow the harsher moments to fade away. At the same time, older women have had more experience with men and have an expanded frame of reference to draw upon. They have been through the entire male-female relationship at least once and often are aware (all too keenly sometimes) of past mistakes.

Where does a girl start?

As usual, by analyzing and understanding the problem she's dealing with in order to apply the most precise solution that will help her achieve her goal. To supply the emotional needs of her man, she must have a clear grasp of what those needs are. To give him what he's missing, she has to know precisely what he lacks. Her greatest source of information is the man himself. Bachelors have a need—sometimes even a compulsion—to tell anyone who will listen exactly what their fears and hopes and apprehensions are. Paul is typical of a man in that position—this is what he says:

"I know it looks good on the outside, Doctor, and I don't want to complain, but I have my problems too. I'm a district manager for a major tire company and I have a good job—I make about $22,000 a year plus all the usual fringe benefits. For a twenty-nine-year-old like me that's not too bad.

"But I earn every penny of it—and more. Let me tell you how it goes. I get up about six-thirty and make it out of the house by seven—it's a forty-five-minute drive to the office, and I try to get there before the phone starts ringing. There's no time for breakfast, so I get some coffee at my desk. I start reading the reports from the day before and pretty soon the calls start coming in. Something's always going wrong in the tire business these days. I try to square things away by eleven when we have our meeting, then it's lunch from twelve to two with the big boys. I hate those lunches, but I don't have any choice —it's part of my job. Then it's back to the office, more problems to fight, and if I'm lucky, I get out by four-thirty to beat the traffic. Or I should say to get stuck on the expressway with all the other middle-management geniuses who are leaving early to beat the traffic.

"When I get home I spend about an hour trying to recover from my day. If I have a date that night, I get ready for it. Most of the time I do have a date and we go out to dinner—my second big meal of the day—and usually I'm so tired I end up eating and drinking too much. I tell myself it's okay because I never drink at lunch—company policy, you know." Paul shook his head.

"If I don't have a date, it's a sandwich from the shop on the corner, or if I feel really energetic, I broil a steak. Since I got out of the Air Force six years ago, I've learned three delicious ways to broil a steak: at 450 degrees, 500 degrees, or shoot the works and put that little knob all the way up to "BROIL"! It isn't exactly gourmet cooking, but it's better than eating out all the time. Sometimes the guys come over and we play cards or we go out and have a few drinks and listen to music. I don't usually try for those chicks in the cocktail lounges—it's just not my style. Then to bed by midnight to make it the next morning."

"That doesn't sound too bad."

Paul frowned. "No, that isn't the bad part of it. The bad part comes when I start thinking about what I'm doing. I oversee twelve tire stores in two states out of a total of 307 stores in fifty states. There are twenty-two district managers, fourteen regional managers, and thirty-seven vice presidents ahead of me —I'm seventy-fourth in line. If I play my cards right, in twenty years I'll be a senior vice president. That means $58,000 a year and plenty more in bonuses and stock options. It's a great chance—I can't afford to pass it up. I couldn't do better anywhere else, *but* it's hard work, plenty of pressure, and a lot of guys fighting for the same thing. It all boils down to one thing. I have everything except . . ."

"Satisfaction?"

"Yeah. How did you know? I have everything in life except satisfaction. I mean, I really can't get excited about getting everybody in the country to roll on a set of Super-Silent Squee-Gee Whitewalls Guaranteed Against Road Hazards As Long As You Own Them. It's a living, but I sure hope there's more to life than that."

What does that mean to a girl?

It means that Paul is ready. He's ready for excitement, glamour, romance. He's ready for the emotional exhilaration that only a living, breathing woman can bring into his life. He's tired of being a super-robot for Super-Silent Squee-Gees and is ready to respond to his inner urgings to be a man.

Every man has his specific set of frustrations, and the woman who wants to marry him must supply exactly what is missing from his life. The best way to find out what he thinks he is missing is to ask him. One quiet afternoon at the beach or after a nice dinner she might say *casually:*

"What are you working toward? I mean, what do you really want from life?"

or

"Are you satisfied with things the way they are?"

or

"Tell me, is your life what you expected it was going to be, say, five years ago?"

These are what psychiatrists call "open-end" questions, and they almost always bring on evasive answers. *Then,* the psychiatrist (or the young lady) asks what is called the "cork-popper." This is the question that no human being can resist answering in full and agonizing detail. No matter how discreet and diffident he may have been up to that moment, this is the query that literally pops the conversational cork. The question is simply: *"What do you mean by that?"* Men (and women) can tolerate any form of mistreatment *except* the possibility of not being understood. Even the shyest, the most retiring of men, will instantly plunge into a clarification when confronted with the magic question, "I don't understand. Can you explain what you mean?" For the woman who needs to be convinced, a few try-outs at ladies' luncheons or cocktail parties should provide ample proof.

What will the man answer?

Each male will give a response based on his own private world, but there will be four unsatisfied needs that all single men have in common. These are precisely the yearnings that a single woman can satisfy at the same time she relinquishes her single status. The deficiencies, in order of urgency, are:
1. Lack of food
2. Lack of sex
3. Lack of love
4. Lack of individual identity
It is *not* a coincidence that these are the same needs which an infant must have satisfied by his mother.

Do infants have their sexual needs satisfied by Mother?

The answer to that one is long and complex but, simply stated, infants have *infantile* sexual needs such as needing to be held, cuddled, warmed, and caressed by Mother. These are the forerunners of adult sexuality and have nothing to do with stimulation of the sexual organs. Adult sexuality, on the other hand, has a lot to do with the sexual organs, as every girl knows.

Can't a man satisfy his own requirements for food?

Yes and no. He can feed himself enough calories to keep his body going. But that's not the problem. The only really satisfying food is calories *plus* good vibrations, calories *plus* warm human emotions. While the most important *physical* experience for every man is eating, the most important *emotional* experience for every man is his relationship with his mother. The girl who can combine the concepts of "food" and "Mother" has constructed a psychological hydrogen bomb that relentlessly wipes out all resistance. The woman who serves real emotional feeling with the entrée is almost guaranteed to get her man. And the best part is, she doesn't even have to be a good cook.

How come?

Well, first, of all, Mother wasn't such a good cook. Not long ago an enterprising bakery set up a display of pies with the notice: "Pies Like Mother Used To Make—$1.00." Next to it was another display featuring: "Pies Like Mother Tried To Make And Couldn't —$1.25." The second offering outsold the first, two to one.

Inside every grown man is the little boy who remembers a kitchen full of the aroma of home-made cookies or frying chicken made just for him by the only woman in his life. At the age of nine he didn't notice if the chicken was a little greasy or the cookies were under-cooked. All that mattered was that Mommy made them.

Even in this modern world where almost everything is for sale, no bachelor can buy food lovingly prepared just for him—and for him alone. That's one reason why the menus for seduction that appear every few months in the slick little magazines are doomed to failure. Those intimate dinners for two by candlelight that look so good in the pictures are more likely to bring on indigestion than orgasm. Joyce tried it both ways:

"How was I to know? It looked great on the cover. It was in one of those monthlies for ladies—something like 'A Dinner To Put Him In The Mood For Love.' I thought, 'Why not?' I cut out the recipes—they looked so beautiful in the magazine—a fellow sitting across from a girl in a hostess gown, eating on a terrace with the lights of Manhattan behind them. I called up Bill, asked him over for dinner, and started getting everything ready. I can still remember the menu: Crabmeat and avocado appetizer, beef stroganoff, asparagus with hollandaise, sliced oranges with shredded coconut and cherries jubilee for dessert. There was red wine and brandy after dinner—out of those big snifters. I'll tell you, it took me four and a half hours just to get ready and I had to borrow the brandy snifters from the florist—he was growing cactus in them. I set the table on the patio outside, and then Bill arrived. Just as the doorbell rang I had a last-minute worry—wasn't that meal a little heavy? But by then it was too late." Joyce threw up her hands.

"I don't know how it affected Bill, but when the crabmeat met the stroganoff in my stomach, the evening ended right there as far as I was concerned. I stopped eating. Bill went on through the whole meal, and I guess he felt pretty good. After the wine and the brandy he was very relaxed. I cleared the table, put some nice tapes on the stereo, went in the bathroom for something to settle my stomach and—I guess I'd done my job too well. The article should have been called: 'A Dinner To Put Him In The Mood For Sleep.' Bill woke up about 2 A.M., just when my dinner was beginning to digest. It was an evening to forget—for both of us."

This kind of plastic impersonal approach to feeding is always doomed to end in disaster. Joyce reviewed some of the psychological principles of combining food and affection and tried again:

"I won't say it was because of that meal—I'm sure it was just another sign that we weren't right for each other—but Bill and I broke up a few weeks later. I did it your way—or should I say 'our way,' with Les, and it was quite an experience.

"I tried to remember what my mother used to make for my brothers, and I copied it as well as I could. I started off with shrimp cocktail, then we had fried chicken with fresh biscuits (not the frozen kind that come in little mailing tubes), wildflower honey, corn on the cob, mashed potatoes with gravy, lettuce and tomato salad with French dressing, and strawberry shortcake with freshly whipped cream for dessert. It was really strange the way things went. Les is in television—he's an assistant producer and he's supposed to be a sophisticated guy. He travels a lot to Europe and knows the best wines and best restaurants. I was worried about giving him something so simple, but it sounded logical the way you explained it." Joyce stopped and pursed her lips.

"Actually everything went wrong. It was raining that evening so we had to eat inside at the dinette table in the kitchen—my place doesn't have a dining room. I burned the first batch of biscuits; you know it isn't as if I make them every day. When he arrived with an orchid corsage, there I was standing over the stove perspiring with my hair in my eyes. I said to myself, 'Joyce, you blew it again!' But I didn't. It was kind of hot in the kitchen by then, so he took off his coat, rolled up his sleeves, and sat down to eat. As he went through each course, it was as if he just didn't believe it. He just kept eating and shaking his head. After dessert—two helpings—he came over and kissed me—sweaty as I was—and I really believe there were tears in his eyes. He said, 'Joyce, nobody's cared enough to cook me a dinner like this since I was ten years old. Thank you.' He really meant it."

"What happened then?"

"Then we went into the living room and talked and listened to records and everything until five o'clock in the morning. It was one of the best evenings in my life. And I'm sure Les enjoyed it too.

"The next morning he sent me three dozen long-stemmed red roses and a beautiful hand-made imported apron. We're going to the mountains this weekend, and I know we're thinking about each other in a different way after that great evening together."

Is the effect of food on a man that *powerful?*

That's just the beginning. Food is the most effective method known of controlling human behavior. The closer food or the feeding situation approaches his earliest experiences, the more unconscious emotional power it exerts. If a woman wants to make herself indispensable to a man she can pull out all the stops and unleash the ultimate weapon—*milk*.

What is unique about milk?

Simply this: from his first moment on earth, the most important substance in the life of every human being is *milk*. Whether he gets it from Mother, a cow, a camel, or a goat, milk leaves an indelible impression engraved on every man's brain. The unconscious concept of milk is a vital nourishing food synonymous with love. When Mother gave the breast (or bottle) she gave love and affection at the same time. For every man the world of the subconscious is ruled by the symbol of milk. Milk shakes, ice cream, later soft drinks and beer (often from a bottle suspiciously resembling a milk bottle), even alcoholic beverages (an Alexander, crème liqueurs, "cream" sherry, that nice milky foam on beer) carry the theme of Mother's milk throughout every day. The six-foot 200-pound man sipping a cup of coffee with cream is emotionally only moments away from the twenty-pound baby happily drinking from his bottle. Perhaps that's why so many professional athletes—who earn their living by playing games—still drink four or more glasses of grade A straight from the cow.

If a woman can establish herself as the *provider of milk* she literally makes herself part of her man's unconscious mind. Even more important, she is unlikely to be displaced by any other female competitor. Nice legs, a good figure, bright conversation, feminine flattery, can turn the head of most men, but not the one whose woman supplies milk and love in abundance.

Exactly how does a girl use this knowledge?

It depends on exactly what she wants. If she is at the stage where she wants her man to marry her, all she has to do is inject enough milk (or milk symbols) into their relationship and wait for the results. Specifically, it works like this:

On every occasion they are together she must provide him with milk (or the symbolic equivalent) in some form. If they go out on a date, after he brings her home, she can invite him in for hot chocolate or coffee *with cream*. It's even better if she floats whipped cream on top of either drink. If he has his favorite brand of "milk"—that is, beer or wine, she should serve it *just the way he likes it*. (After all, that's the way Mother served her beverage.) Ice cream is a fine substitute, and the most effective ice cream is that made with her own hands—in one of those little crank freezers. Remember, Mother made all her milk herself—or at least baby thought so.

What if the man doesn't like milk?

That's no problem, usually. Most men have shifted their emotional attachment from actual white liquid milk to common milk substitutes like coffee, tea, or beer and wine. But one thing to remember—the closer a girl comes to supplying the original beverage, the more control she is bound to exert. Milk chocolate, pudding made with milk, and cream custard have more unconscious influence than a glass of beer or a cup of coffee.

The rare man who cannot tolerate milk in any

form whatsoever is a more complicated situation. Because this often reflects a complete denial and renunciation of the mother-child feeding relationship, it may leave a girl nothing to build on. Certainly all the facts have to be considered, but a man who totally rejects milk is a questionable prospect for marriage.

Every item of food (within reason, of course) will be much more effective in establishing an emotional attachment if a girl can make it herself. In this era of "convenience foods" with instant potatoes, twenty-second rice, pre-jelled puddings, and cake mixes that taste like the cardboard box they come in, the girl who is willing to take a little extra time has a tremendous advantage in the emotional sweepstakes. A woman who feeds her man a slice of buttered freshly baked bread can almost set her own wedding date.

She feeds *it to him?*

Yes, if she really wants results. Hand-feeding is an emotionally supercharged technique known to animal trainers, primitive tribes, and mothers of finicky eaters. There is a quirk in the operation of the human mind that tends to make people think they themselves provide everything they have or acquire. A fellow who eats in a restaurant forgets about the kitchen full of people who make his meal possible. The man who is served dinner by his girl usually doesn't quite make the unconscious connection that she prepared every morsel with her own little hands. Almost every woman has had a man innocently ask (usually after she has slaved for hours in the kitchen), "Did you make this yourself?"

The most ferocious lion, after a period of hand-feeding by his trainer, becomes docile and submissive —but only toward that individual. In the animal unconscious mind, the trainer has taken the place of the one being even the king of the beasts respects—his mother.

If a woman takes every opportunity to hand-feed, she will be amazed at the power it gives her—she will literally have her man "eating out of her hand."

After dinner, as she serves coffee she can break off a bit of chocolate cake she has baked (*milk* chocolate), and pop it into his mouth. "Here, try this. I just made it." Another opportunity comes with men who linger in the kitchen while dinner is cooking. The girl who warns, "Now, don't touch anything until it's ready" will be lucky to get an invitation to the wedding of the one who smiles, "Why don't you taste some of this?" as she pops a bit of dumpling into her future husband's mouth.

Even dinner at a restaurant holds opportunities for someone who is alert. The girl who says, "Here, have some of mine," and feeds her date a forkful of steak from her own plate is miles ahead of the other young ladies in her league.

The final touch is the "message that lingers." Every time she serves a meal, she should wrap up some part of it for the man in her life to take home—and the more milk it contains, the better. The next day when he's back in his own surroundings with an icebox full of frozen dinners and cottony white bread in plastic bags, that big hunk of home-made apple pie or heaping dish of lasagna reminds him as nothing else can. It tells him there is someone who cares about him, who wants him to be happy, and is willing to translate her feelings into the basis of life itself, food, *just for him.* Even the slowest thinker gets that message fast.

What about sex?

In the complex process of making the man you have chosen choose you, sex takes over right where food leaves off. A man's need for the right kind of food blends almost imperceptibly with his need for the right kind of sex. By a strange coincidence, both of these needs originate at the female breast.

There is no other structure of the human body quite like the breast. In a miracle of diversification it is designed to please everyone. It provides nutrition for babies, sexual excitement for men, and sexual satisfaction for women. The primary needs of human beings—calories and orgasm—revolve around these two wonderful glands, the female breasts.

Every boy baby has his first contact with a woman at the breast of his mother. Even more important, feeding time is also loving time. While he nurses, Mother whispers to baby, caresses him, and otherwise showers him with affection. He gets the message: food and love go together and both come from a woman. From that moment on, the breast has an almost irresistible attraction for every man. Twenty-five years later, reinforced by male sex hormones coursing through his veins, female plus sex plus breasts becomes the driving force in his life. But the baby confusion still remains.

Confusion about what?

Most men are drawn to large breasts by the mistaken idea that more breast means more milk. The fellows who looked at breasts every day at meal-time at the age of six months now spend a dollar a month to gaze at magazines with center-folds of young ladies with mammoth mammary glands. In the unconscious mind of every man alive, breast *and sex* means milk, and milk means love, security, and everything that goes with it. (The man who calls his girl, "Honey," "Sugar," "Sweetie-pie," and other variations on the theme of groceries is telling her the real story.) To a woman, sex means an expression of love for the man she loves *and* a means of providing herself with love, security, and everything that goes with it. The way she handles the sexual part of her relationship with a man not only determines whether or not she will marry him, but has a lot to do with their sexual happiness after marriage. If she can provide him with total sexual satisfaction—meeting his deepest emotional needs at the same time she provides him with the maximum physical gratification—the only possible result can be a lifetime of happiness for both of them. In order to succeed at this formidable task she must be aware of two factors.

What are they?

First, she has to understand how men really feel about sex. The sexual drive in men is a mystery to many men and virtually every woman. The few women who have correctly guessed at what men really want from sex have gone down in history for their achievement. Helen of Troy, Madame Pompadour, Marie Antoinette, and a few others have changed the course of history because they divined the true nature of male sexuality.

What do men need from sex?

Ironically, the answer to the riddle is available at any secondhand bookstore for about $1.98. Every college endocrinology textbook describes the production of the male sex hormone, testosterone, by the testicles. This hormone acts directly on the brain to produce intense sexual feelings. The more hormone accumulates, the wilder the sexual drive. By some yet unknown mechanism, orgasm and ejaculation act on the brain and associated endocrine glands to reduce sexual longings. Every man develops his own "sex cycle" —for most males, forty-eight hours without orgasm in some form results in noticeable physical discomfort.

Do men really become uncomfortable without sex?

Yes. That's one of the major differences in sexual feeling between the boys and girls. Lack of sexual activity produces frequent involuntary erections (sometimes under embarrassing circumstances, like at the office), a feeling of pain and heaviness in the testicles, and after extended periods of inflammation of the prostate gland. Prostate trouble is no fun— there can be a continuous puslike discharge from the penis and a lot of pain. Speaking of pain, sexual excitement in men, unless it leads to ejaculation, can swiftly become intensely painful. A strong erection rapidly proceeds to throbbing and aching of the penis, among other things. What it all adds up to is, sexual feelings in men are far more compelling and urgent than they are in women. When a man has an erection, there is no putting it off until tomorrow night—it's a question of right now or suffer. Which leads directly to the next thing a woman has to know about male sexuality.

What's that?

As far as men are concerned, the most powerful incentive on earth is sex. Men will suffer unbearable privation, they will fight, they will kill, as long as they get the girl in the end. From a commercial point of view, sex sells everything from shaving cream to foot powder. The implied message is always the same: "Use our product and it will lead to orgasm with the girl of your choice." Sometimes the slogan is updated to: "Use our new improved product and it will lead to new improved orgasm with the girl of your choice." (Imagine what to expect if the girl uses the same product.) By comparison, green stamps to a housewife, medals to a general, and merit badges to a Boy Scout are mere confetti. But if an incentive is going to work, it has to be awarded at the right time. The general gets the medal *after* the battle, the housewife gets her stamps after the purchase, and the smiling lifeguard on TV gets the girl *after* he buys the mouthwash. Sex between men and women is inevitable; proper timing is what makes the difference between happiness and despair.

Then premarital sex is all right?

Every girl has to decide *that* question for herself. But right or not, premarital sex in the sense of sexual attraction is unavoidable. Sexual interaction is usually well under way by the fifth grade, when the kids are playing kissing games at birthday parties. Actual sexual intercourse looms on the scene somewhat later, but by the time a girl is close enough to a man emotionally to consider marriage she is also close enough to consider sex—in all its forms.

For some women the solution is easy—because of religious convictions or other reasons they must postpone intercourse until the ink is dry on the wedding certificate. Although probably no more than ten percent of adult females feel this way, they are entitled to make the decision they feel comfortable with. For the other ninety percent, the alternatives are somewhat more hazardous although potentially rewarding. Sex, in its fullest meaning, if used constructively, can be a girl's most effective tool in achieving a durable and satisfying marriage.

How does she go about it?

By blending the desperate urgency of the male sexual drive with the incentive principle and using the combination to provide what no other woman can offer: genuine sex. The difference between ordinary everyday sex and genuine sex is the difference between a genuine hundred-dollar bill and a well-executed counterfeit. Both banknotes look the same, but only one is really satisfying and has lasting value. Counterfeit sex, like counterfeit money, superficially resembles the real thing. The mechanics are the same, the sensations may often be similar, but counterfeit sex buys nothing—*genuine* sex buys lasting happiness. The right kind of food feeds the spirit while it nourishes the body. Genuine sex satisfies the deepest emotional needs at the same time it provides sexual gratification. Any normally equipped

woman can provide counterfeit sex—only the one
woman in a man's life can provide genuine sex.

Is there really a difference?

Yes. Most bachelors have more of the counterfeit
variety than they can handle. And regrettably, sex,
like any other sport, if played too often or too dili-
gently, can lose its value. Listen to Al's point of view:

"Man, if somebody had told me this back in college
I would have died laughing. Now it's happened and
I can't even work up a smile."

"What do you mean?"

"Well, it's really crazy. I'm the manager of a temporary help agency—you know, 'Rent-a-secretary,
rent-a-receptionist, by the hour-week-or-month.' I
must have thirty gals a day go through my office and
I can take my pick. For the first year, it was a different one every night. I thought I'd go out of my
mind. But now it's the *same* girl every time. And I'm
really going out of my mind!"

"The same girl?"

"Yes. The same girl. Same body, same routine, only
a different face and a different name. I mean, they
all look alike to me now, and even worse, they all
sound alike and they do the same things. I can tell
you the script for tonight and for next week in advance. We have dinner, go back to my place, I make
a couple of drinks while she's slipping into bed. I
join her, we go through the same routine, first me,
then her, we tell each other the same lies . . ."

"Which lies do you mean?"

"You know. 'You were great, Baby!' and she tells
me, "Oh, you know exactly what a girl wants!' Once I
got so bored with it, I said, nicely, 'Wow, that was

really terrible.' This chick just smiled and purred, 'Yes, I thought it was so perfect . . .' The worst part is the next morning when I wake up, look at that girl lying beside me, and think, 'Ugh! Why did you do that again?' "

"Do you know the answer?"

Al smiled. "Sure, I do. I think it's time for me to find a girl who cares about me—at least one who remembers my name. Yeah, I think that's a good place to start. From now on, if they can't remember my name, I'll just take 'em right home."

How does a girl go about providing genuine sex?

She begins by keeping her man in a constant state of low-level sexual excitement. A few women do this instinctively—they call it "keeping a man interested." This form of premarital sex is socially approved, legal in public places, and if used properly, can make life immeasurably more enjoyable for everyone.

How does it work?

The basic idea is body contact. Many primitive tribes rarely communicate in those abstract symbols we call words. They do most of their talking with their hands —*by touching each other*. Hand language is a thousand times more effective in getting the message through. Those sweet nothings whispered into a man's ear are carefully evaluated and filtered through millions of brain cells before they reach their target and do their job. A touch or a caress can by-pass the brain almost completely and speed to the spinal cord where it triggers the appropriate reflex in an instant.

The advantages are obvious and can even be measured in the laboratory:

A male subject is connected to recorders measuring heart rate, blood pressure, and breathing rate. His girl friend sits across the table from him and says,

"Tony, you know I love you."

There is a one-second delay followed by a very moderate rise in heart rate, an insignificant increase in blood pressure, and no change in breathing.

Now she sits on the couch next to him, puts her head on his chest, her arm around his neck, and holds his hand. She doesn't say a word. Instantaneously, his heart rate increases, blood pressure shoots up, and breathing rate almost doubles. Although most laboratories are not currently equipped to measure it, Tony is probably well on his way to having an erection at that moment as well.

The important point is that a powerful physical change has been triggered in Tony as a direct result of his girl's action. He literally has no control over his response—whether he wants to or not, he must react. There is no chance for a reluctant man to reflect on the consequences or the wisdom of what is happening. Even more effective is the subliminal effect of touching. The man who is constantly touched affectionately by his woman *unconsciously* develops a feeling of warmth and attachment—whether he wants to or not. In this competitive world, the woman who knows literally how to handle her man has an immense advantage.

What are some subliminal ways that a woman can do this?

Those women who touch men instinctively provide the best demonstration. When they walk up to their man, they put an arm around his waist or lay a hand on his chest. They may touch him on the shoulder gently or quietly take his hand. Women who understand this idea without even thinking about it caress their man exactly the way a mother touches the baby she loves. Every human being understands that. No physical gesture is wasted. Helping him off with his coat at the movies, loosening his tie when he's tired, unlacing his shoes and putting on his slippers, all contribute to making *unforgettable* mental impressions. The girl who gives her man a back-rub after a hard day at the office does more for herself (and him) than a whole week of afternoons at her hairdresser.

What about the man who doesn't like to be touched?

A girl should listen carefully to a man like that because he's telling her something important. The male who rejects physical closeness before marriage is not likely to seek it after marriage. Unless the woman is looking forward to a lifetime as the disappointed pursuer of a reluctant little boy, it might be a good idea for her to change partners—before she gets married, when it's easier.

Of course, there's the other side of the coin. The girl who is constantly fussing with her escort, brushing imaginary lint from his lapels, fixing his hair, and tucking in his handkerchief is playing another game. She is impersonating another kind of mother—the kind he can do without. If he is any sort of man, he will arrange to do without her as soon as he can find a replacement. It shouldn't take him very long.

How else can a woman use sex before marriage to her advantage?

Back to the incentive principle. Almost every imaginable manifestation of sex works to a woman's advantage except the act of sexual intercourse. Up to and including the moment of orgasm, she has all the cards. Immediately *after* orgasm in the male, the entire balance of power shifts to the man. During every preliminary sexual stage she intensifies her control of the relationship—the orgasmic explosion shatters her power into useless fragments.

All too many married women have had the experience. "As soon as Jim reaches his climax, he doesn't even know I'm there—he just rolls over and goes to sleep." Because the penis is linked directly to the brain (via the spinal cord), as soon as the physical tension is released by orgasm, the emotional tension dissipates as well. Along with it vanishes any influence a woman might have on a man's thinking. After intercourse men think of women as desexualized beings—the way no woman under the age of ninety ever wants to be thought of.

On the other hand, when he is desperate to discharge his sexual excitement, a woman—and what she can offer—becomes the center of a man's entire world. He will promise her anything—from a mink coat to a new stove. If she insists, he will deliver it in advance—then and there—just so long as he can find a way to be comfortable again. *After* intercourse, if she asks for a cigarette, he may be too indifferent to get up and bring her the pack from the dresser.

What does that have to do with getting married?

Everything. For the woman who really wants to be sure to marry the man she has chosen, the motto might be, "Promise him anything, but deliver it the night *after* the wedding." Premarital sex is like gasoline—delivered drop by drop, it provides the power that brings man and woman together. Scattered indiscriminately, it can catch fire and consume any chance for marriage or future happiness. The woman who loves a man almost always wants to express her love to the fullest—and that means sexually. But if she gives herself completely—to the point of intercourse—she destroys the most important incentive to marriage that exists. So many women do it the other way. They provide their men with unlimited sex before marriage and very limited sex after marriage. Based on an understanding of the human mind, the most effective way for a woman to guarantee happiness in marriage is to refuse complete sexual satisfaction before marriage and *never* refuse it after marriage.

But isn't "waiting until after we're married" old-fashioned?

That's really beside the point. Being "modern" and "sophisticated" isn't necessarily the highest goal in life. Finding happiness for herself and making her man happy rate much farther up on the scale. Realistically, the man who has every possible need satisfied, emotional, social, sexual, has no wish to marry. The girl who gives him everything leaves herself out.

Then how far should she go?

As far as she wants to. The kinds of sexual activity that no one ever seems to describe more specifically than "making out" provide ample room for partial sexual gratification. This includes every form of foreplay short of intercourse, including the euphemistic "petting to climax," or more precisely, mutual masturbation to the point of orgasm. As everyone who has experienced it will testify, these techniques are satisfying up to a point but will never replace the real thing.

But isn't that kind of sex harmful?

No. Actually the best preparation for a full sexual life is all the reasonable varieties of sexual behavior. Sexual play to the point of orgasm makes sexual adjustment after marriage easier and more satisfying by reinforcing the sexual reflexes.

Are there any disadvantages to withholding complete sex before marriage?

Yes. Some men react violently unless they have it all their own way. They insist on sexual intercourse on their terms as "proof" that a girl "loves" them. The woman who uses the incentive approach may lose this kind of man as a prospect. In many cases losing such a character then and there is easier than getting stuck with him as a husband later on.

Another disadvantage is that restricted sex is harder on the woman than unlimited sex before marriage. She must use tact, diplomacy, and restraint. She must constantly remind her man that she is not refusing sex—she is *simply postponing it*. She must emphasize by word and deed that it is only a matter of time before it happens. In that sense, the word "NO" should never appear in her sexual vocabulary. Much better is, "Not just now," "Perhaps next time," or "Let's wait just a little longer." Any suggestion that the decision is final must be avoided—the man must always feel that he has the power to change her mind.

There is another problem, too. As every girl knows, women have sexual feelings and sometimes it's hard for them to wait for a far-off wedding day. Under some circumstances, even a month can seem a long, long time. But for the woman who wants to tip the psychological scales incontestably in her favor, this is the method that works.

But isn't the girl who withholds sexual intercourse exploiting her man?

And isn't the man who insists on intercourse as a condition of their relationship exploiting the girl? Any woman who views the sexual incentive concept as a "man-trap" is in for a disappointment. No male in his right mind can be coerced into marriage just for the privilege of enjoying that one big night which has been denied to him. The woman who uses sexuality in a constructive way is determined to guide herself and the man she has chosen into a happy and mutually rewarding marriage. If that's exploitation, there should be more of it.

What if a woman doesn't want to hold back sexually?

Then she doesn't have to. Particularly in this most important and intimate part of her life she must follow her own feelings, provided she is aware of the hazards involved. Some women may be surprised to discover that the risks aren't the ones she heard about in those moral lectures. Unwanted pregnancy and venereal disease can usually be avoided with a little intelligence and common sense. The real danger is giving away the one thing that can't be replaced— her competitive edge over other women.

The woman who is too willing sexually begins to be like all the rest of the girls in the temporary help agency. As a matter of fact, she often finds herself providing her own version of "temporary help"—and like anyone else in that business, she can be replaced.

There is something else. Establishing a mutual satisfying sexual relationship is probably the most difficult task two people ever undertake. To add that strain to all the other strains of the premarital period may be just too much for the couple to manage. The problems of achieving mutual orgasm, avoiding frigidity and impotence in the initial stages, and competition from outside parties, may be more than the budding emotional ties can stand. But as usual, the final decision is up to the woman, and if she wants sexual intercourse at that stage, she can still use it to help achieve her goal.

How?

In two ways. First, she must be the best possible sexual partner. At the same time she must retain the incentive idea by making sure her man knows it won't last unless they get married. This kind of emotional tight-rope walking can be hard on everyone and is not a game for amateurs. It requires sensitivity, understanding, and a subtle feeling for knowing when to stop—and not stop. The woman who is having a complete sexual relationship with a man sometimes panics when marriage seems to be getting farther away instead of closer. If her reaction is the Chinese laundry approach—no tickee, no washee—the ticket in this case being the marriage license, she may lose the tickee, the washee, and a potential husband all at once. Sex outside of marriage is like throwing a steak to a tiger—easy to give, but hard to take away.

One effective technique is for the girl to arrange a separation at the most satisfying point in the relationship. Sometimes a trip does the trick. If she calls time out and leaves for two weeks in Tahiti, it gives a man a chance to feel what he will be missing. When she comes back, the time is ripe for a serious discussion of marriage.

How does a girl go about satisfying her man's need for love?

By providing it in a form that no one else can duplicate. Every single man has one big problem that causes him endless unhappiness. His world is deficient in love. He has no source of uncritical admiration and understanding. Everyone he deals with wants something from him—usually more than he is willing or able to provide. His boss wants more profits for the company, his secretary wants more time off, his customers want lower prices, and his competitors want him to go bankrupt. Even more discouraging, whatever he may accomplish usually has a limited life expectancy. If he manages to become Salesman-Of-The-Year, his title expires on December thirty-first at midnight. Then the struggle starts all over again. If he finally works himself up to $30,000 a year, there is always the fellow across the hall who gets $31,500. Everyone in his life, in some way, is always evaluating him and finding him wanting. This is a woman's golden opportunity—if only she will take advantage of it.

What does she do?

The very best thing a woman can do for her man— and for herself—is to fulfill the role of a loving noncritical companion in his daily struggle through life. The world that the average man faces becomes more materialistic and more impersonal every day. The threats that assail him are increasingly difficult to ward off. If his woman provides an inexhaustible supply of reassurance and consolation, the only result can be happiness and security for them both. It can all be summarized in one sentence: *No matter what happens, the woman should side with her man.* In every dispute, no matter what or with whom, she must be the one he can depend on. When his boss fires him, he can turn to her. When the customers buy from someone else, she reassures him *and* helps him to do better. His battles are her battles and his problems are her problems. She is never too tired or too busy to pitch in with encouragement and help. Even if the whole world turns against him, he must feel that he can count on her. There can be only one woman in his life who can play that role, and when a man finds her, there is nothing in this world that can keep him from marrying her.

You mean a woman should never correct a man even when he's wrong?

Wrong is a relative word. From earliest childhood, there was never a shortage of women to explain to a man how he could improve. First there was Mother, then older cousins, aunts, and maybe big sister. A dozen years of teachers took over where they left off, followed by a horde of girl friends. Over his short lifetime, everything from his table manners to his knowledge of current events has been taken apart and exposed as woefully inadequate. The average man absorbs an unbelievable dose of criticism every working day. It starts in the morning on the way to work:

Bus driver: "Can't ya read, Mister? Ya gotta have the exact fare!"

Boss's secretary: "Mr. Heller is very unhappy with you today."

Boss: "Listen, you're going to have to get a tighter grip on this operation. It's not going right!"

Switchboard operator: "Unless you have the area code, I can't put the call through."

Restaurant hostess at lunch time: "I'm sorry. I don't have any record of your reservation."

Waitress: "Can't you see how busy I am? You'll
have to wait your turn, Mister!"

Clerk at department store: "I don't care what
your wife said—we don't exchange merchandise
after ten days."

Television commercials: "You have dandruff, your
breath smells bad, you smoke too much, you're
catching a cold, you're getting a headache,
you're too fat, you're getting bald, your sweat
smells bad, your feet smell bad, you're getting
old."

Modern man is bombarded with reminders of how
defective he is. The girl who is smart enough to remind him how perfect he is can only win his undy-
ing loyalty and love.

Will every man react that way?

Only about ninety-nine percent of them. The remaining one percent of the male population belong to
that tiny minority who mistake kindness and gener-
osity for weakness. Somehow they have slipped
through the net of the primary selection process, and
it is well to discard them before the final stage—
marriage. For the dog who bites the hand that feeds
him, the next stop is the dog pound. For the one
man in a hundred who doesn't appreciate being
treated with love, it's back to the human dog pound
—to join that pack of perpetual bachelors who are
doomed to wait in vain for someone to adopt them.

Is there any other need a woman who wants to get married must fulfill?

Yes. Unless her man is one in a million he suffers from acute lack of individual identity. He is social security number 352-91-6492; his place on earth is just before number 352-91-6493, and just after number 352-91-6491. He eats from a Melamine plastic dish, wears polyvinyl plastic shoes, and carefully knots his nylon plastic tie around the collar of his polyester plastic shirt—just like fifty million other men just like him.

Every man cringes at the prospect of being just another name on the organization chart, just another blank face jammed into the 5:15 commuter express, just another helpless victim creeping through the tangle of used cars on the freeway. Unfortunately, in our world of mass-production there is no way for him to be unique. Even "custom-made" articles are all stamped out of the same mold. He can buy a little label for his suit that says, "Made especially for . . .", or he can buy a brand of cigarette that costs a dime more and is only smoked by 9 million other men instead of 14 million. Modern man has lost his individual identity in every way but one.

Which one is left?

The relationship with his woman—*if* she handles it right. Ten hours a day everyone tells him he is no better than anyone else. A perceptive woman devotes as much time as she can to insisting that there

is no man on earth like her man. She says it by
word and by deed.

The words can go something like:

"Dick, I never thought I would ever find a man
like you."

"But you understand things so much faster than
anyone else."

"I feel more relaxed with you than anyone I've
ever met."

"There is nobody in the world like *you*."

The deeds reinforce the words, like making things
just for him. This is the occasion for a hand-knitted
sweater or a handsewn necktie. Even a hand-
embroidered pillow slip will do. The object doesn't
have to be a work of art, but it must be a unique
object—the only one in existence—made especially
for him and for no one else.

*Will filling these four needs in a man guarantee
that he will marry the girl?*

Regrettably, there are no guarantees where human
beings are involved. But if a woman actually supplies a man's need for food, for sex, for love, and for
individual identity she is well on the way to making
all the other women in the world superfluous as far
as he is concerned. If she has selected the right man
and carried out her program as planned, there will
be only one unanswered question on her mind. She
can clear that up anytime:

"I've been meaning to ask you, darling, shall we
have a big wedding or just the family?"

12

ALTERNATIVES TO MARRIAGE

Should a girl get married?

That's the question Louisa was discussing. She is the dean of women at a well-known Eastern girls' school. As she began, she laughed:

"Doctor, when I was in my twenties—more than forty years ago—asking that question didn't make any sense. We always assumed that the only girls who *didn't* get married were the ones who *couldn't* get married. Every red-blooded American girl spent years rehearsing that hundred-yard dash from the high school graduation ceremony to the wedding chapel. Why in those days if one of my girl friends had told her mother she didn't want to marry, it would have been a family emergency. Mother would have plopped an ice bag on her head, put a mustard plaster on her chest, and sent her kid brother running to the corner to fetch the doctor. Every healthy girl got married and *that* was *that*. But things have changed."

"How do you think they have changed?"

"Well, for one thing, when I was growing up most girls chose matrimony not just because they wanted to but because they *had* to. Society simply had no

place for a woman alone. I should know. It took me
a year to find a decent job after I left teachers' college, and I had to take the only one I could get. It
was a one-room school in Arkansas and paid all of
three hundred dollars a year plus all the milk I could
drink from the town cow. If I hadn't been so determined to teach I would have married the first man
who came along, out of sheer frustration!"

Louisa was lucky—at least she had an education.
The average girl in those days had three choices:
work, stay home, or get married. The job opportunities were not exactly the kind that swept a girl off
her feet. For an intelligent capable girl, long hours,
low pay, and lack of any chance for advancement
were, to say the least, unappealing.

What about staying home?

Staying home was a little worse. Louisa tried that,
too:

"After a year in Arkansas, I just gave up. I had to
cut the wood for the school room stove myself, pump
all the water, and I drank so much milk finally just
looking at a cow made me break out in hives. I
moved back in with Mother." She shuddered.

"I cleaned house, washed dishes, ironed sheets,
and did all the things that Mother was getting too
old to do. I had no money, no friends, and less of a
future than I did when I was an exile in Arkansas. It
was Mother, me, and two old maid aunts. One
afternoon we were all sitting on the back porch
drinking tea and as I looked at the three of them I
realized I was seeing myself thirty years from then.
I packed my bags that night and went to New York

to stay with a girl friend." Louisa looked at the floor. "I hate to admit it, but I got married six weeks later."

Things have changed a lot since then.

How have they changed?

These days no girl ever has to get married unless she wants to. With intelligent planning she can live her entire life as a free agent—well, almost. Abby tells what she did. In her early thirties, slightly overweight, she had a round face and a ready smile. Her expensive gray tweed skirt and red turtleneck sweater were set off by the heavy gold chain she wore around her neck. The impression she gave was one of intelligence, poise, and success.

"Doctor, don't ask. I must have answered that question a thousand times already."

"What question is that?"

" 'You're such a nice girl. How come you never got married?' "

"I really wasn't about to ask you that. But as long as you brought it up . . ."

She smiled and shook her head good-naturedly. "Just can't beat you psychiatrists, can I?"

"The idea isn't to beat us."

She was serious in a flash. "Of course you're right. Let's get down to business. I decided not to marry when I saw what happened to my mother. My father died when I was five, and she was left without a penny to support six kids. She couldn't even sew on a button without pricking her finger and we really went through some hard times. I can remember when I was six going to the freight yard to pick up the coal that fell off the coal cars so we could burn it in the fireplace in the winter time. After a couple of

years of struggling she couldn't take it any more. She
took a job doing the only thing she knew how to do."

"What was that?"

"Being a wife. My mother was a beautiful woman."
Abby blushed. "I guess I take after my father—he
was the smart one. Anyhow she got married to a man
she didn't love just to give us all a home and a chance
to grow up right. That was when I decided I never
wanted to be in that position."

"What did you do about it?"

"I worked my head off in high school and got top
grades. Then I tried to pick a career where a woman
could compete successfully with men. It wasn't easy
to find one. In case you haven't noticed, this is still
a man's world." Abby clenched her teeth.

"It's okay, Abby, no one's arguing with you."

"I'm sorry, but you'll see in a moment why I'm getting so worked up. So what is there for a bright
nineteen-year-old girl? I considered all the possibilities. I wanted a job where I could be totally equal
with men—physically and emotionally. I needed something where there wasn't too much competition. Being a singer or dancer was out—there are just too
many young hopefuls and not enough hope to go
around. Driving a bus or running a ranch wasn't for
me, although I knew that some women did those
things. An airline pilot sounded pretty good—I mean
I knew I could qualify if I tried—but men just won't
let a woman into certain fields—it must trample on
their vanity. You haven't noticed any ladies flying
those jumbo jets, have you?"

"I must say I haven't."

"And I also realize my chances were best if I could
find the kind of job where I didn't have to give direct
orders to men. There is something about being
bossed by women that goes against a man's grain."

Was Abby right about men?

She was pretty close. Most men have never gotten over those first fifteen years of being ordered around by a woman—their mother:

"Henry! Pick up your toys!"

"Where have you been? I've been worried sick about you! Go straight to your room!"

"Listen, unless you eat all your carrots you can forget about the cherry pie for dessert!"

When the same man, twenty years later, is called on the carpet by the lady vice president, it brings fifteen years of resentment flooding back to the surface. Women can make it in business and industry, but the going is tough. Abby's careful plan tried to avoid all the bumps in the road. She continued:

"I finally decided to be a court reporter. If I could learn to take dictation at two hundred words a minute, I'd be able to write my own ticket. All a court reporter has to do is sit in the courtroom six or seven hours a day, five days a week, and take down everything everyone says. The pay is great—about fourteen thousand dollars a year—they get all the legal holidays off, and usually it's civil service. And there are more jobs than qualified people. So I did it. For three years I worked days in a real estate office and studied court reporting at night. Two years after that I passed the exam and started working for the municipal court. But I didn't stop learning. I went to college at night and took every course in law and business I could find. Three years later I opened my own business—public stenographer. Now I have nine girls working for me and I do most of the private court reporting in the entire county. I finally made it."

"Finally made what?"

"I have everything I could ever get from marriage —and much much more. I have money—last year I made thirty-three thousand dollars—I have financial security—my business gets bigger every year, I have a house, a new red Mustang, I just put in a swimming pool, I take a month's vacation every year— next month I'm going to Hong Kong—and most of all I have the satisfaction of knowing I can make it in a man's world."

Can any woman do what Abby did?

Sure, if she's willing to make the sacrifices. Abby gave up a lot to get her house, her new red Mustang, and her yearly trips. All those years working days and going to school nights when other girls were working days and going out nights cost her something. Now, at thirty-three, she is getting close to the point of no return when it comes to marriage. Not only is she losing her motivation for marriage but, realistically, she becomes less attractive to men as each year goes by. She knows the score.

"I'm satisfied with the deal I made. I know I'll never be in the spot my mother was in—selling out just to keep her kids eating. I also realize—I don't kid myself, Doctor—that any chance I might have had for marriage is slipping away day by day. I mean, I can read the scales and I see that I'm putting on a little weight. But more important, it's getting harder for men to relate to me. I was having dinner with a fellow last week and the headwaiter interrupted us. He rushed up to my date and said,

'I have an urgent phone call for Mr. Abby!' Poor Don's face got as red as the lobster on his plate and he blurted out, 'I think you mean *Miss* Abby—I mean, just plain Abby—I mean, her!' It was an important message from my office about the schedule for the next day. Would you be surprised if I told you I never saw Don again? I didn't." Abby frowned.

Are there many girls like Abby?

More and more every year. For the first time in a century the chance exists to escape from what many women consider to be a dead end: marriage. A lot of females are at least trying it on for size. Not every woman who side-steps matrimony commits herself as fully as Abby did. Sally had a different plan.

Sally was petite, not much over five feet tall and probably weighed ninety-five pounds at the most. Blond hair and intense green eyes gave her the image of somebody's sister in a television situation comedy. But she also had a lightning-fast mind that kept her two steps ahead of most of the men she came in contact with. Let her tell her own story:

"I went to a woman's college and I had a lot of time to observe and to think. By the time I was in my junior year I knew I'd never have any trouble getting married. I was popular with boys and I liked going out, but there were some things that held me back."

"What, for example?"

"Let's say I'd taken the 'easy' way out and gotten married as soon as I'd finished school. All I'd have to do would be run a small restaurant, a boarding house —convertible into a motel on weekends and holidays when relatives come to visit—and a hand laundry with super service: 'your shirts back in one hour on request.' Besides that I'd have to be a comparison shopper, an expert on nutrition, and a clinical psychologist. Oh yes, I almost forgot. I would have to handle public relations for the entire family and have a flair for catering—'we guarantee satisfaction, individuals or groups up to twenty-five people. Short notice our specialty.'

"Then we come to sex. A wife should be a combination mistress–companion–sexpot–love-slave while remaining basically wholesome. If she makes it in that department, she is rewarded with a houseful of children. She then has a chance to expand all her far-flung operations—catering, laundry, restaurant, and human relations—to accommodate the new arrivals. After about forty years of this form of entertainment, her husband retires. He stays home and watches TV and do you know what *she* does? She just keeps cooking and cleaning and ironing and thinking up new ways to keep *him* from getting bored. I don't think four years of college is enough preparation for all that!" Sally laughed.

"It isn't quite that bad, Doctor. I know being a wife and mother can mean the real fulfillment of being a woman. During the five years I've been in the business world I can't avoid recognizing that every man who is successful *and* happy owes the biggest part of it to his wife. Those guys who are honest are the first to admit it. And the prospect of creating new human beings and preparing them for a meaningful life on their own—that's the most wonderful thing any person can do. But when you analyze logically what a wife has to tackle, it can be kind of overwhelming."

"Is that why you decided not to get married?"

"No, that's why I decided not to get married *right away*. I knew I could have any one of a dozen careers—and I knew I could make it really big. So I

wanted to give it a try before I made a choice. I
didn't want to have any regrets either way. So I
had my career and I was a smashing success. Actually
too successful."

"Too successful?"

"Yes, sir. I was a car-leasing tycoon. Don't laugh."

"I'm not laughing."

"My first job after college was working for a finance
company, and I got to see their figures on car
leasing. You know, things like how much it cost them,
their profit, and all that. They were really stupid—I
mean they missed the whole point. So I flew to De-
troit, talked one of the small auto companies into
setting me up with their cars, and built it from there.
I leased autos for twelve percent less than anyone
else in the business and later on I expanded into
trucks, buses, and everything else. At the high point
of my career, I had nine offices in the state and
over a hundred employees. The last year I was in
it I made almost a hundred thousand dollars. Then I
decided it was time to retire."

"How come?"

"Well, it wasn't the money. I started worrying because the job had me hooked. I was literally drunk
with power. I went on a three-week vacation and
had to come back after five days. I needed that "fix"
every morning of walking into my executive suite
and seeing my private secretary sitting there typing
away. I was even going to get a *male* secretary, but I
caught myself in time."

"What were you trying to prove?"

Sally grinned and nodded. "That's exactly the
question I asked myself, Doctor. Then I knew it was
time to quit. Well, I didn't really quit. I sort of ar-
ranged a merger."

"A merger?"

"Yes. A year after I left the finance company, I hired away one of their young vice presidents. He was a brilliant guy, and he helped me build up my company literally from nothing. He helped me in a lot of other ways, too, if you know what I mean. I guess it's a feeling that women have, Doctor, but when I first asked Jay to move to my company I knew he was the man I would marry. I retired—or better, switched careers—he took over as president, and we merged. He got me and the company, I got him and everything else I really wanted. When I want to kid him sometimes, 'Well,' I tell him, 'Jay, my last deal was my most profitable one.' "

"What does he say to that?"

"Jay's too smart to answer. He just nods and smiles."

Can any woman do what Sally did?

Yes. The results may not be as dramatic and the figures may not be as impressive, but any woman can try her hand in the world of commerce. She can have an experimental career and function as an independent woman to see how she likes it. If it's her cup of tea, she may want to go all the way like Abby or "merge" like Sally. Or she may choose from several other rewarding alternatives.

What are some of the other alternatives?

One of the most popular is "legal bigamy." If applied correctly, this solution is infinitely flexible and gives everyone, husband, wife, and the business world, just what they want. A woman who takes this route simply gets married to her husband *and* her career at the same time. She divides her attention between her responsibilities according to their needs and *her* needs. When the family needs more attention, the job gets along with less. When the husband and kids are doing well on their own, she can plunge deeper into her job, But it takes careful planning to make legal bigamy work right.

What kind of planning?

It has to be a job that dovetails with changes in family responsibilities. A woman has to be able to drop it at any time and then pick it up a month or a year later without missing a beat. Ideally it should pay well enough to make it a real job, not just a hobby, and it should be challenging enough to hold her interest.

Are there any jobs like that?

More than most women imagine. Gloria found one and there are dozens of others. Listen to what Gloria says:

"Doctor, I really found my own job out of desperation. I worked before I got married, as a secretary to a television producer. It was an exciting, glamorous, fascinating job. I met all the top personalities in show business and it paid fairly well too.

"I really wanted to make TV a career and even work my way up to production if I could. But then I met Larry, went right out of my mind for him, and we got married. After six months of marriage, I almost went out of my mind for another reason. There was, like, nothing to do. The big event of my week was a trip to the supermarket.

"Every Thursday morning I said to myself, 'Gloria, what sensational development awaits you today? Will coffee be on special at sixty-nine cents? Or will it be "Hawaiian Week" at Sav-A-Bundle Markets with a free ten-cent orchid for every lucky lady? Or maybe you can drink your troubles away with those free samples of Orange-Vite Punch in two-ounce paper cups?' Actually it was the Orange-Vite that saved my sanity."

"How was that?"

"I got talking to the girl who was handing out the samples and I discovered a new career. She went to different markets sampling different products. She worked for an agency who made the deals with each of the food producers and they paid her three-fifty an hour plus car expenses. She could work every day in the week or as little as once a month if she wanted to. I got myself hired that same afternoon and was working the next day. It's such a great job I almost feel guilty about having it."

"Why do you like it so much?"

"Aside from the obvious reasons, I get to talk to a lot of people, I never get bored, and I have the best of both worlds. I see all the other housewives wandering through the market wishing they had something to stimulate them and I'm it. But when the day is over, I fold my little card table, put away my cheese puffs, and go home to Larry. What a deal!"

But what if a woman can't get a job like that?

There are plenty of others. Women with training in special areas can work as registered nurses for a day or a week at a time. Substitute teachers are almost always in demand. Any woman who wants to can train as a practical nurse and in a few months use that as her *reversible* escape route from marriage. Even the woman with no previous job experience can find her niche with a little advance planning. Short training periods can qualify her as a teacher's assistant or office worker. Once she can type, file, or take elementary shorthand, getting assignments from temporary help agencies should be no problem.

But these are dead-end jobs, aren't they?

That's the idea. Practical nursing, substitute teaching, or temporary office assignments give most of the advantages of a full-time job without encroaching on a woman's regular life. Marlene sums it up neatly:

"Being a substitute teacher works out just fine for me, Doctor. I work only when I feel like it or when I need the money. When I think I'll explode if I stay home another day, I call in and tell them I'm available. After a few weeks of teaching school I really appreciate what little angels my own children are by comparison. Besides, just knowing I don't have to worry about a future in the job makes it so much better. The school board lets me do almost as I please because they realize they need me more than I need them."

However, there is one very special requirement for success on a part-time job.

What's that?

A good name for it is "controlled schizophrenia." (The term "schizophrenia" comes from two Greek words, *schizein,* to split, and *phren,* mind.) In using this technique a woman carefully splits her thoughts and energies between her job and her husband. When she is working she may be oblivious to everything else. The moment she returns home, her job becomes a million miles away. When she lets her marriage invade her occupation, everyone suffers. Even more important when her working life begins to intrude on her relationship with her husband, it's time to get things under control. Beverly made that mistake:

"I got home late from work at the hospital one night, Doctor. I'm a surgical nurse and I work about four days a month. We had an emergency come in and I'd been on my feet for twelve hours straight. When I got home Ben was sort of irritated. He hadn't had any dinner and he'd had to put the kids to bed himself. He said some angry things and I just blew my top. I shouted, 'Listen, I can earn my own living anytime! Who needs you?'

"Well, I just took one look at the expression on his face and I knew the answer: *I did!* When I calmed down I told him so. Golly, I can always get a job, but I'll never find another man like Ben!"

That's the hazard of controlled schizophrenia. If the job begins to take over the marriage, the woman must be willing to push the little button that says: DESTRUCT! and dispose of her career once and for all. She has to be the final judge as to whether or not it's worth the sacrifice. But a job, after all, is only a job and a good husband is a living, breathing, loving human being. Some women are even willing to settle for a husband who belongs to someone else.

How can they do that?

The French call it being a mistress. In those nineteenth-century romantic French novels, the mistress is a slightly mysterious, enticing figure who dashes in and out of the luxurious boudoir one step ahead of the suspicious wife. In modern times it doesn't work that way, although the mistress is still prominent on the socio-sexual scene.

Naomi is a good example. She is forty-two, with raven black hair and dark eyes. She is thin and subdued and doesn't look much more than thirty-five. She chuckles:

"The funny part of the situation, Doctor, is that I never thought of myself as a mistress. Why I don't own a single pair of black lace panties! The closest I come to that image is a peek-a-boo nightie that the girls in the office gave me as a joke on my birthday." Then she became serious.

"But this is my problem. Arthur—the Senator— doesn't even know I'm here today. He thinks I'm out shopping. I've been his personal secretary for almost eighteen years and for the last fifteen I've been . . . well, I guess you'd call it his mistress. His wife has been an alcoholic ever since they got married twenty years ago, and there's never really been anything between them emotionally or as far as sex is concerned. Arthur and I have grown close over the years and he spends at least five nights a week at my apartment. He's becoming more important in the Senate each year, and anyone in public life who wants to be reelected can't even think of getting a divorce. I never married anyone else because I love him—and I know he loves me. If something should happen to his wife

—and it could—you know how alcoholics are—then I'm sure we'd get married."

Is that kind of relationship common?

More common than the average person realizes. It is truly amazing how many attorneys, physicians, dentists, and leading executives have developed emotional and sexual relationships with their secretaries and female assistants. In many cases they have become closer to them than to their wives. Arnold is more bitter than most, but he expresses a common attitude when he says:

"Listen, Doctor, I feel closer to Edna, my assistant, than I do to my wife. Edna has been fighting in the front lines with me for over thirty years. While she and I were struggling to hold the company together with our bare hands, my wife was out there buying fur coats two at a time and playing Lady Bountiful with the 'Friends of the Symphony Orchestra'—with my hard-earned money. Can you blame Edna and I if we share a little more than just an office with each other? I honestly believe she's the only woman in the world who really understands me—and cares about me."

What does a woman get out of being a mistress?

In many cases the answer to that is obvious. To most "business wives," their role means a unique opportunity to share an exciting life with the man they love. Instead of taking the chance of finding the right man among the salesmen and the office boys, they start right at the top. They also expect—and many of them find—financial security in the process. Most men provide well for their office mistresses, making sure they have a liberal pension and often cutting them in on stock options and "inside" deals. Besides many women find an inner satisfaction in pre-empting a very desirable man from a wife who considers herself socially and intellectually superior.

As Naomi said, "My father was a steel worker and I only went to business college, but I know I've given Arthur more happiness in one day than his high-society Radcliffe wife has given him in those entire twenty years."

But there is one factor more prominent than all the others.

What's that?

Few women deliberately set out to become office mistresses. Most of the girls who choose this alternative to marriage simply find themselves drifting into it over the years. Usually it's a case of a man and a woman who work hard on the same project—a business or a professional practice—growing closer emotionally as the man's wife grows more distant. Before they realize it the mistress and the husband are trapped in the relationship. Frequently both of them find it a pleasant sort of entrapment and don't struggle too hard to free themselves.

If they enjoy it so much, why doesn't the man just get a divorce and do it right?

Maybe they are doing it "right"—for them. As Naomi said, "I've often wondered how it would be if Arthur finally got a divorce. I really don't think things could be any better between us. The way things are now, I have the best of everything: independence, security, and a feeling of accomplishment. I couldn't ask for any more."

Isn't a mistress just a sexual opportunist?

Not really. The gril who barters her way to the top sexually is in a different category. She is usually a cold hard planner who selects her target with calm deliberation. Once she has gotten everything she can from a man in the way of privileges, promotions, and opportunities, she throws him away like a disposable beer bottle and moves on to the next victim. The greatest hazard these ladies face are their willing male victims who promise everything and deliver nothing. Like every relationship built on exploitation, both participants usually end up with exactly what they bargained for. Some women become mistresses for almost exactly the opposite reason.

For the opposite reason?

Yes, out of self-sacrifice, or what passes for self-sacrifice. These are the girls who are weighed down with overwhelming personal responsibilities. It may be an ill mother or an n'er-do-well brother who demands their constant time, money, and attention. They spend so much time as family social workers ministering to the sick, getting relatives out of jams, and advancing money that they have no energy left over for their own lives. Many of them find the role of a "part-time wife" or mistress rewarding enough and far less demanding. Very often they choose men who are in about the same situation as far as "family responsibilities" are concerned. These girls are totally different from the free-home-trial variety of mistress.

What's a "free-home-trial mistress"?

Recently more and more men and women have been moving toward a "try-before-you-buy" approach to marriage. Instead of the usual preliminaries to wedded bliss, they select a more demanding approach. Gwen describes it frankly:

"Doctor, Ernie and I have been married three years now and I still think it was a good idea."

"What was a good idea?"

"Living together before we got married. You know, neither of us were kids even then—I was twenty-two and Ernie was twenty-six and it wasn't exactly the first relationship we'd ever had. That old dating routine right out of the nineteen-forties just didn't turn us on."

"Dating routine?"

"Sure, you know what I mean. It starts with going to the movies and a goodnight kiss. Then it's necking in the car and maybe something really daring when the roommates aren't home. When the engagement ring finally changes hands it's time to sneak away for a wild weekend at a motel and then a beautiful wedding with all the trimmings. That's terrible!"

"In what way?"

Gwen raised her eyebrows. "In the worst way of all! The poor kids who do it that way end up having as little in common with each other as the plaster bride and groom sitting on top of their seventeen-layer wedding cake. I think our way is different."

"Which way is that?"

"Just as soon as Ernie and I really got interested in each other, we rented an apartment together. It was exactly like being married only we could change our minds anytime. After about six months we just decided we liked it and we got married."

"How did you happen to 'just decide you liked it'?"

Gwen's face turned bright red. "Uh well, uh, to tell the truth I thought that six months should be enough for Ernie to make up his mind and I sort of told him, 'Now or never, sweetheart.' I mean, every man needs a little encouragement, don't you think?"

Is being a free-home-trial mistress really a good idea?

There are some obvious disadvantages. First, it's far from romantic. The girl is treated about the same as a vacuum cleaner from a department store: 'No risk, no obligation, test in the privacy of your own home. If not satisfied in thirty days, return for a full refund, no questions asked.' There is also an obvious lack of the mutual trust and confidence that builds strong marriages.

The second defect is more serious. Playing house has absolutely no value in predicting the final outcome of a man-woman relationship. Like many vacuum cleaners, most of the important defects don't show up until the trial period is just a distant memory. Both parties are on their best behavior, and their housekeeping arrangement is sometimes just one long drawn-out date.

Problem number three is particularly hard on the girl.

Which one is that?

If her first stint as a mistress doesn't lead to marriage, then she usually tries again. If that effort comes to nothing, she may be impelled to try another go-around. By the time she's set up housekeeping with three men in eighteen months, a lot of people—including some prospective husbands—might think she's just in it for kicks. Most girls don't want that. And there's where the big pitfall comes in. Gwen tells the rest of her story:

"I guess I ought to be completely honest with you, Doctor. Ernie wasn't the first fellow I lived with. I was the mistress—I guess that's what you'd call it— of three other men before that. By the time I got around to Ernie, I was feeling just a tiny bit desperate. I couldn't see myself with two fellows a year for the next five years, if you know what I mean. Maybe if I'd been in a better position I would've held out for a little more than Ernie." Then Gwen shrugged her shoulders and smiled. "But, when you come right down to it, who knows about those kind of things?"

Being a mistress on the installment plan can be an ordeal. Like most installment buying, it isn't so much the original cost as the upkeep.

Do many women deliberately set out to become mistresses?

Not usually. The pathway to mistresshood usually is studded with missed opportunities, regrets, attacks of indecision at the most critical moment, and many sleepless nights. It isn't exactly the kind of life a woman would plan for herself. But for a small group of women it may be the only solution they can choose.

Again, as Naomi put it, "For some of us, Doctor, half a man is better than none."

Then there are some women who can't even bring themselves to that point.

Who are they?

Those are the honorary "aunts." The sister or daughter who just never got around to marrying may become an auxiliary member of the family. She helps raise the children, takes care of anybody who gets sick, and in general, is there to do whatever has to be done.

Almost everyone can remember one of these kindly, hard-working, somewhat tragic figures hovering around the edges of the family as they grew up. The honorary aunt was very popular with the husband since he saved the expense of a maid. The wife was delighted to have her because it made her housework go faster. The only defects were the ones that were obvious to the victim—the girl who never married. She was condemned (mostly by herself) to watch everyone else enjoy what she really never had to deny herself.

Fortunately the rising expectations of modern women have just about eliminated this as an alternative to marriage. It's just as well because it wasn't much of a solution anyway. Nowadays women want everything that everyone else has and they are entitled to it. This concept has brought some apparently new life styles into existence including the professional non-wife.

What's a "professional non-wife"?

A professional non-wife is a woman who is determined to be a woman in every sense of the word without ever having to become a wife. Sprinkled around the country are a small number of ladies who feel this way, especially in places like New York, San Francisco, Miami, and Chicago. The underlying theme of their life is best expressed by Maureen, who is one of them. She is thirty-five with short brown hair. Her Italian knit dress is expensive and well-cut, her snake skin shoes match her bag. Her medium height and ample proportions give her an appearance of compactness. She speaks crisply:

"I don't see, Doctor, why a marriage license has to be the ticket of admission to the good things in our society. I want everything I can get from this world and I shouldn't have to marry to qualify for it."

"It doesn't look as if you've done so badly, Maureen."

She fingered the strands of her pearl necklace. "No, I haven't, and that's just the point. I'm as smart as any man and I've been willing to work to prove it. I'm in the printing business and I have the most modern and efficient printing plant in the Southwest. I have a town house just a few blocks from my downtown office, I have a summer place on the Gulf, I have a T-Bird for town and a Maserati for the country. Beyond that I have over a hundred thousand dollars invested in stocks and bonds." Her lips tightened. "What do you think of that?"

"I think it's a notable accomplishment for such a young woman."

She smiled. "Thank you."

"I mean, you've acquired a lot of material things in a short time."

The smile faded.

"Yes, but that's only part of it. I have a full social life including friends of both sexes. I'm the vice president of the National Graphics Association—that's the printer's trade group. They wanted to make me secretary, but that's a woman's job."

"Maureen, there's only one question that bothers me. Did it ever occur to you that maybe you were trying a little too hard?"

"No, Doctor. This is the kind of life I want. I couldn't be happier. I never have to depend on any man for anything. If I'm going with a man and I get tired of him, I just find another one. I don't even think about 'What if I don't get married?' Can't you see I've solved the problem? I don't *ever* have to get married. What can a man offer *me?*"

Is Maureen right?

Maybe—at least as far as Maureen is concerned. Apparently the only thing her money and success haven't brought her yet is children. So far no one has discovered a way to print babies on a printing press. But some single women are even overcoming this problem.

How are they doing it?

For the past five hundred years or so most unmarried women considered pregnancy to be a biological disaster area. A menstrual period that was a week or two late was about as welcome as a case of typhoid.

But things have changed. A few unmarried girls are becoming pregnant more or less deliberately and trying to raise their own children. But a few wrinkles remain to be ironed out. Pamela describes one of them:

"I thought long and hard before I had my baby, but I haven't regretted one moment of it. I'm proud to be both mother and father to my little girl!"

"What happens when you go to work? Don't mother and father leave baby at the same time?"

Pamela frowned. "I have to admit that's one of the problems. But I'm working on a solution. You can't expect me to solve all the problems in the first year, can you? I mean, it's hard to be a pioneer."

But what if a single girl doesn't want to go through the usual steps to become pregnant?

No problem. Modern social innovators have come up with a solution for even that kind of dilemma. Now a determined young lady can completely bypass the time-honored ritual of fertilization by the male and still have the kind of child she wants. The precedent-breaking technique is called the "pseudo-parthenogenetic family."

What's a pseudo-parthenogenetic family?

For decades scientists have known that females can become pregnant without being subjected to a shower of sperm. Under proper conditions, the egg can actually "fertilize itself." For example, if a single frog egg is pricked with a bloody (frog's blood) needle, it can develop into a fully mature frog. The same sort of thing is possible with a rabbit. There is a drawback, however—all offspring are sterile females. Up to now the technique has not been perfected in human beings, although modern research is directed at such exotic concepts as fertilizing an egg outside the woman's body and implanting it in the uterus of another woman where it can develop into a mature full-term baby. But the female freedom-fighter doesn't have to bother with such far-out ideas. Social upheaval has come to her rescue.

How come?

As the number of children available for adoption, especially those from minority groups, has increased recently many local adoption agencies are changing the rules. Now a single woman can adopt an infant. The girl who is determined to have *everything* a married woman has—except a husband—has a clear track ahead. Provided she can meet the minimum requirements—and many single girls can—she is eligible to have her own child. It isn't exactly parthenogenesis, but it's the next best thing.

Shouldn't a child have both a mother and father?

Certainly. But there are thousands of lonely lovable kids in this world who will never have anyone except the director of the orphanage unless the adoption rules are stretched a little. From a practical point of view a child who is racially mixed, handicapped, or past the "cute" stage doesn't have much of a chance in the competition for nice acceptable middle-class parents. Growing up with a mother who loves you, even if she never got around to marrying, is better than standing around on visiting day drawing circles in the dust while the other kids get picked to live in a new home. It also gives a woman who can't or won't get married a chance to fill her life—and the life of a child—with what everyone needs more of: love.

Are there any other alternatives to marriage?

A lot of others have been suggested. In the constant quest for a formula that will guarantee happiness between men and women, virtually every combination and variation of the male-female relationship has been tried somewhere. In many parts of the world, an acceptable marriage is still based on the concept of two or more wives to each husband. Polygamy is a cornerstone of the Moslem faith, and millions of such marriages bring satisfaction and security to both men and women.

As recently as 1890 many Americans routinely took more than one wife—as part of their belief as members of the Church of Jesus Christ of Latter Day Saints, better known as the Mormons. As with most plural marriages, these relationships were marked by outstanding devotion, fidelity, and mutual dedication. Those who have experienced it will testify that the man with two wives and twelve children tends to feel more responsibility and involvement, not less. In these marriages, both wives help each other keep house and raise the children. Just as important, a baby with two mothers rarely suffers from lack of love and attention. Polygamy has never been actually made illegal in the United States—it has simply been made unbearable.

It's legal for a man to have more than one wife?

Yes, as long as he does it consecutively. If he goes through the flimsy formality of getting a divorce or annulment, he can have half a dozen wives. In effect polygamy is tolerated in our culture if the parties can prove monogamy's a failure. If she plays by the same self-defeating rules a woman can have seven or eight husbands. But things are beginning to change. There are a few intrepid pioneers who are once again experimenting with plural marriage—only they don't call it that.

What do they call it?

The socially acceptable title is group marriage. In this revival of a very old idea, everyone is married to everyone else. Three men may be married to two women or five women to two men or two men and two women. The household is usually operated according to polygamous guidelines. Everyone pitches in to support the group, keep house, and raise the children all together. There are some theoretical advantages to consider and some hard practical problems to overcome. Incidentally, most of those who undertake group marriage are simultaneously rebelling against modern society, which adds an additional burden to their experiment. So far there are no recorded cases where the town druggist, the vice president of the bank, and the local judge have combined their families into a homey little marital group. When and if this should happen, the results will be sensational in more ways than one.

Are there any other problems with group marriage?

There are some very knotty problems. If a couple decides to leave the group after a few years, which baby belongs to which couple? If one of the husbands or wives dies, assuming they have accumulated (or inherited) property, who gets what? Because there is no provision in our society for the group marriage the complications can become endless. For most women alone, group marriage and polygamy are not worthwhile to consider as solutions. They are fascinating social experiments interesting to sociologists and psychiatrists, and philosophers, but still potentially hazardous to those who engage in them.

13

WIDOWS HAVE
SPECIAL PROBLEMS

Do widows really have special problems?

Yes, without any doubt. In the split second when a woman becomes a widow her position in society is permanently and dramatically altered. Many Hindu ladies never had to face that problem. In place of the usual Western funeral, the deceased husband was cremated in a roaring mountain of logs. At the peak of the blaze, the new widow was expected to leap into the center of the bonfire to join her husband in his next life. This quaint custom, known as suttee, was in many ways a perfect solution. Indian wives usually did everything possible to prolong the life expectancy of their spouses, there was no economic burden of widows left behind, no loneliness for the survivor, and no chance for social and sexual marooning of the woman who stayed behind. There was only one little problem.

What was that?

The senseless and idiotic waste of human life. Simply because her husband was unfortunate enough to die, a woman, more or less willingly, threw away her own existence. Cruel, barbaric, and inhuman, one form of suttee was outlawed in 1826. The other form remains legal and is extensively practiced in every country of the world, being most popular in the United States.

What form of suttee is that?

The emotional variety. Most women are prepared, one way or another, for every role they will play in their lifetime except widowhood. Every year over 500,000 American women of all ages lose their husbands to the Grim Reaper. All too many of them respond by leaping *emotionally* into the grave with him. It just doesn't have to be that way.

What can a woman do?

She can try to analyze her plight, understand it, and cope with it effectively. Probably the most frustrating aspect of being a widow was expressed by a woman who experienced it. Jane lost her husband three weeks before she came to my office:

"Doctor, I have a Master's degree in sociology, I've raised four children, I worked as a supervising social worker for twelve years and I'm forty-one years old. Not one of these experiences has helped me in any way to solve the mess I find myself in. Is there anything I could have done in advance to make it easier on me—and my children?"

Most newly-made widows learn their roles the hard way: by on-the-job training. There is a better way.

What's the better way?

By preparing for the day before it comes. But the better way isn't the easy way. Our society has conditioned its members to think at the most about two months in advance. A man buys an air conditioner in June, fixes the furnace in October, and does his Christmas shopping December twenty-fourth about six P.M. Modern women can't afford to be so casual. The average woman who is married today is almost certain to be widowed at least once in her life and at an earlier age than ever before.

Why is that?

For one thing, modern men are killing themselves. The combination of cigarette smoking, unbearable nervous tension, drinking (especially when combined with driving), breathing bad air, and heart attacks, cuts like a sword through the ranks of middle-aged males. More and more women are finding themselves standing alone with the deed to a cemetery plot in one hand and an insurance policy in the other.

Two other advantages which women have over men tend to work against them.

What are they?

First, women generally live longer than men. It seems that just being a female, in some mysterious way, offers spectacular protection against heart disease. The female sex hormone, estrogen, as it flows through a woman's veins wards off the heart conditions that strike relentlessly at their husbands. In fact, it is a medical curiosity to diagnose a heart attack in a woman before the menopause.

The second advantage that modern widows have is even more ironic. In the old days most ladies who lost their husbands usually had two choices: they could turn to dressmaking or move in with relatives to survive. Nowadays with social security, company pensions, veteran's benefits, and life insurance, the second most important problem is solved for many widows. Most of them are able to get along on their own. But the number one problem of how to *enjoy* their lives remains. Of course there are always a few exceptions.

Who are those?

The exceptions are women who find that the same event that makes them widows—the death of their husbands—also moves them toward happiness. A small proportion of wives who longed for some way out of an unhappy marriage—other than divorce— suddenly find their dream come true. What they could not accomplish in ten years of wishful thinking is done in an instant by a tiny blood clot blocking the narrow arteries of the heart muscle. Ironically, most of these women find themselves more unhappy than before.

But shouldn't they be delighted?

Theoretically. After all those years of, "If only something would happen to get me out of this mess . . .," something does, and they find that instead of being relieved and delighted, they tend to be depressed and even despondent. They forgot to consider one little detail: *guilt*.

There is a quirk in the mind of every human being that psychiatrists call "megalomania." It is a childish delusion that every adult clings to based on the silly idea that a person's thoughts influence the outcome of a given event. For example, many gamblers actually believe that they can influence the entire destiny of the universe to make the dice or roulette wheel stop on the number that will leave them nine dollars richer. Deep down in her unconscious mind every woman who has wished for her husband's death is afraid that, like sticking pins in a voodoo doll, her thoughts had something to do with stopping the heart of another human being. Fortunately for all of us, it just doesn't work that way. But believing it does work—even unconsciously—can trigger the guilt that can bring on months of depression and anxiety when death occurs.

What percentage of widows have to deal with a problem like this?

Close to one hundred percent. At one time or another virtually every woman has wished that her husband were dead. It usually comes in a flash—during a bitter argument, after a disappointment, on discovering his sexual involvement with another woman, or simply because of the dreadful monotony of daily life with a dull man. It may range all the way from an idle wish—"Hmm, I wonder what it would be like without Tom," to the naked thrust: "I hate you! I wish you were dead!"

Months—or years—later when it finally becomes a

reality, a woman is left with the insistent unconscious feeling that her thoughts and words somehow brought about the dreadful event. Most widows could be spared a substantial part of the suffering they go through if only they were aware of this unconscious state of affairs. The antidote to their guilt is merely the truth. Fortunately for all of us, no human being has the power to commit murder simply by thinking the thought. It also pays to remember that there is no crime which we have not committed in our minds. At one time or another every child has wished for the death of his or her parents and every parent has wished (at least unconsciously) for the death of his or her children. The very fact that there are still almost four billion of us strolling around the planet is conclusive evidence that thoughts, no matter how "wicked" they may be, are still not lethal.

What's the biggest problem a widow faces?

That's hard to say because everything happens at once. Donna describes it well:

"It was like the bottom dropped out of everything. I was sitting home sewing one afternoon, waiting for the children to come home from school, and the telephone rang. It was the State Police to tell me that Roger had been in an accident. I was frightened enough when they told me, but then the man said, 'I'm going to have one of the officers stop by your house in a few minutes.' Then I knew he was dead. And the funny thing is, I wasn't frightened any more —I was just numb. It was as if I were standing two feet away from myself, watching everything, and saying: 'Don't worry, this isn't really happening. It couldn't happen this way.'" Donna shook her head. "But it did.

"The next four weeks were just a blur. I was forty years old, mother of two children, wife, I mean, widow, of a successful businessman and all of a sudden I had to run the house, think about the business, be mother and father, worry about the will and the estate, take care of the funeral, and keep myself from falling apart. It was very very hard but somehow I did it. And I know you're going to think I'm foolish for saying it but looking back at it—that was almost a year ago—it was easier than what I'm going through now."

"What are you going through now?"

"That's just it, Doctor. To be painfully honest, the role of the 'grieving widow' is easy to get used to. Everybody feels sorry for you and wants to help you —at least with advice. But when all the commotion is over and you have to take your place as a woman again, things suddenly get harder."

In what way do things get harder?

Probably the most difficult part about being a widow —after the first weeks or months of turmoil are over —is the sexual marooning that has occurred. At certain periods in her life every woman finds herself more or less sexually isolated. For some girls it happens during the college years, for others, unhappy marriages interfere with their chance for sexual happiness, divorce paralyzes many women sexually, and some simply prefer to remain single. But for a widow, sexual marooning cuts the deepest and the swiftest. One evening she is Mrs. Walter Miller with all her sexual needs provided for (more or less), without any serious sexual conflicts (more or less), and looking forward to a lifetime of sex with her husband. The next morning she is Mrs. *Harriet* Miller. Sexually she remains the same, her needs remain the same, but as one widow remarked cynically, "Overnight my husband was rendered totally and permanently impotent by death."

Grim but true. The new widow finds herself instantly deprived of any socially acceptable means of sexual gratification whatever. Yet her sexual requirements remain the same or even increase.

Her sexual needs increase?

Strange as it seems, it can happen that way. Darlene tells how it affected her:

"My husband died about two years ago in a fire at his plant. I was twenty-eight then and we had been married about six years. When they brought me the news I just collapsed. The doctor gave me an injection and I went to sleep. I woke up about three o'clock in the morning with the wildest desire for sex I've ever had in my life! Even when Dick and I were first going together I never felt anything like that. I swear, at that moment I would have traded anything just for a chance at an orgasm. I never knew what 'crawling the walls' meant until that night. I couldn't stand it any longer so I finally masturbated and managed to get to sleep again. When I woke up in the morning, I couldn't have cared less about sex and it was that way for the next month or so."

"What happened to your sexual feelings after that?"

"Well, about a month later they came back slowly and gradually. It was almost like being thirteen years old again."

Was Darlene's experience unusual?

Not really. Many widows go through approximately the same thing. Because the sexual urge is one of the basic primitive urges that affect members of the human race, in moments of stress or fear or isolation, a sudden overwhelming surge of sexuality can occur. A woman who knows about it in advance can deal with it easily and at the same time avoid guilt. For the woman who is unprepared the discrepancy between what she feels—wild passion—and what she is supposed to feel—grief—can cause a lot of unnecessary suffering. Even more important, these overwhelming sexual impulses don't always occur in the middle of the night. They can happen in the minister's study after the funeral, in the lawyer's office or at a meeting with the banker. The woman who understands their true nature realizes that they have no relation to the man who may be present and can control them before she does something everybody may be sorry for.

What can she do about them?

The most important thing is expecting them. If a girl can say, "Oh, yes. That's what they were talking about," she's won half the battle. Usually that's enough to give her control of the situation. If it still persists, Darlene's solution, masturbation, may be a satisfactory *temporary* solution to a *temporary* problem.

What about the next stage—when all sexual feelings disappear?

During the first few weeks of widowhood most women couldn't care less about sex. They are so busy trying to put the pieces of their lives together they barely have the time to get through each day. Usually about the fourth to tenth week after a husband's death, and frequently in response to a specific experience, the first twinges of sexual feelings come creeping back.

Most often the experience consists of being thrown together with a familiar man—perhaps one who has helped her through the recent difficult days. A quiet moment together, a sudden flash of tenderness, a surge of feeling, and there is the almost forgotten rapid heart beat, the pleasant restlessness, and the slowly-building tension that signal the start of sexual excitement. It happened to Eileen:

"I was just beginning to think I had everything under control and I was preparing myself for a nice quiet life. After all I was fifty-two and Henry had passed away about two months before. Ward, our—I should say—*my* insurance agent was over that evening explaining some details of Henry's insurance policy. Now Ward has been a friend of the family for at least twenty-five years. He never married and we all just considered him like a cousin. He had been so helpful since the funeral and there he was at ten o'clock at night trying to do even more. I just felt so *close* to him. I got up from my chair and sat down next to him on the couch. He must have sensed how I felt because in a few moments he just folded up the policies and said, 'Eileen, I'm so sorry to have kept you up so late. Let me come back tomorrow when you've had a chance to rest. What about, say, eleven in the morning?"

"How did you feel about that?"

"Honestly?" Eileen's tongue slowly went around her lips.

"Certainly."

She smiled. "I was as mad as I could be—then. I felt miserable and rejected. But by the next morning I realized what a wonderful man Ward was. He must have been through the same scene—and worse—with a thousand widows in the past twenty-five years and he knew exactly what was best for them when their feelings started getting out of control. It's been six months since that evening and Ward comes over for dinner at least twice a week now. I don't know if anything will come of it but if I ever decide to marry again, I could do a lot worse than Ward."

Some widows aren't so fortunate.

What happens to them?

Many men know that widows, like divorcées, tend to be emotionally vulnerable in the first months of their widowhood. For these sexual vultures, a widow in distress is fair game. They feed on her weaknesses and exploit her sexually. Since such sexual encounters are generally impulsive and emotionally supercharged, they yield a bumper crop of unwanted pregnancies and overwhelming feelings of guilt. Emotional reactions the morning after range all the way from, "Whatever made me do *that?*" among the more sophisticated, to "I've never been so ashamed and humiliated in my whole life. I feel so *terrible!*" Most important, it never has to happen. The widow who is forewarned can carefully avoid high-risk situations and undependable companions.

What are some high-risk situations?

Most obviously those where she is alone with a man after dark in an emotionally stressful situation. Evening conferences or meetings at home or at someone else's house or "just a quiet talk" at a quiet little restaurant are likely to end up in someone's quiet little bedroom. Undependable companions include men married to other women—like her best friend's husband. Some married men think they are a divine gift to widows and rely for protection on the assumption that the new widow will be ashamed to complain to their wives. That of course, is the key. To the hopefully straying husband, sometimes a casual remark like, "I wish Evelyn (his wife) were here to enjoy this with us, don't *you*?" *He* doesn't but he usually gets the message.

By far the best way to deal with the sexual reawakening that occurs as widowhood becomes a way of life is gradually to blend it into her new existence.

How does a widow start off on her new life?

Carefully. Her first task is to analyze—with painful honesty—her old style of living. The sooner she can go through the process of self-evaluation and self-revelation, the sooner she can begin to live again—or in some cases, to live for the first time. First she must face the hard fact that emotionally and sexually a widow can neither go backward, nor remain the way she is. The irresistible forces of time and the changes in the world around her compel her to progress. After she understands that the next step is easier.

What's the next step?

Preparing a short list of questions with very short and very frank answers. It goes something like this:

1. Was my marriage really happy? (Only two possibilities: Yes or No)
2. Did I really find sexual satisfaction with my husband? (Again, Yes or No)

Provided the answers to #1 and #2 are "No," then the next question becomes:

3. Am I willing to do what is necessary to start from scratch to build a new relationship with men?

If the answer to #3 is "No," it's time to look for a rocking chair, a shawl, and a big furry female cat. If the answer is "Yes," an entire lifetime of excitement and enjoyment is about to open up.

What if the answers to #1 and #2 are "Yes"?

Then question #2½ is: "Do I want to have the same thing again?" If the answer is "Yes," question #3 is, "How do I go about reproducing the same relationship with another man?"

If the answer to #3 is "Yes" in both cases, what does the woman do next?

Nothing. Absolutely nothing. Every surgeon knows, the minimum period for a surgical wound to heal is six weeks. The natural defense mechanisms of the body require that long to act. When it comes to emotional wounds—such as losing a mate—the same rule applies. If a woman can simply survive during that period, she is well on the way to starting her new life. If she is too happy too soon a widow is looking for trouble.

What kind of trouble?

Inappropriate cheerfulness in someone who has suffered such a loss doesn't mean that she will get away without being unhappy. It merely means that she has postponed the time of her unhappiness. The phenomenon is called "delayed mourning," and it happened to Sylvia:

"I couldn't believe it was true, Doctor. Leo and I had been married more than thirty years and yet when he died, I only felt sad for a couple of days. I was almost sixty and I thought, perhaps when you get to be this age, you stop feeling things. Was I wrong! About ten months later I had a terrible depression—I couldn't even get out of bed in the morning. I just didn't want to live any more. I dragged along for three weeks that way until my sister-in-law came to visit me one afternoon. We were talking about it and all of a sudden she looked at me and said,

'Do you think, Sylvia, it could have something to do with not feeling sad when Leo died?' I just couldn't help it. I burst out crying and I must have sobbed for hours. By night I felt a lot better and the next day it was all over. I guess you just can't put off the inevitable."

Sylvia was right. When it comes to being a widow there is such a thing as being *too* brave.

Does doing nothing apply to everything else in a widow's life during the first six weeks?

It should, as much as possible. Immediately after an automobile accident the victim may feel amazingly well—no aches, no pains, no disability. Then within a day or two all the symptoms begin to build up. The person who heeds the doctor's advice to rest and relax comes through in much better shape than the one who tries to carry on life as usual.

Becoming widowed is an accident, too (except for those rare cases where it is self-inflicted). The ordeal profoundly disturbs a woman's mental and emotional equilibrium and *all* postponable decisions should be postponed. That applies to things like financial transactions, selling a house, moving to a new town, and most important, taking advice.

What happens after the six weeks are over?

Then it's time to start making decisions. If a widow prepares her list of questions about her future, after about a month and a half of mulling the answers, she should be ready to arrive at some conclusions. For the woman who is relieved to be released from the responsibilities of marriage and is anxious to spend the rest of her days by herself, as one cynical widow put it, "In peace and freedom without men," her job is over.

For the woman who wants to re-join the human race it's a different story. She has her work cut out for her.

What does she do first?

More important is what she doesn't have to bother doing. She doesn't have to decide whether or not she wants to remarry. That's one of the few advantages of being a widow. Unlike the nineteen-year-old who really has no socially acceptable alternative to marriage (legal or common-law), the widow can take her relationships with men pretty much the way she wants to. Unless she is particularly young or particularly attractive she may be relieved to find that society has lost interest in her sexual behavior. No one pays much attention to her reputation or her morality. One of the ironies of the professional moralists is their preoccupation with the sexual lives of young erotically attractive girls.

Why is that?

The underlying reason isn't hard to uncover. An individual who takes a morbid interest in the sexual activities of other people and looks in their bedroom windows to check on them usually winds up in the penitentiary. On the other hand the expert in "moral guidance" who has the same morbid fascination with what other people are doing sexually but hides behind the mask of "morality" still gets his kicks. Fortunately most moral crusaders can't get worked up about what widows are doing—or not doing. Perhaps they can't stretch their own little erotic daydreams to include mentally undressing widow ladies. This makes women whose husbands have died one of the few groups in our society immune from the sting of these self-righteous gnats.

But shouldn't a widow get married if she's going to engage in sex?

Maybe she should and maybe she shouldn't but the decision must be up to her. The point is that most of the *compelling* reasons for marrying—social acceptability, legal transfer of property, protection of the children—are no longer prominent considerations. Her own future happiness is—and for the rest of her life will continue to be—number one on the list. For some widows that means marriage is obligatory. For others, it will be optional. A small group of women may sensibly choose sex without marriage—if that is really best for them.

When would sex without marriage be best?

Helen's case might be a good example: Tall, blonde, suntanned, she strode confidently into the office. Sliding gracefully into a chair, she brushed her hair from her eyes and spoke in a calm low-pitched voice:

"Doctor, I think I'm one of your exceptions. I'm fifty-nine now and I lost Jack, my husband and . . . and, well, let's say, my inspiration, about six years ago. I'm a writer—I write articles and books about all kinds of wild animals and I travel a lot. I do my own photography and background material and I love it. I guess that's one of the things that's kept me going." She stopped a moment, cleared her throat and went on:

"I lead a funny kind of life. I just came back from six months in Tanzania and I didn't exactly stay at the Hilton. I lived in the bush where my animals live. I'm leaving next week for Australia to do a feature on the wallaby—the kangaroo's cousin. I know for a fact that there is no man near my age who could all of a sudden start living in native huts, eating caribou meat, and walking fifteen miles a day through the tall grass. I'm not willing to give up my way of life because really it's all I have left of what Jack and I built up. So I deal with my sexual problems the best way I can."

"What do you do?"

"Let me be honest because that's why I'm here. I've been traveling with my husband for almost twenty-five years. I know men around the world. There are airline pilots in Nigeria, ranch owners in Australia, men with plantations in Brazil. They've grown up with Jack and me and many of them have lost their wives over the years. We have a lot in common—not to mention our loneliness—and sex with them is really the best solution to our mutual problems. We don't harm anyone, we make each other's lives a little happier, and that's really the whole idea, isn't it?"

Is Helen right?

She may be right as far as Helen is concerned. But her approach wouldn't necessarily be best for everyone. Dorothy looks at it from a different point of view:

"Maybe my real problem is that my marriage was too perfect. With Neil it was as if we were just one person joined together. I know that I could never have the same thing with anyone else and I just don't want to settle for 'being married.' I'm still young at forty-three and I need sex but that's all I want— not the responsibilities and burdens of marriage. I have my boyfriends and we get along well with each other—but they're friends and it can never be anything else."

What about the widow who wants to remarry?

She has some unique opportunities that never existed for her before. Take for example the widow over forty. When she was twenty, she was usually restricted to marrying a man near her own age. A fifteen-year-old boy didn't appeal to her and a man in his thirties was "just too old."

By the time she is in her forties, all the mathematics have changed. Although a man her own age might still be fine, she has the realistic option of selecting a chap whose emotional age exactly meshes with hers. A fellow who is ten or even fifteen years older might be perfect. On the other hand, a man in his thirties has some undeniable advantages.

You mean it might be good for a woman to marry a younger man?

There are certain obvious benefits. A younger man is likely to be in better physical condition than someone ten years older. More important he will probably be in better sexual condition. For most men, sexual potency gradually declines with age. When a fellow says glumly, "I'm not the man I used to be," he doesn't mean on the golf course. The fact that sexual slowing down is basically emotional rather than physical is of slim consolation to a woman. If the erection isn't there, it just isn't there.

In contrast, once the fear of pregnancy is past and the burdensome day-to-day responsibilities are behind them, many widows find a sudden permanent increase in their sexual needs and desires. Vicky made that amazing discovery:

"I was forty-two last month, Doctor, and I've been widowed for two years now. I'll be honest with you. When George was alive, sex just didn't mean that much to me. Once a week was more than enough and sometimes just going to bed would give me a headache. I guess I didn't reach an orgasm more than a quarter of the time." She shrugged her shoulders.

"All of a sudden, boom! I just can't get along without it. If one night goes by without intercourse, I literally start shaking. And masturbation isn't enough —I need a man. I went with a lot of men before I found Clint—and I didn't even want to go out with him at first. He's thirty-five and divorced and talk about coincidences, his ex-wife is the way I *used* to be! Every night at bedtime instead of giving him what he needed she'd give him a list of symptoms. Now you know a man can't get any satisfaction out of that. It's really perfect for both of us. He gets what he never got before—a satisfying sex life—and I get the same plus a chance to make up for twenty years of being a dope. I never knew it could be this good!"

There are other advantages besides. As time passes the biological and sexual ages of Vicky and Clint will come closer together. By the time she is sixty, he will be fifty-three and perhaps beginning to slow down sexually a bit as she begins tapering off. Because survival in men is directly related to age, a woman is less likely to become a widow the second time around if she marries a younger man. The final fringe benefit is the increased maturity and experience in life that an older woman brings to a younger man.

Does every man have to slow down sexually as he grows older?

Certainly not. But until the majority of men take advantage of the opportunities to preserve their sexual functioning, a widow has to assume that an older man will be less potent than his younger competitor.

Are there any drawbacks to choosing a younger man?

Yes. One of the biggest is other women. A younger and presumably more desirable man has more women after him. Unless a woman is willing to work constantly to be at her best, she may find the years beginning to count against her. On the other hand, every woman is really always competing emotionally and sexually with every other woman for her man. That's the way the game is played.

Of course there is a possibility the man will suddenly change his mind and decide he really wants to be married to a young girl. But that can happen to almost any man at any age and statistically it is not really a significant risk.

Then there is social disapproval. The old hens at the supermarket may start clucking: "Did you know that Charlotte's husband is *younger* than she is?" This is always accompanied by a widening of the eyes and a sucking in of the breath as if they had just swallowed an egg instead of laying one. Most of them would be delighted to have a man of their own—of any age.

What should be the difference in age if a woman decides on a younger man?

It depends on the circumstances and the people involved. In general a woman over forty-five can reasonably select a man up to seven years her junior. Between forty and forty-five she should think twice about the whole idea. Under the age of forty, the balance shifts and a man the same age or older becomes more appealing. Of course everyone is different and in the final analysis, each woman has to make up her own mind.

What are the advantages of marrying an older man?

The first advantage is the one that has appealed to fathers of young girls over the centuries: an older man is usually better able to support a wife. For the woman who isn't as interested in sex as she used to be, an older man can be less demanding sexually. But he may also tend to be more demanding emotionally and usually becomes more rigid and inflexible as he grows older. For the woman who wants to build a new and rewarding life for herself the combination of little sex and lots of demands may rapidly become uncomfortable. A widow should use all the flexibility and freedom her new state brings to improve her life. If she feels she can find greater happiness with a younger man than with an older man, she must have the confidence to implement her own decision.

What's the next step for a widow?

Realizing the power her new situation gives her. No matter how much she loved her husband, once he is gone, she has the responsibility to make the very best life she can for herself—and her children. Sometimes becoming a widow is the golden opportunity to get what she really wants out of life. It can be the second chance that so many people wish for and so few ever actually reach for when it becomes available. Trudy was one who seized her opportunity:

"For a long time after Glen passed away, Doctor, I just sat around feeling sorry for myself. I have a college degree but my major was philosophy. Where does a middle-aged slightly over-weight lady philosopher find her true role in life—in the space age? Toward the end there I really started getting depressed. I had to take tranquilizers in the daytime and sleeping pills at night."

"You said, 'toward the end.' What happened?"

Trudy smiled. "In spite of the sleeping pills I just couldn't sleep one night, so I got up and turned on the late late movie. It was a terrible picture—about a man sticking pins into bugs. But there was a fantastic commercial that really stuck a pin into me. It described a program for retraining people with hard-to-use college degrees as teachers. It showed a retired army officer, an engineer, and—of all things—a widow, who took courses on the side and started teaching almost immediately. I couldn't sleep at all that night but it wasn't from nerves—it was from excitement. At one minute to nine in the morning I called the number they showed on the screen and by ten o'clock I was down there filling out the forms. All my life I have wanted to be a teacher—and now it's come true. And just because somebody stuck a pin in this big lazy bug."

Trudy is only one example. Many widows have been able to fulfill their secret ambitions with ease. Most of them have the time, the money, and certainly, the patience to take them into any career they really desire. Physical and vocational therapy, practical nursing, teaching, medical assistant, secretary, newspaper reporter (at least on a local weekly), social worker, and a thousand other interesting useful jobs are all within the reach of many widows. Sometimes just working in a dress shop or the neighborhood grocery a few hours a week are enough to inject meaning and activity into a widow's life again.

How does a widow start to do something like this?

As before, doing nothing for a while is sometimes the best way to begin. After the hard first six weeks are over a short trip to gain a little perspective into her old way of doing things may work wonders. It doesn't have to be a tour of Europe or the Orient. A few days in the country at a quiet spot or a long weekend at the beach may be enough to see things as they really are. Then once she has some idea of what she wants to do with her life, careful reading of the daily papers to turn up clues, calls to the local social service agencies, a check with the Board of Education, and following up all the leads that come from the original inquiries usually lead her where she wants to go.

What about volunteer work?

It has its place. Sometimes it's a good way to try a new career without actually getting involved in it. Working as a volunteer in a hospital gives a woman some idea of what the rest of the jobs are like. Being a teacher's helper gives her an inside look at a teacher's life. But volunteer work never gives the same rewards, emotional and financial (both of which are important to most widows), as being a professional in her own field.

Does the same thing apply to younger widows?

Even more emphatically. Too many younger widows, those from thirty to forty, succumb to the temptation to "keep the family together." They act as if their husband were going to walk in the door at any moment. The truth is—he isn't. The gallant young mother struggling to bring up her children alone makes a grand plot for a TV series. In real life, it doesn't play nearly as well.

How come?

Because everyone gets cheated. A mother is a mother and no matter how good she is at that, she can't be a father, too. Even more important, as every woman knows, a memory is no substitute for a man—especially at night after the lights are out. A woman who throws away her own happiness and that of her children, as some kind of vague noble sacrifice, will never have their thanks or anyone else's. The best thing any young widow can do for her children is to find them a good father—and find herself a good husband in the process.

At first it may be difficult. Getting back into circulation requires, among other things, leaving the children with a baby-sitter while Mommy has dinner with her date in a nice restaurant. Sometimes she may have to leave them at home while she goes out sailing, playing tennis, or just basks on the beach.

Is it all right for her to do that?

She isn't doing it just for her own entertainment. If she keeps her goal clearly in mind, she will be working hard for the benefit of the entire family. It can help a lot if she explains to her children exactly what she is doing and why she is doing it. Claudine had her misgivings when she first attempted it:

"Doctor, I really didn't know where to begin. Like, how do you tell a four-year-old that you're looking hard for a man to take the place of his Daddy particularly when all he knows is that his Daddy doesn't come home any more? It took me over a month to get up the courage to try it."

"How did it go?"

"I was amazed. I didn't know there were so many practical-minded four-year-olds in this world. I sat Timmy down on my lap after his nap and I asked him:

" 'Timmy, how would you like to have a new Daddy?'

"He wrinkled up his little face and said, 'Naw. I want my Mommy!'

"That shook me for a minute until I realized what he was trying to say. The poor kid thought I was going to leave him and put a strange man in my place. I said,

"'What I mean is, how would you like a Mommy *and* a Daddy too?'

"He smiled, said, 'Okay,' jumped off my lap, and turned on television."

"Then what happened?"

"That was it. He never mentioned it again. Whenever I went out after that I just told him I was looking for another Daddy so he would have a Mommy *and* a Daddy, too. He would always smile when I left and keep on playing with the sitter. Once in a while the next morning he would ask: 'Did you find me a Daddy yet?' I'll tell you, Doctor, we can certainly learn a lot from our children."

Basically the way children react to the idea of a new father hinges on how their mothers explain it to them. If the new man is presented as someone who will bring love and unity to the family their cooperation is almost certain. On the other hand if they expect him to draw their mother's affection away from them, things may be pretty tense for all concerned. As usual honesty is the best policy and the youngsters usually come through with flying colors.

What if a child refuses to accept the situation?

Then most of the time it becomes a question of taking the unpleasant medicine to prevent an even more unpleasant disease. The widow who sacrifices everything to martyr herself for her seven- (or seventeen) year-old child may find her reward indefinitely postponed. The grateful offspring is unlikely to say on its twenty-first birthday:

"Gee, Mom, thanks for staying single for me. I sure appreciate it. Have a nice old age."

Usually it goes more like this:

"Gee, Mom, you're getting so old. How come you never found another guy to marry? Say, can I have the keys to the car?"

Is it important for an older widow to marry again?

Yes. A woman over the age of forty is almost certain to deteriorate emotionally (and sexually) if she is out of emotional (and sexual) circulation for too long. Even worse, the older she gets the faster the deterioration proceeds. Human beings are sexual beings and without the constant stimulation of regular and frequent sex they tend to fade and dry up.

Why is sex that important?

Because every woman is equipped with a complex set of sexual structures designed for a specific purpose—and that purpose goes far beyond reproduction. Every experience of sexual excitement and orgasm affects every organ and tissue of the body. In a normal person the nervous and circulatory changes that accompany intercourse are beneficial to the muscles, the heart, the adrenal glands, the pituitary gland, the thyroid, and last but not least, the brain. Even more vital, the older widow who is experiencing full sexual gratification with a man she loves looks forward to every new day with excitement and anticipation. That in itself is worth every bit of effort it requires for her to function again sexually. As a wise old physician once said: "If all the benefits that come from sexual intercourse could be compounded into a tablet, it would be the most powerful and wonderful medicine in the world."

But how does an older woman get started?

First by making the decision. Sometimes that's the hardest part. A fifty-one-year-old widow expressed it this way: "I know what you say is true, Doctor. I have to start being a complete woman again. But it's hard to pick up where I left off thirty years ago. Do you actually mean I have to start *dating* again?"

Many widows have the same reaction at the beginning. When the question of dating comes up they immediately think of the anxiety and turmoil of their late adolescence. It brings back memories of waiting around at parties, hoping a boy will ask them to dance, wrestling matches in the rumble-seat of roadsters, and wistfully wishing for a bid to the Junior Prom. But every widow should realize that a lot of things have changed since those days, including her own sophistication and her ability to feel at ease with men. Besides, she has the widow's secret weapon.

What's the widow's secret weapon?

Her invisible advantage over other women is her understanding of men. Many spinsters think of men as strange beasts, most divorcées have left marriage with bad feelings, but most widows have just spent twenty or so years in a close, affectionate relationship with a man. They know what men like, they know how to please men, they know how to adjust to male whims and peculiarities. Even more important, every single man knows it too. From a man's point of view, a widow is the ideal wife whose virtues have been proved in actual use. Tom describes it well:

"Doctor, I'm an attorney. I'm fifty-six years old and I've practiced law for thirty-one years. Every time a client of mine asked my advice about getting married, I always told him to look for an attractive widow. I used to say, 'Widows make the best wives. They already know what marriage is about and they take a man the way he is. They can whip up an apple pie, sew a button on your shirt, and snuggle you into a warm bed all in the same hour. They know how to run the house, save your money, and make you a happy man.' If I had it to do over again, I'd marry a widow in a minute!"

"Does your own wife know how you feel about widows?"

"She ought to, Doctor. Her husband was my first client and a year after he passed away Louise and I got married. We've been happy from the first day—and that was twenty-five years ago next week."

There are other pleasant surprises when a widow starts going out again with men. Jeanette really wasn't prepared for them:

"One of the things that made me so unhappy when Jim died, Doctor, was that he was just getting ready to enjoy life. He'd worked hard ever since he was twenty—and he and I were just getting ready to do all the things we'd been looking forward to."

"For example?"

"Well, the children were on their own and we really had no more financial responsibilities. We were just starting to loosen up a little, eat at nice restaurants, planning to take some trips, and Jim was going to do something he'd wanted to do for years—he was going to buy a big sailboat. And then at the last moment, he had his heart attack and got cheated out of everything."

"How about you?"

Jeanette looked surprised. "Me?"

"Didn't you get cheated out of everything too?"

She nervously patted her skirt, smoothed her hair, then looked up. Now there were tears in her eyes. "I guess you're right. I was looking forward to all those things and now I've lost my chance. I'm not complaining but I gave up so many things over those years."

"Maybe you still have a chance to enjoy them."

Three months later Jeanette was back. She had lost some weight, her hair was back to its original auburn color, and she had a glowing tan.

"What happened?"

"Nothing very much, Doctor. I just thought over some of the things you said and I decided there was no reason I couldn't enjoy everything Jim and I had planned together. I know he would have wanted me to. So I put myself back in circulation and in the past few months I've been to all the places we planned to visit—only instead of Jim, I'm there with Frank."

"Who's Frank?"

"Why he's Jim's cousin from Illinois. He's two years older than Jim and I'm amazed at how much alike they are. In fact one of the reasons he moved out to California when he retired was to buy—of all things, a sailboat."

"Then that explains the suntan?"

Jeanette grinned. "Of course. And it explains the smile, too."

Is it right for a widow to become so friendly with her former husband's friends and relatives?

Not only is it all right but often it is the best thing she can do. The precedent was set several thousand years ago in the Bible, in Deuteronomy 25:5: "If brethren dwell together and one of them die, and have no child, the wife of the dead shall not marry without unto a stranger: her husband's brother shall go in unto her, and take her to him to wife, and perform the duty of a husband's brother unto her."

While a woman may not be eager to marry her brother-in-law, the basic concept has undeniable wisdom. If a widow can find her next husband among close friends of her deceased husband or even (if she likes) among his family, she avoids most of the unknown elements of a brand-new relationship. Sometimes over the years an informal emotional bond has been built up between them which provides a good framework for marriage. For this kind of relationship to be successful, a widow should apply the same rigorous evaluation to an old friend as she would to a man she has just met. The real value of considering an old friend as a possible husband is that both his virtues and his faults are right there on the surface where they are easy to see.

Then a widow does have a chance to be happy again?

Certainly. Of all the categories of women alone—single, divorced, and even those women who are alone though married—the widow is best prepared for a full rewarding new life. Most widows know how to make a happy marriage. All they have to do is take a deep breath, plunge in, and start doing it.

14

SECRETS OF MALE SEXUALITY

Is it true that sex is only for married women?

It might be true if the marriage license was what started the sex hormones surging into a woman's bloodstream. But that's not the way it is. Every female, married or not, is assaulted by massive doses of estrogens (and progesterones) about the age of twelve. From the moment of her first menstrual period, if not before, she is every inch a fully functioning sexual being. Except as far as society is concerned. For the next ten years or so, every time she has a sexual urge she is supposed to cross her legs and grit her teeth. By some bizarre twist of logic, the emotional and biological release that is available to every other being on earth—including teenage boys —is denied to her. Even when she passes the magic age of eighteen (or twenty-one depending where she lives) unless the ink is dry on the marriage license, no woman of any age is supposed to even think about sex. It isn't fair.

Then sex without marriage is okay?

It depends on who's deciding. *In most states it is a criminal offense for any woman to have sexual inter-*

course *unless she is married*. If she is convicted of fornication, cohabitation, or adultery she can spend the best years of her life behind bars. Fortunately this primitive and discriminatory law is not enforced —if it were, many young ladies would go straight from college to the penitentiary.

But if the law isn't enforced, it doesn't mean much, does it?

Except that it's there. The quaint old custom of branding adulteresses with an artistic letter "A" isn't done any more either although there is a modern-day legal equivalent.

What's that?

In most parts of the country a woman who has been divorced from her husband is granted custody of their children. However, if she engages in sexual intercourse while the children are still living with her, the judge who granted the divorce is empowered to *take her children away from her*. Instead of having the first letter of the alphabet engraved on her forehead, she is branded an "unfit mother" for all the world to see. No one has ever explained why expressing herself sexually as a human being disqualifies her as a mother. By coincidence, it was sex that made her a mother in the first place. If the whole idea isn't crazy enough at that point, there is one man with whom she can have unlimited sex without running any legal risks. Ironically that is often the only man in the world she has no sexual interest in whatever—her former husband. But it's single women that have to take most of the pressure.

How is that?

After being forced to deny her sexuality for ten years or so, the single woman is suddenly compelled to perform or else. The same judge that could have sent her to jail for having sexual intercourse before the wedding can break up her marriage if she doesn't have sexual intercourse afterward. It's all completely legal—refusal to "consummate" a marriage is adequate grounds for annulment. The woman is the same, the sexual act is the same—only in one case the magic wand of matrimony has been waved by the justice of the peace. Sometimes it gets unbelievable. Take a girl who marries at noon. If she "does it" in the A.M. she is a criminal. If she "doesn't do it" the same afternoon, she is a failure as a wife. It's like expecting a girl who has never been allowed in the kitchen to walk off with first prize in the Pillsbury Bake-Off. She'll be lucky if she knows how to put a cake in the oven. Widows and divorcées face the same problems but in a slightly different way.

Which way?

A woman whose husband dies is suddenly precipitated into a whole new world. After years of marriage (usually) and some degree of sexual satisfaction and security, she is forced to start all over again and this time at a disadvantage. While she has been on the sidelines for five, ten, or twenty years, a lot of rules of the game have changed. In many ways it's like the retired movie actress who suddenly needs money and has to launch a come-back. On the first of the month a woman may be preparing breakfast for her husband. On the thirty-first she finds herself trying to decide whether to kiss a strange man good night on the first date. It isn't easy.

Divorce has its problems too. As husband and wife drift apart emotionally, they also drift apart sexually. Sometimes sexual gratification goes first, sometimes it goes last, but in divorce, it nearly always goes. Both the widow and divorcée live under the shadow of uncertainty—will they be able to find sexual happiness with the next man who comes into their life?

What's the solution?

When it comes to sex, the first step toward any solution is knowledge. Whether a woman is preparing for marriage, trying to readjust to life without her husband (deceased or divorced), or searching for sexual satisfaction *without* marriage, she desperately needs to know all she possibly can about the innermost sexual secrets of men. She needs to know what men feel sexually, what they expect sexually, and what they fear sexually. Once she is armed with this information, she can face virtually any sexual problem with confidence.

Where can a woman get this knowledge?

Usually not from men. As almost every female over the age of twelve has learned, males are funny when it comes to sex. Most of them live in a dream world where every man is super-potent and relentlessly determined to bestow his favors on each passing damsel. Every penis is supposed to be a stick of phallic dynamite perpetually prepared for record-breaking performance. An entire magical cult has been built on the exotic erotic daydreams of adolescent boys. It features electric beds, child-women with glowing-pink plastic skin, and occasional glimpses of forbidden pubic hair. These strange cults have their own emblems, T-shirts, and heroes. They even have a vast mythology of imaginary sexual conquests. To the perceptive woman, all this adds up to one thing.

What's that?

Most men are sexually insecure. The he-man image, the sexual bravado, the folklore of the Don Juan or Casanova, is an elaborate defense against sexual uncertainty. What no man will ever admit to a woman—and rarely admit to another man—he confides daily to his psychiatrist. In hundreds of research studies, in thousands of personal interviews, in dozens of extended scientific observations, it has become apparent that the average man feels himself at a decided disadvantage sexually. So much of his sexual behavior is designed to cover up, to compensate for his deficiencies—real or imagined.

Whose fault is male sexual insecurity?

Certainly not the man's. Objectively speaking, when it comes to sex, men have been given a tough row to hoe. The outcome of each act of intercourse depends almost totally on the performance of the man. To make matters more difficult, it all hinges on his ability to obtain and maintain an erection. No matter how skilled he may be sexually, unless his penis is transformed from a flabby appendage into a rigid conduit for spermatic fluid, sexual satisfaction for either partner is impossible. Whether he likes it or not, his sexual success and to a great extent his emotional satisfaction in life depend on the fragile function of his phallic magic wand. As if that were not enough to worry about, most of the time the reaction of his penis is beyond his conscious control. If it works correctly, he doesn't know why—and he doesn't really care. If it doesn't work correctly, he doesn't know why either but *he cares*. Most male sexual problems are intensified because of adolescent experiences.

How come?

Between the ages of fourteen and eighteen an unbelievable amount of testosterone, the male sex hormone, is produced by the testicles and the adrenal gland. As it gushes into the body it seeks out the two primary target organs, the penis (and testicles) and the brain. The result is an almost constant preoccupation with sex accompanied by persistent powerful erections. Virtually all teenage boys masturbate regularly and enthusiastically—the performance of some of them is truly impressive. Many males at this stage are capable of three, four, and five ejaculations in a row, *barely losing their erection between orgasms*. Once they start to have intercourse, some can maintain nearly the same level of orgasmic activity—at least in the beginning. To make matters worse, even though their sexual capacity declines somewhat into the early twenties, many men are still capable of three and four orgasms nightly until the third decade.

Why does such impressive potency "make matters worse"?

Because for the rest of their sexual lives men tend to look back on their early sexual experiences as a *standard of performance*. Deep inside, every man thinks he should be as dynamic as he was when he was twenty. Every night he is unconsciously (or consciously) measuring the hardness of his penis and the intensity of his excitement against his recollection of "How it used to be." In that way he is his own worst enemy.

Why?

Because, along with all the other things it is, sexual intercourse is also an athletic performance. It requires skill, practice, and coordination. It also requires self-confidence. Imagine how a baseball player would perform if every time he were up at bat he began to reminisce about all the home runs he *used* to hit. Every man suffers from sexual fears and if a woman understands those fears and knows how to resolve them, she can help herself and her man.

What are men afraid of sexually?

There are six major Fears of Male Sexuality—some conscious, some unconscious:

1. Not being able to have a strong erection.
2. Losing the erection either before intercourse or before ejaculation.

3. Ejaculating too quickly (premature ejaculation).
4. Not being able to have another erection promptly after ejaculating.
5. Not being able to satisfy a woman.
6. Being compared unfavorably with other men when it comes to penis, potency, or sexual skill.

These fears can overwhelm a man and paralyze him sexually or they may fade until they are no more important in his life than his golf score. It all depends on one person.

Who's that?

His woman. To a man, his sexual partner is really two beings in one. Potentially she is the source of erotic excitement, almost unbearable pleasure, and the ultimate in emotional satisfaction. She can also be a cruel antagonist who with a word or a look can annihilate his chances for sexual satisfaction. Ron went through it:

"I guess it was what you doctors call a 'learning experience,' but I'll tell you, I never want to suffer like that again. Even now, six months later, I get the creeps just thinking about it."

"What happened?"

"Well, it all started out so great. I met this chick at a party—I guess it was about a year ago—and we clicked right away. She was a model and I guess she just dug me." He smiled. "And when she found out I was an actor's agent, it probably didn't hurt at all either.

"Well, anyway we started going together and pretty soon sleeping together. She moved into my place and for about a month or so it was great. I mean, she just couldn't get enough sex. Actually that was the problem."

"What kind of problem?"

"I never thought the day would come—after all I'm only thirty-four—but I couldn't keep up with her. We'd have intercourse say, twice, maybe three times one evening and then about two o'clock in the morning she'd wake me up asking for more. After about three weeks of that I just couldn't go it. I mean, fun is fun but, I mean, who's built like that? Then things really got bad. No, they got terrible." Ron shivered as he said it.

"She started saying things like, 'What's the matter, big boy, can't you keep it up?' Doctor, there's no way for a man to answer a question like that. Even worse, pretty soon not only couldn't I *keep* it up, I couldn't even *get* it up. Man, was that a bad feeling!"

"What did you do then?"

"What could I do? I just moved her back into her own apartment. It was a bad scene. The night we broke up she started telling me how really bad I was in bed and how much better all her other boyfriends had been—including a lot of the guys I worked with down at my agency. Wow, I just wanted to jump in the river. Then I made the big mistake."

"What did you do?"

"I tried to prove she was wrong. I went on a campaign to make it with every good-looking chick I could find. Ohhh, was that terrible!" Ron winced.

"I picked girls up everywhere and just tried to show the world I could still do it. And the harder I tried, the worse I got. I remember this gal I met on a movie set. She was a script girl or something. We went over to my place, got into bed—in those days I was trying to set records in that department too. I used to make it from the doorway to the bedsheets in under five minutes—but that was all I ever accomplished the whole evening. Anyhow, I just couldn't get an erection no matter what she did or what I did. I was like, paralyzed. After about half an hour, she just got up and started dressing. As she walked out the door she looked back at me and said, 'Listen, I know it's none of my business, but are you sure you're used to doing it with *girls?*'"

Ron held his head with both hands. It took him several months of treatment plus the devotion of a girl who really cared about him to allow him to function as a man again.

Can a woman's attitude make that much difference?

A woman's attitude makes *all* the difference. It is the brain and not the penis that decides whether or not erection is going to occur. If his woman turns off his brain, there is nothing left to turn on his penis. Sometimes this can be hard for a woman to understand.

Why?

Because her sexual needs are almost exactly the opposite of a man's. No woman ever has to be concerned with that dual physical-emotional challenge of obtaining an erection. It doesn't stop there. The man must maintain his erection until the penis is deep within the vagina. Imagine urgently trying to unlock a door as the key is slowly going soft in your hand. But once an erect penis is in place in the vagina, the balance of sexual power shifts. With simple friction, the man is almost certain to reach an orgasm and ejaculate. The woman must concentrate her energy

and attention on making sure she will not be left behind. It is almost as if each participant had one half
of the lucky ticket and neither of them could win unless they put their pieces together. That's where a
woman's sexual responsibility comes in.

A *woman's sexual responsibility?*

Yes. For the past hundred years in the United
States (and most European countries) the emphasis
has been on encouraging men to provide sexual satisfaction to women. Long treatises have been written
about complex techniques of "foreplay" to make sure
that a woman is "ready." Men are constantly reminded to prod their ladies to the peak of passion before even attempting to please themselves. Behind
these detailed instructions is the veiled threat that if
a girl fails to reach a climax it is probably the fault of
her partner.

Isn't that true?

No, half true. The other side of the picture is the
woman's duty to provide the best possible emotional
setting for her man to excite and satisfy her. By giving
him the strongest possible erection, the widest range
of stimulation, and the greatest feeling of sexual
security, she makes her own gratification almost certain.

How does she do that?

She begins by banishing the six Fears of Male Sexuality. The first fear is the most important one—fear of

not having a strong erection. Unless she handles this one right, a woman may never get around to dealing with the other problems. She must enter the situation radiating confidence that her man will succeed. By word and deed she has to let him know that everything will go well. Lois tried it both ways:

"I guess Larry had some bad experiences before and since then he's always worried about being able to have an erection. At first I tried to play it light— and it wasn't a good idea. I said things like, 'Well, let's see if we can set a new record tonight.' or 'Wonder how your reflexes are doing?' I learned one thing fast."

"What was that?"

"A man's sense of humor ends at his belt buckle. When it comes to potency, there's no joke that's funny. Whenever I tried to be casual, everything stopped right there. So I switched tactics and adopted the 'good vibrations' approach. I just assume that everything will go right. When we start to have intercourse now I act as if there is only one way that things can go—the right way."

"Does it work?"

"It's starting to."

Lois had the right idea. In the erection department, mental state is the vital ingredient. But there is a way to facilitate impulses from the brain to the penis by reinforcing them with impulses from the penis to the brain.

You mean there's a special way to stimulate a man's penis to help him have an erection?

No, there isn't. In spite of the panting ladies who write coy little books telling exactly where and how to

squeeze the penis the real facts are quite different.
The woman who wants to give her man the most
pleasure doesn't need a road map of the male sexual
organs. All she really needs is an understanding of the
male mind. *The technique she uses to touch him
physically is not nearly as important as the technique
she uses to touch him emotionally*. It works like this:
detailed instructions on manipulating the penis by the
usual exotic methods are all a waste of time. They
may impress women but to a man they mean very
little. Most adult men have been masturbating for ten,
twenty, or thirty years and they have tried all the possible variations of stimulation techniques. If ingenious
variations themselves would do the trick, a man
wouldn't need a woman—he could do it all himself.
Actually the erotic effect of having his woman caress
his penis is ten percent physical sensation and ninety
percent the excitement of knowing that she cares
about him sexually and wants to help prepare him to
enjoy intercourse with her. If this combination of sensations and nervous impulses and anticipatory excitement bombards the brain effectively, a firm hard
erection is almost inevitable.

What about the second fear of male sexuality?

The antidote to fear of losing an erection depends on
establishing enough sexual momentum to carry the
man through to successful completion of intercourse.
If the emotional stimulation (combined with physical
sensations) gets him off to a flying start, there is little
chance he will falter before the finish line. If a man
begins with a good erection which is constantly reinforced, he (and his partner) can usually forget about

fear number two. But it has to be done right. A fly on the bedroom wall might see it this way:

A man and a woman are lying in bed together. She has just turned out the light:

Man: Uhm, do you feel like, you know, doing it tonight?

Girl: Huh? Oh, yeah. Sure (She rolls over toward him) Are you ready?

Man: Uh, not exactly.

(They embrace.)

Girl: Ready yet?

Man: I suppose so.

Girl: (Cheerfully) Well, let's get on with it!

The man begins intercourse with a half-hearted erection and in three or four minutes loses it.

Girl: What happened?

Man: (sheepishly) Gee, I don't know. I guess I'm too tired or something.

Girl: (Smiling) Don't worry. We'll try it again tomorrow night.

Even flies can do better than that.

A woman who really wants to help her partner must make him feel that she wants him. If she embraces him eagerly, rubs against him, kisses him warmly, and gives the unmistakable impression that she can barely wait for him to begin, neither of them is likely to be disappointed. Women who know confide that one of the most effective aphrodisiacs is simply a soft sigh of appreciation at the right moment. It is the female equivalent of wild applause.

Then should a woman pretend to be sexually excited even if she really doesn't feel that way?

It should never come to that. At most she may have to anticipate her own sexual excitement by a moment or two and communicate her eagerness to her partner. She will usually be rewarded promptly. If she lets him know how much he is pleasing her—or about to please her—his own enhanced enjoyment can be transmitted to her a few moments later. When she gets right down to it, the woman is only pleasing herself. The better she makes her man perform, the more *she* is going to enjoy intercourse.

What else can a woman do to make her man more potent?

She can utilize one of the best kept secrets of the human race: *every man, deep inside, has the wish to be taken over sexually by a woman.* Over and over again men tell their psychiatrists—but never their girl friends—"If only she would be more active sexually. If only I could get *her* to take the initiative once in a while." Many male sexual daydreams revolve around the fantasy of being seduced by a sexually dominant woman. In movies and plays (written by men) the theme of a sexually aggressive woman is constantly repeated. In that mirror of inner sexual longings, pornography (written almost exclusively by men), at least half the fairy tales involve women who force men to copulate with them.

Why do men like to have women take over sexually?

There are several reasons. First, most men fear sexual rejection. If the woman makes the first move, there is no chance they will be rejected. Second, the idea that a woman finds him exciting is extremely stimulating to every man. Third, simply being close to a woman who is "turned-on" turns on most men. The combination of three different forms of stimulation makes even the meekest fellow a tiger in the bedroom. All a woman has to do is translate her knowledge into action and things begin to fall into her lap.

What does she do?

Instead of being passive, she becomes active. *She* kisses her man. *She* undresses him. *She* begins the caresses of *his* sexual organs and if she really wants to drive him wild, takes his hands and unmistakably shows him what *she* wants him to do with them. If she feels like going all the way, when it is time for intercourse (and with this method it won't take very long) *she* rolls on top of him.

The fascinating thing that stands out when the woman takes over is that the *physical* contact is the same. Whether the woman is on top of her partner or beneath him, the penis remains in contact with the vagina in about the same way. When the man kisses the woman or the woman kisses the man, the lips touch each other in the same way. The only thing that changes is the *idea*—and of course, that's what counts.

The same thing holds true for other sexual varia-

394

tions. When a woman takes a man's penis into her mouth, realistically speaking, it is difficult for him to distinguish between those sensations and the ones provided by the vagina. (From a scientific point of view, the vagina actually stimulates the receptors of the penis in more ways than the mouth could ever hope to.) The thing that sends most men out of their minds when a woman performs fellatio on them is the idea that she is driven by an overwhelming sexual desire for them.

Then all a woman has to do to have perfect sex with her man is to dominate him sexually?

It's not quite that easy. The real enemy of happiness in sex is monotony. Expectation, anticipation, and pleasant surprises add a supercharged element to the sexual life of any couple. But the same old thing every time soon loses its power to wipe out the six sexual fears of men.

What about the rest of male sexual fears?

The third one is really the most difficult. Premature ejaculation is one of the most frustrating and depressing symptoms any man can have. Even worse, it is a two-edged sword: at the same moment it drops the curtain on a man's sexual pleasure, it deprives his partner of her chance at orgasm. Although accelerated ejaculation is basically an emotional condition, there are some relatively simple things a woman can do to help.

The process of ejaculation and orgasm in a man is extremely complicated but the timing is controlled by a balance between nervous impulses that speed orgasm and those that hold it back. If the woman does anything to increase the stimulation of her man, she only makes his problem worse. If she does things that help suppress orgasm, she prolongs his sexual staying power.

What can she do?

Anything that cuts down on the intensity of sexual excitement without destroying her man's erection. Simple things like keeping the bedroom lights burning brightly and lying as still as possible for at least thirty seconds immediately after the penis is inserted into the vagina can be helpful. Then she can try a technique that has been used successfully in China for at least three thousand years. She merely reaches down and cradles the man's testicles *gently* but firmly in her hand. As soon as he reaches the point where he is about to lose control and swiftly bring the evening to a conclusion she carefully tightens her grip on the testicles and pulls downward *very gently*. If done skillfully, the ejaculation will be rapidly and completely blocked. It is wise however for the girl to tell the man in advance what she is going to do and why she is doing it. Male castration fears being what they are, any sudden clutching gesture in this direction can swiftly end a beautiful relationship.

There is another benefit to this Chinese method. After it is used successfully several times a conditioned reflex may be built up and simply holding the testicles gently slows ejaculation. The method is effective up to the "point of no return."

What's the "point of no return"?

The mechanism of orgasm in the male is like a sling-shot. Tension builds gradually under control until the maximum pressure is reached. Once the rubber band is released, from that point on, everything happens by itself. Once orgasm begins, and every man can sense that moment instinctively, nothing in the world can stop it. (Many unwed mothers can testify to the truth of that observation.) The goal of everything a woman does is to prevent a man from reaching the "point of no return" before he (and she) are ready.

Another element on her side is time. Simply stopping intercourse for a moment or two stops the stimulating impulses and allows the inhibitory ones to dominate. However since the real cause is emotional, the real treatment is psychiatric and anything else is simply a means of postponing the inevitable.

The next fear is, in some ways, the opposite of premature ejaculation.

Which one is that?

A man's fear that he will be unable to have another erection promptly after ejaculation. The best answer to that one is reality. Women must understand that they have a colossal advantage over men when it comes to orgasm. After his orgasm the sexual equipment of every male must recover before another orgasm is possible. In spite of his wishes or the demands of his girl, there is no erection, no insertion, and no ejaculation until the waiting period is over. Women, on the other hand, can go from one act of intercourse to another without even taking a deep breath. (It doesn't mean of course, that a woman will have an orgasm each and every time but she can at least go through the mechanics of copulation.) The woman who has as many as six or eight climaxes in a thirty minute period of intercourse may find it hard to understand why her partner has only one orgasm and has to wait forty-five minutes before he is even back in service again. That's just the difference between men and women.

Of course that explanation doesn't necessarily make men feel any better about it. They still suffer (and the word is *suffer*) from feelings of inferiority and anxiety about not being able to snap back as promptly as their buddies claim to be able to. (Most of the time their buddies do just as poorly—the difference is they lie better.)

Since there is no way a woman can change the physical design of men, her best bet is to adapt her feelings to her man's capacity. It doesn't do either of them any good if she wants to begin again in four minutes and his inner time clock is set for forty. Under those circumstances discretion is the better part of valor and it is best for the woman to let the minutes slip by gracefully. Some women however have a special problem that complicates things further.

What kind of problem?

They suffer from orgasmic impairment. Through no fault of their own, because of underlying emotional obstacles, they find it difficult or impossible to reach a climax during intercourse. The woman who never approaches orgasm, in some ways has fewer problems than the one who *almost* gets there after fifteen minutes of trying hard—only to have her partner ejaculate then and there and wipe out any hope of orgasm for her. Jan knows how frustrating it can be:

"You know, I used to tell myself, Doctor, 'If he could only keep it up another five minutes or so, I *know* I could have a climax!' And believe me, I've tried."

"What did you try?"

"Mostly things that didn't work. After Ed ejaculated, I would still be excited and I always tried to rush him to give it another try. I wanted to do it again before the feeling went away—I always thought it was just a matter of getting enough stimulation. It almost drove poor Ed out of his mind. He would try before he was ready—sometimes only ten minutes after we'd just had intercourse—and he was beginning to lose confidence in himself. He started saying things like, 'Gosh, Jan, maybe you need a man who can give you what you really need from sex.'"

"What happened then?"

"Something very strange. Ed had some high blood pressure or something and the doctor gave him some medicine. One of the side effects was he couldn't ejaculate—at all. He could have intercourse for an hour or even two hours without ever having a climax. And that's when I found out what orgasmic impairment is all about."

"What do you mean?"

"I would never have believed it if you had told me but even after an hour of sex—non-stop—I still felt as if all I needed was another five minutes to have an orgasm. It still didn't come. Then I realized it must be an emotional problem. I was just mentally postponing it each time until it was too late. Now I'm ready to get down to business and find out the real reason I can't get what I want from sex—and from Ed."

Then what can a woman do specifically to help a man over this fear?

She can simply reassure him by word and deed that she doesn't expect him to repeal the laws of human physiology. Sometimes a sentence or two is enough:

"Listen, Mel, why don't we just rest for an hour or so and then we'll both be able to enjoy it more." or

"Let me fix us a cup of coffee and we can try again in a few minutes."

The tactful lady will stretch a "few minutes" into about three quarters of an hour.

Under unusual circumstances, there are some men who are ready for intercourse again almost immediately. Especially in the early days of a new relationship or after a long separation (or sometimes without any obvious reason) potency returns promptly after ejaculation. Then the most appropriate response is for the girl to allow herself to be overruled by an insistent partner accompanied by an insistent erection.

What's the next sexual fear of men?

Not being able to satisfy a woman. After he passes the hurdles of obtaining and maintaining an erection, controlling the timing of his ejaculation, and responding again the next time around, a man may still be plagued by the gnawing fear that he is not really supplying his woman with what she wants out of sex. That's the reason so often men are compelled to ask a girl: "Did you . . . I mean, were you able to . . . uh, was it the way you wanted it?" In spite of the veneer of self-confidence that every male wears, deep inside there is still the feeling of competition with every other man when it comes to sexual prowess and technique.

The woman who wants to bring sexual happiness to her man (and herself) stops this fear before it starts. After intercourse she simply lets him know how much she enjoyed his efforts. Sometimes a look or a gesture is enough. For the man who needs more reassurance, a few words are sufficient. The key to success is to provide the encouragement *before* he asks. In this area, praise given voluntarily is ten times more valuable than the kind that has to be asked for.

What if the woman doesn't reach an orgasm?

Intercourse isn't a kind of sexual slot machine with the jackpot being awarded for super-sensational orgasms. The woman who withholds praise from her partner because she doesn't reach a climax is only compounding her problem. One essential ingredient in her sexual plan is a strong erection on the part of her partner. If she intensifies his sexual fears, her prospects for satisfaction will fade before they start. On the other hand, if she isn't attaining sexual gratification from most of her attempts at intercourse, both she and her man need to sit down for a frank discussion of their mutual problems. Most of the time those discussions are best held in the living room, the patio, or the psychiatrist's office—if it comes to that. The bedroom is probably the worst room in the house for a serious discussion of sexual problems.

Why is that?

The bedroom—and the bed—is the most emotionally charged setting any human being ever occupies. That is where humans are conceived, some of them are born, most of them get together sexually, and many of them die. The same words that can be spoken casually in the kitchen take on an ominous and sometimes overwhelming significance in the room where really serious things happen.

Does a woman have to reassure a man every time they have intercourse?

Well, he worries every time. If she is willing to tell him, convincingly, that he is, sexually, the only one for her she will be well on her way to making sure that *in every way* she is the only one for him. Which leads directly to the last major fear of male sexuality.

What's that?

The fear of being compared unfavorably with other men when it comes to the size of his penis, his potency, or his sexual skill. Nearly every man is haunted by the specter of being displaced by someone else who surpasses him sexually. The woman who makes this fear come true loses that man once and for all. No matter what she says or does, once she plants the seed of sexual insecurity in his mind, there is no turning back. The real tragedy is that the damage can be done unintentionally. Sometimes a word, a look, even a careless gesture, can strike a man in this most sensitive of all areas. Denise will never forget how it happened:

"I'd been going with Hal about six months and we were talking about getting married. We went away for a weekend to make our wedding plans and—well, I just don't know what got into me, Doctor. We'd just finished having intercourse and I noticed that one of Hal's testicles was much smaller than the other. I said to him, 'Gee, I never realized that you were built that way. Is everything all right?' It was like I plunged a knife into his heart. He turned around and there was real hatred in his eyes. He just got dressed, drove me back into the city at midnight, and I never saw him again. I cried for days and I still don't know why it hurt him so much."

Denise got her lesson in male anatomy too late to save her relationship with Hal but hopefully in time to avoid the same mistake the next time.

Generally one testicle appears larger than the other since it is carried lower in the scrotum. This is part of the asymmetry of the human body. (Females usually have one breast which is slightly larger than the other. This rarely upsets anyone except teenage girls when they first notice the difference and go-go dancers who sometimes get comments from the customers.)

Most men don't worry about the discrepancy in testicular size unless a woman points it out to them. Then they may panic, particularly if they have other problems at the same time.

Denise went on:

"I tried everything I could to make it up to Hal. I even went to see his mother to try and understand what had happened. After she told me about his childhood, I knew there was no chance. He had what they call 'undescended testicles.' Until he was about fourteen, they never came out of the abdomen into the scrotum and he was always afraid he wasn't going to be a man. He took shots for years and finally they came down but he never got over it. And of all things I had to ask him about *that!*"

Even more hazardous is any comment about the size of a man's penis.

Why is that?

All too many men still are sensitive to the myth that there is a connection between the size of a man's penis and his ability to satisfy a woman. They interpret any remark about the dimensions of this organ as a direct reflection on their manhood. Chuck was a good example:

"I know, Doctor, I shouldn't let something like this bother me but I just can't help it. I mean I've been around long enough to understand that the size of my penis has nothing to do with how I am sexually. But . . ."

"But?"

"But I still can't get away from it. The other night I was undressing in front of Carol, my girl, and she said, 'Gee, it sure looks small that way, doesn't it?' Well, I didn't have an erection or anything but I never thought of myself as small until then. And that night at least, I stayed small. In spite of anything Carol or I could do, there was no chance of getting an erection. My penis just lay there and sulked all evening. What can I do?"

"Why don't you have Carol come in and talk it over with me—if she wants to?"

About a week later Carol appeared as scheduled and went through a cram course in male sexuality.

The following week Chuck arrived for his appointment, beaming.

"Well, Doctor, I don't know what you taught Carol, but I learned a lot myself."

"For example."

"For one thing, I always suspected—but I never could be sure—that the size of the penis in its relaxed state has no relation to its length when it's erect. I mean, even if a man looks small to start with he may be normal or even larger after erection. She told me how you explained that in some men, before erection, most of the penis is retracted into the body, making it appear to be undersized. Those men whose penises are all outside the body appear to be more generously endowed. When erection occurs, everything is out there where it belongs. But the next part is the best."

"Which part is that?"

"That's the part that Carol told me privately—the part she *didn't* learn from you. She let me in on a secret of female sexuality that really blew my mind. And since then, my potency has never been better!"

"What did she say?"

"Nothing really medical, but it did the trick. After she explained everything that you told her she leaned over to me and whispered, 'Anyhow, honey, a girl would rather be tickled than choked . . .'"

Even more damaging is any criticism of a man's potency.

How come?

Because to a man, potency is a sexual never-never land. When it comes right down to it, no man really knows what a satisfactory standard of sexual performance is. Is it three times a week or three times a night? Can he satisfy a woman better by having intercourse with her twice for thirty minutes each time or once for sixty minutes or four times at fifteen minutes? Were the other men in her life better or worse? Is she really satisfied with his sexual abilities or just too considerate to tell him the truth? No man can ever be sure of the answers to these questions—he places his total sexual confidence in the hands of his woman —and only *she* knows.

The woman who really wants to find lasting sexual satisfaction will tell her man what he needs to know in the way he needs to know it.

How does she do that?

By telling the truth *subjectively*. If she insists on providing a *scientifically accurate* answer to each of his questions, it might go something like this:

Man: Well, was it all right for you this time?

Woman: To tell the *truth*, I thought you slowed down too much at the end. When I was married before my husband was a lot better at it. I think he had harder erections too.

Man: (turning pale) Gee, maybe there's something wrong with me.

If there isn't something wrong with him then, there will be the next time he tries to have an erection with the lady scorekeeper who shares his bed with him.

How does a woman tell the truth subjectively?

By being honest without making unnecessarily painful comparisons. Sex after all is not mechanical and computerized (at least not yet) and emotional feelings still mean more than making all the orgasmic lights flash every single night. For example:

Man: Well, how was it this time?

Woman: (leaning over and kissing him) Wonderful! Just wonderful!

Man: (glowing) That's good. Maybe I can even do better next time.

While, strictly speaking, his erection may have only been seventy percent as hard as seven sessions ago and her orgasm may have registered only six on a scale of ten, by reacting positively and with encouragement, the woman almost guarantees that he *will* do better next time. When it comes to sexual intercourse, in a sense, the man is the manufacturer and the woman is the consumer. By receiving his product with enthusiasm, she encourages him to constantly improve it.

What about sexual skill?

One of the best-kept secrets of all time is the real value of "skill" in lovemaking. Over the centuries thousands of books have been published describing in agonizing detail various positions, maneuvers, flexions, rotations, and permutations guaranteed to result in super-stereophonic psychedelic sex. As generations of eager readers have discovered to their dismay, there is one little defect in the cookbook approach to sex—it just doesn't work. The center of all sexual feeling is the brain—not the genitalia. The sexual organs themselves—penis, vagina, and clitoris—are no more than sensitive receptors which perceive changes in touch and pressure during intercourse and transmit them to the brain. Strangely enough, the genitals don't even have to be stimulated for orgasm to occur. As every man—and many women—know, a sexual climax can occur spontaneously during sleep where the sexual organs aren't even involved—the entire cycle of reflexes begins and ends in the brain. Thus the whole concept of solving sexual problems by caressing the penis or manipulating the clitoris according to instructions is doomed to failure *with one vital exception.*

What is the exception?

If the participants interpret the emphasis on technique as an earnest attempt to please one another, it can make a difference. Symbolically, the woman who takes the time and effort to bring greater enjoyment to her man will end up stimulating him sexually. Not so much because she has pressed the right buttons at the right times but because he responds emotionally to her extraordinary display of affection and understanding.

On the other hand if a television set is tuned to the wrong channel, no amount of manipulating the antenna can set things right. Even the most exciting and sexually skillful man alive cannot satisfy a woman unless they are both on the same emotional wavelength. Erotic ecstasy depends not so much on what the couple *feels as how they feel about each other.* Unless they share true sexual excitement—which is ninety-nine percent emotional—no set of massage lessons, no matter how scientific, will bring them true satisfaction.

Once a woman realizes the full enjoyment of sex is substantially independent of sexual technique she can stop searching for "magic fingers" and settle down to enjoy the relationship with her man. The confidence that this realization brings makes it possible for her to reassure and encourage her partner and prevent him from falling prey to the fear that he is depriving her of that last little tingle. It can also help her deal with the problems of impotence.

What's the most common form of impotence?

Premature ejaculation takes the dubious honor. It is also the form of impotence that most dramatically underscores the emotional basis for sexual failure. The man with early ejaculation is normal in every other way—he has a good erection, intense sexual excitement, and performs well. Too well. Some men with this condition may respond dramatically to a sympathetic woman but sooner or later their difficulty is bound to return unless they are willing to face the problem where it begins and ends—within their own mind.

What about a man with copulatory impotence?

The man who loses his erection either before intercourse starts or after intercourse begins but prior to ejaculation *superficially* suffers from a lack of sexual stimulation. Either he is not receiving enough excitatory impulses from the brain or he is originating enough negative impulses to block erection. Almost invariably this condition is a result of his own underlying emotional problems *but* his woman can help by increasing the intensity of the external sexual stimulation.

How does she do that?

By understanding a little twist of male sexual behavior. Going back to the fifth fear of male sexuality,
fear of being unable to satisfy a woman, one of the
most exciting experiences a man can have sexually is
"turning a woman on." Every psychiatrist, every pros-
titute, and every producer of pornographic films understands this clearly. The most successful prostitutes
simulate a lady being driven out of her mind with
wild passion. (It isn't easy, as those girls who do it
twenty times a night will wearily testify.) But the
gent whose wife or girl friend receives him with all
the enthusiasm reserved for a headache commercial
appreciates every little wiggle and moan that he
thinks he is responsible for. The most successful pornographic films depict a relatively sedate female gradually being whipped up into an erotic frenzy by an
obviously delighted gentleman. Virtually any woman
who understands this can treat many forms of copulatory impotence successfully in the privacy of her
own bedroom.

Specifically what does she do?

Everything she possibly can to intensify that flood of
stimulation from the outside to the brain and thence
from the brain to the spinal cord. It all begins with
direct touch stimulation to the sexual organs. As usual,
there is no magic technique, no "secret genital hand-
shake." What a woman *does* is not as important as the
fact that *she cares enough to do it*. Given the encouragement, most men will tell a woman exactly

what they want done and where. The penis, scrotum, the perineum (just behind the scrotum) can all be amazingly responsive under the right circumstances.

The woman who takes her man's hand and places it over her clitoral and vaginal area may be rewarded by seeing him have an immediate erection. Merely the *idea* that she wants to be excited by him is almost unbearably exciting to him. In the same way, if she takes one of her breasts and gently places the nipple in his mouth, many reluctant penises lose their reluctance at that specific moment.

Does this approach work every time?

No. In sexuality, nothing works every time. Precisely because human beings are not machines, repeating the same old manipulations over and over again is doomed to failure. But there is no cause to be concerned. Because of the tremendous range of heterosexual activity, no two experiences of intercourse need be identical. This is where oral sex can play a role.

Is it all right to do that sort of thing?

That is a decision everyone has to make for herself. Apparently most men and women have decided it is all right because at least seventy percent of those past the age of puberty engage in cunnilingus and/or fellatio.

Isn't that dirty?

Not really. The normal human mouth contains far more deadly bacteria than either the normal penis or vagina. Strictly from a medical point of view, mouth-penis and mouth-vagina contact is far more hygienic than mouth-to-mouth sex. But of course there are more considerations than bacteriology.

What are they?

First, the potential that oral sex has for helping a man who is impotent. A woman who adds fellatio—or stimulating a man's penis with her mouth, lips, and tongue—to her sexual repertoire usually finds that it makes a dramatic difference in her partner's ability to obtain and maintain an erection. The very fact that mouth-penis activities have a "forbidden" quality for most people adds to their allure and drives the man's brain to wildly intensify the impulses to the erection and orgasmic centers in the spinal cord.

Second, cunnilingus—mouth-clitoral or less commonly, mouth-vagina activity—has an almost explosive effect on male potency. But the effect is intensely magnified if the woman follows the most erotically satisfying sequence.

Which sequence is that?

If during the preliminary stages of intercourse she gently guides her partner's head toward her clitoris while nudging her pubic area toward him, virtually every man will react with an erection. The idea that his woman eagerly wants him to do what he may even have been afraid to suggest is overwhelming. As the woman becomes sexually excited in response to this very direct stimulation, he will find that her excitement *excites* him. If she gently stimulates his penis with her fingers simultaneously, a durable, firm erection is virtually assured.

Shouldn't she take his penis into her mouth at the same time?

If he really has problems getting or keeping an erection, probably not. As most women suspect, the penis is not nearly as sensitive to touch as the clitoris or labia and can respond better to pressure and friction from the fingers. Some impotent men find fellatio at that moment too distracting. There is also a practical problem.

What's that?

A woman who is performing fellatio can't do something even more exciting at the same time. She can't talk with her mouth full.

There is no rule that says intercourse must be conducted in complete silence. If a lady constantly (or from time to time, as the case may be) tells her partner how good he is making her feel and what she wants him to do next and what she is going to do to *him* next, their mutual sexual feelings can only intensify. The wonderfully exciting sighs and moans and insistent requests as orgasm approaches play an essential role in maintaining a man at maximum sexual performance.

Then is fellatio really a good idea at all?

It certainly has its place as a sexual preliminary and there is one important fringe benefit. It is the only method of exciting a man that *partially* by-passes the brain and works directly on the penis to produce an erection. As a result, the woman who uses fellatio in a particular way can often cause an erection in a man who would otherwise be totally impotent.

How does it work?

It has been known for years that placing the non-erect penis in a partial vacuum quickly brings on an erection. Blood is drawn into the collapsed veins and venous sinuses of the organ and erection ensues. A woman who is willing to put forth the effort can frequently produce the same result.

If she places her mouth firmly over the penis and produces a strong suction, followed immediately by complete relaxation, the penis should immediately enlarge slightly. As she continues, alternately increasing and decreasing the suction, both participants may be rewarded with a relatively good erection. As one young lady said, "Doctor, it isn't the same artificial respiration I learned in First Aid Class, but under certain circumstances, it can be life-saving."

Is there anything else a woman can do for this type of impotency?

Yes. Once a satisfactory erection appears, she can guide the penis gently and swiftly into the vagina. Active pelvic thrusts on her part will stimulate the brain at the same time the vagina is stimulating the penis. Every man wants to feel that his woman is eagerly interested in what he is doing and not just waiting until he is finished so she can watch the eleven o'clock news. If the erection begins to falter after intercourse begins there are a few other possibilities.

For example?

She can carefully close her legs and gently squeeze the vagina around the penis. She can reach around and stimulate the testicles and perineum with her fingers while everything else is going on. And most important, at any time she can do any of the thousands of little things that will spontaneously occur to her during the exhilaration of intercourse.

In dealing with impotence, success breeds success and in spite of the basic emotional conflicts that bring it on, the man whose woman helps him overcome it may gradually find—to his surprise and amazement— that his condition has one day just disappeared.

What about absolute impotence?

The man who, in spite of everything just can't get an erection before intercourse, suffers from absolute impotence. Most of these men have gone through hours and hours of having their penises manipulated—without any real results. The only trouble is the stimulation is being applied at the wrong end—it's the brain that needs the excitement. Most men with absolute impotence will find that the wisest—and most rewarding—solution is to find a psychiatrist who understands their problem and is eager to help them. After the man and doctor begin to make *some* progress, the woman can make her contribution. As usual in sexual matters, there is always the exception.

What's that?

The morning erection. The majority of men with absolute impotence awake at least occasionally with a firm, sometimes even rigid erection. For a long time this was considered to be a reflex response to the full bladder that accumulates during the night. Actually the erection is the result of night-long unconscious sexual fantasies. Most men awaken, get up and urinate, and usually by the time they are back in bed the penis is fast asleep too.

An otherwise impotent man who awakens with a morning erection sometimes can strike a decisive blow for potency by having intercourse then and there. If his woman is cooperative—and for her own benefit she should be—with a minimum of preliminaries the penis should find its way into the vagina. Vigorous intercourse with ejaculation following as rapidly as possible is essential.

Why is it so important to hurry?

Because almost every man with absolute impotence also is absolutely despondent. He usually has given up hope of ever having normal intercourse. By proving to him that fully satisfying intercourse is possible, his woman can break the chains of despair that bind down his potency. Having super-instant sex a few times in the early morning or even in the middle of the night is a small price to pay if it will help a man to ultimately give the woman what she wants—any time.

Is there anything a woman can do for a man with retarded ejaculation?

Not really. This relatively rare condition is particularly resistant to the kinds of things a woman can do herself. On the bright side it usually responds fairly quickly to treatment by a psychiatrist who understands the underlying emotional condition.

Then it's really worthwhile for a woman to go to all this trouble just to help a man sexually?

No, if she were just going to help a man *sexually*. The woman who restores a man to top sexual performance is also helping to restore him to normal emotional functioning. And most important of all, she is providing herself with a sexual and emotional partner who is perfectly attuned to her needs, her hopes, and her desires. And that, after all, is what the relationship between men and women is really about.

15

SEXUALLY MAROONED
MARRIED WOMEN

Do married women get sexually marooned too?

It can happen. As every girl who has read the fine print in the marriage license knows, there is no guarantee of sexual satisfaction or your two dollars back. The basic challenge of finding sexual happiness is the same after marriage as it was before. Unless a woman is constantly alert, getting married may be nothing more than an expensive way to ruin a beautiful (sexual) relationship. Claire knows how it feels:

"Doctor, if anyone told me that a wedding would change sex from a pleasure into a chore, I wouldn't have believed it. I still can't believe it but it's happening to me."

"What do you mean?"

"Well, Norm and I have only been married eleven months and we're starting to taper off already. On our honeymoon, we had intercourse twice a day at least and sometimes more. I never knew people could do it that much!" Claire's cheeks reddened. Then she frowned.

"And now we do it so little! First it went down to once a day, then a couple of times a week and I fig-

ured it out last night—if it keeps petering out the
way it is, in seven weeks we just won't be doing it
any more. I thought things would be different!"

"Different in what way?"

"I knew having a happy marriage wasn't easy but I
thought I could at least have all the sex I wanted. I
mean I didn't go through that big ceremony to do
what I'm doing—I mean what I'm not doing—I could
have just gone into a convent or something!" Claire
threw up her hands.

Is Claire's case unusual?

Not really. Many women alone are dismayed to find
that getting married isn't the final solution to all their
sexual problems. Unless they are constantly alert they
may simply exchange old familiar problems for new
and more baffling ones. The unique feature that can
make marriage so attractive before the wedding can
make it so frustrating afterward.

What feature is that?

Sexual exclusivity. From the wedding day onward
both husband and wife agree to restrict *all* their sexual activities to each other. The wife grants the husband a total monopoly on her sexual services and the
husband dedicates his entire sexual production to his
wife. The marriage ceremony is actually a tight little
legal agreement with no loopholes. The language is
precise and unmistakable: "Till death do us part!"

In a sense every honeymoon is a mental trip to Las
Vegas. When they plunk down the two dollars for the
marriage license, blushing bride and self-conscious

groom are really betting all their chips on each other —sort of a turn of the sexual roulette wheel. If they win they win big—a lifetime of mutual sexual happiness. If they lose, a woman may find herself more sexually marooned than when she was fifteen years old.

Why is that?

At least at the age of fifteen she could tell herself it was only a matter of time before she found sexual happiness. But if she's twenty-three, married, and unable to make sex work the way it should, excuses are harder to find. It doesn't help any when she thinks back and realizes how much time and effort she devoted to the selection of her brand new husband.

There's another "advantage" of being married that can work against her too.

What's that?

The fact that marriage puts the stamp of social approval on sex. For so many people the most exciting word in the language is "forbidden." When sex had to be snatched in secret moments in the back of a car; when intercourse was only possible in a five dollar motel on the outskirts of town, every sensation was supercharged. The fellow who couldn't wait to get his hands on his girl friend on a date, now that he's married can't wait to get his hands on the evening paper. Sex before marriage was an exciting contrast to the hum-drum pressures of daily life. After marriage, unless a woman is vigilant, sex can become just another of the demands of matrimony.

As one young lady complained, "All I did was walk down the aisle in a long white dress and suddenly sex changes from something that blows your mind into just another item on the list of things I've been putting off all week!" When that happens, a woman is well on her way to becoming sexually marooned . . . though married. But there's a brighter side too.

What's that?

For the girl who isn't willing to let matters take their course, marriage gives some unique sexual opportunities as well. The principle of sexual exclusivity can work in her favor by freeing her from the anxiety of sexual competition with other women and giving her a chance to forge a permanent emotional link with her man through sex. In the bargain she also receives (hopefully) a long-term sexual partner who will enthusiastically cooperate in making sex best for both of them. If she is really lucky she can get the most important ingredient of them all: love. This most profound and durable of all emotional bonds gives sexuality relevance and meaning and can make each successive sexual experience better than the one before.

When should a married woman suspect that she might become sexually marooned?

If she waits until the final stages of marooning, the condition will diagnose itself. But by then it's often late to do anything about it. To be able to do herself the most good she has to pinpoint the problem before it gets out of hand. There are some obvious danger signals that she can be alert for. If her husband shows any of the following six signs, her sexual future can be in jeopardy:

1. "Too tired" at bedtime to do anything but drop off to sleep.
2. Fascination with the late late movie on television which keeps him up until his wife is safely in dreamland.
3. An unusual interest in his job requiring overtime, night work, or extended trips.
4. A preference for twin beds after several years of sleeping in a double bed.
5. Sudden criticism of his wife's sexual responses.
6. Subtle neglect of his personal appearance.

Most women detect these changes promptly and immediately misinterpret them.

How do they misinterpret them?

They put the cart before the horse, sexually speaking. They assume the reason for their husband's indifference is another woman. It usually doesn't work that way. *First* he loses interest in his most convenient source of sexual gratification, his wife. *Then*, when his sexual deprivation becomes acutely uncomfortable, he goes to the trouble of looking elsewhere. To the average man, arranging a little sexual action on the side is expensive, time-consuming, and demanding. Listen to how one fellow feels about it:

Earl is thirty-one and has been married six years.

"Listen, Doctor, looking back on it, I never really wanted to do it. If Ethel hadn't cut me off every time she got mad at me—and that turned out to be most of the time—do you think I'd get into the mess I'm in now? I'm an accountant and I know how to figure out how much things cost. I've been seeing Sherri for six months now and I've had to put out almost $2,000—$1,845.00 to be exact, plus a few odd cents. You know when you have a girl on the side she expects a little extra attention. Besides Sherri's a model and has good taste." He nodded approvingly.

"Did you get your money's worth?"

Earl thought a moment. Then he shook his head. "Taking everything into consideration, I don't think so. I took Sherri to a lot of places that made three or four hundred percent on the food and five hundred percent on the drinks. That's too much. Besides in six months I've had intercourse with her thirteen times. That works out to $141.92 each time—I think that's really out of line."

"You do?"

"I know, you're going to say we accountants measure everything in money but it's not true. I just like to know what I'm spending. Besides it was such a nuisance making up all those excuses and taking cabs everywhere when I've got two cars. But the reason I'm here has nothing to do with money at all."

"What is it?"

"I love my wife and I'd rather find a way to be happy with her. That's why I got married in the first place." Earl thought for a moment, then added, "Besides, playing around isn't as much fun as I thought it would be."

Once sexual marooning occurs every woman knows for sure.

How does she know?

Basically sexual marooning happens when a woman wants intercourse more often than her husband is willing to supply it. There are, of course, exceptions. The young lady was in her early twenties, very pretty and very upset:

"Doctor, I'm sure that I'm sexually marooned and I just don't know what to do about it. I've only been married two months and I don't want it to get out of control."

"What seems to be the problem?"

"Well, I enjoy sex at least three times every night and my husband can only do it twice. What should I do?"

The best course for that anxious newlywed was to count her blessings. The object of sex in marriage (or anywhere else) is not to squeeze the maximum number of orgasms into the minimum number of minutes. One satisfying sexual experience each night is better than three before breakfast just to fill up the record books.

Generally speaking when sexual intercourse happens less than once a week a woman can count herself among the sexually deprived. Just as important is the quality of the sexual relationship. If a woman finds intercourse unrewarding more than fifty percent of the time, she is being short-changed sexually.

What can a married woman do to avoid becoming sexually marooned?

The very best tactic is to stop it before it starts. The majority of wives who find themselves stranded sexually have been willing (perhaps unconsciously) partners in the crime. Rosemary explains it clearly; she is about thirty-five, attractive and neatly dressed.

"Oh, Doctor, if I only knew ten years ago what I know now!" She squirmed uncomfortably in her chair.

"What do you mean?"

"I mean I threw away any chance I ever had for enjoying sex and I did it because I was stupid!" Tears streamed down both cheeks. Rosemary shook her head. "I'm sorry, I don't mean to cry but it was all my fault."

"Let's see what really happened, shall we?"

She wiped her eyes quickly and continued. "My mother told me, from the time I was six years old that sex was nasty and dirty. She used to warn me all the time, 'Never let any man use you for his own lust!'"

Rosemary smiled weakly. "And that, Doctor, was only the beginning. So when I married Sandy, my husband, ten years ago, I was perfectly programmed for failure. Oh, I did all right for the first few months. I had the sexual feelings of all those years dammed up inside me and I just let myself go. I was the way a wife should be—I was ready any time for anything. And I enjoyed it. I guess that was the problem. After about six months I started feeling guilty and I'd find little excuses for not having any sex. I don't have to go into details—I'm sure every woman uses the same dreary alibis. I kept remembering more and more what my mother had told me and it really poisoned my mind. And when we did have intercourse, I would only let Sandy touch me through my pajamas. It got to the point where he and I were really hating each other. I was afraid he was going to ask for sex and he was afraid I was going to turn him down. It wasn't a very exciting relationship. Then the inevitable happened."

"Another woman?"

"Of course. I was surprised it took him so long to get around to it. He endured my stupidity more than two years—I don't think we had intercourse two dozen times in that period. At first I was relieved, then I got depressed, and now I'm furious!"

"At him?"

Rosemary shook her head sadly. "No, Doctor. That would be too easy, wouldn't it? I'm furious at myself because it's my fault. My mother was wrong about so many other things, why should she have been right about sex? If her sex life was dirty and nasty it was because she made it that way. I know how wonderful sex can be because for the first year of my marriage that's how it was. Now what can *I* do about it?"

It took Rosemary a long time and a lot of suffering to bring herself to face sexual reality in her marriage. The deep wound of sexual marooning she suffered was self-inflicted. She happened to use the excuse of her childhood experiences but when a woman decides (even unconsciously) to exile herself sexually from her husband, there is never a shortage of justifications.

For example?

The list is as long as the Tokyo telephone directory. Sometimes the wife "just doesn't feel like it tonight" —and every night. Occasionally a woman suddenly becomes hypersensitive to the presence of her children or in-laws in the house during intercourse. Ted has a typical complaint:

"Listen, Doctor, what do I have to do, take my wife to the moon?"

"For what?"

"To have a chance for some sex. Even if the kids are asleep and all the doors are locked, Ellen keeps telling me, 'What if somebody hears us?' Most of the time she won't even let me get started and if I do she stops me just at the wrong time and whispers, 'Shhh! Wait a minute—you're making too much noise!' What can I do? Insulate myself with foam rubber? I mean, it has to make *some* noise. It seems a little phony to me anyhow, Doc. Before we got married you could've heard her in the next county. Now she wants it sound-proofed!"

Sometimes a woman who doesn't want to say "no" simply engages in sexual guerrilla warfare. Some of the techniques are ingenious. A woman with four children may wait until a moment before her husband reaches his orgasm to ask: "Do you remember if I took my birth control pill tonight, honey?" Almost as effective is the lady who at the most passionate moment clutches her husband's arm and whispers loudly, "Henry, I think somebody's trying to break in downstairs!"

In his own fumbling way, Henry was trying to break in downstairs but he will soon give up and another wife will be sexually marooned at her own request.

How does a woman avoid this kind of situation?

By using "the wives' secret weapon"—only it isn't that much of a secret. In the basic writings of every religion (Moselm, Christian, Jewish, Buddhist, and Hindu, among others) there is a reminder to wives never to refuse their husbands sexually. Long before modern psychiatry, wise and observant religious and cultural leaders recognized that self-styled sexual marooning was the first step in the deterioration of the family. In some religions the wife who arranges to have intercourse with her husband *every* night is singled out for special praise and respect. Although not every modern woman may be motivated to go that far, it makes sense for her to at least be available whenever her husband needs her.

Should a wife have intercourse even if she doesn't feel like it?

That's a tough question. If a woman sincerely expects her husband to get his sexual satisfaction from her exclusively, it seems only fair that she deliver what she has promised. It's something like a hotel that guarantees room and meals to its customers, shuts down the kitchen without notice and then complains when the guests go across the street and eat in a cafeteria.

As one husband put it, "I don't know what my wife thinks I am. When I need sex and she won't give it to me, what am I supposed to do? Go out behind the wood shed and masturbate like I did when I was twelve? If she doesn't want me to run around with another woman, she has to keep me occupied at home. I know I'm forty-four but I'm not ready to take the oath of chastity just yet."

The most effective weapon any woman has to guarantee her husband's sexual loyalty is keeping his sexual tension at the lowest possible level. If he finds constant satisfaction at home he will be unlikely (and from a physiological point of view, *unable*) to find it elsewhere.

*Then all a wife has to do is make herself sexually
available every single night?*

Not quite. She must live up to the spirit as well as the
letter of the sexual part of the marriage agreement.
Ted had other problems besides the acoustical ones:

"Finally Ellen got over her idea that we were having sex in an echo chamber. The next deal was, 'You
can have me anytime you want but don't expect me
to get involved.' It was sort of, 'Here, take my un-
resisting body and do what you will with it.' It was
about as exciting as making mad love to one of those
life-size inflatable dolls. I kept wondering when she
was going to spring a leak and go flat on me."

On the other hand that doesn't mean that the ideal
wife has to dress each night as a Roman slave girl and
help her husband re-enact his adolescent fantasies.

What's the solution?

Sexual intercourse in marriage is a warm spontaneous
communication between comrades in life. It is the
most expressive way of saying, "I love you." A woman
who wants to succeed as a wife will use every bit of
her knowledge and determination to make sure that
nothing interferes with the rhichness and fullness of
her sexual relationship with her husband. Sometimes
it can be a hard job.

In what way?

Besides self-inflicted marooning, there are many other
obstacles to sexual satisfaction for a married woman—
some of which she never even knew existed when she

was single. One of the common problems is geographical marooning. Some husbands have jobs or businesses that compel them to be away from home for weeks or months at a time. The solution is hard and easy at the same time.

What is it?

So far no one has invented a way to have sexual intercourse by mental telepathy. For sex to happen the parties have to at least be in the same room. If it comes down to a choice between sexual marooning and a job that requires constant traveling, unless the wife is willing to give up sex, the job has to go. Fortunately there are few occupations that can compete successfully with sexual intercourse.

You mean a man should give up a good job just to have more sex with his wife?

A job is only a place to work. If husband and/or wife are being deprived of the most important part of their marriage, what good is the best job in the world— and all the money that goes with it? Besides the alternatives aren't particularly attractive.

What are the alternatives?

For the husband and wife, they are pretty much the same. For the man, masturbating in a hotel room while his wife masturbates in an empty house leaves a lot to be desired. Another possibility—sexual opportunism —is probably even less attractive. More traveling husbands than anyone realizes have an "arrangement" with their wives. When the husband is traveling he takes his sexual satisfaction where he can find it. With his wife's knowledge and permission, he picks up young (and not so young) ladies in bars, cocktail lounges, and other assorted establishments.

Why does a wife allow this?

Most wives who agree to this arrangement feel they are being understanding and cooperative. Maybe so, but there is such a thing as being *too* understanding. Equal sexual rights for the lady of the house would require her to dispense her favors generously to parking lot attendants, delivery boys, and the old man who cuts the lawn—at least until her husband gets back. Few men are *that* understanding. For the woman who is unwilling to share her husband with the hat check girl, there are some effective solutions.

What can she do?

She can do what Beth did. Beth is thirty-seven, dark, and slender. She is wearing a pale blue pants suit and smile.

"You seem happy today."

The smile brightened. "A couple of months ago, Doctor, nothing could have made me smile. But I've learned a lot since then."

"For example?"

"Well, the most important thing is a woman doesn't have to accept things as they are—especially when it comes to sex. If she uses her wits, she can make things any way she wants them. *I know*." Beth set her jaw firmly.

"What happened?"

"Herb, that's my husband, is chief auditor for a national company. He's worked for them since we were married fifteen years ago. For the past four years he's had to travel about one week out of every month.

"At first it wasn't so bad but about a year ago I was unpacking for him after a trip and I found a woman's panties in his suitcase. Well, we had a big argument and finally he admitted being with other women on his trips. He said he couldn't get along without any sex at all for that long a time and that was that. I didn't want to break up my marriage—I mean, everything else was fine so, like a dope, I gave in. I just told him never to mention it to me again. And to unpack his own suitcases."

"Did he ever mention it again?"

"Yes and no. He never said a word but three months ago I—well, I'll just say it. He brought home a case of gonorrhea. That was just too ugly! I threatened everything but he was adamant. He apologized but all he would do was promise to be more careful next time. And I decided there wasn't going to be a next time."

"What did you do?"

"I planned a little melodrama. Maybe it was cruel but I felt I was fighting to save my marriage. I love Herb, but Doctor—*gonorrhea?*" Beth shook her head emphatically.

"When he got home from the next trip there were a few surprises for him. It took me the whole afternoon to prepare but it was worth it. When he came in the door, I was wearing my tightest jump suit and I made sure it wasn't quite zipped up. When he put his arms around me he noticed my bra was unhooked in the back. He got a kind of funny look on his face but he didn't say anything. Then he saw the cigar ashes in the ash tray—he doesn't smoke—and he looked at me. He realized my lipstick was smeared—he'd been too shocked to kiss me himself. By that time he was in a daze and he sat down. That's what I'd been waiting for."

"What happened then?"

"Nick, the boy who works at the gas station—he's about nineteen—came in the back door. For some reason, he and Herb never got along."

Beth began to laugh. "I know I shouldn't laugh but Nick said his lines so perfectly! He rushed in the door and yelled, 'Hey, Beth-Baby, turn back the sheets! Your lover-boy is here again!' I thought Herb would faint! His face got bright red, Nick, according to plan, raced out the back door and Herb just sat there gnashing his teeth. It was beautiful!"

"Then what happened?"

"Nothing. It was a quiet weekend. Monday, Herb left for work early and called me at lunch time very nonchalant—or I should say, *imitation* nonchalant. He said, 'Listen, Beth, I've got great news. I've just been made vice-president in charge of accounting. Why don't we go out to dinner tonight and celebrate? Oh, and by the way, that means no more traveling.' I couldn't resist it, Doctor. I guess it was revenge that made me do it."

"What did you do?"

"I said, 'Why that's wonderful! I'll see you tonight, Nick, I mean *Herb!*'"

The wedding ceremony stipulates, "To have and to *hold* and "to hold" doesn't mean by proxy.

Can't marooning sometimes be a physical problem?

It certainly can. A good example is menstruation. The average woman, if her period lasts six days and comes every thirty days, spends at lest twenty percent of her time menstruating. If she and her husband refuse to consider intercourse during her period, she condemns herself to being sexually marooned during one-fifth of her life. In a certain sense, she never functions fully sexually until the menopause. There is another complication. For reasons no one really understands, many women feel their strongest sexual urges during their periods. The time when they need sex the most is just when they are denied it.

Should a woman have intercourse during her period?

She and her husband have to make up their own minds about that. But they deserve to know the scientific facts.

Menstruation is a normal event in the life of every woman. Instead of being the "curse of womankind" or "the monthly sickness," it is a sign of glowing good health. The time to start worrying, as every single girl knows, is if a period *doesn't* come. The menstrual flow is *not* blood. It is a combination of mucus, clots, and tissue fluid mixed with coagulated blood. It is so harmless that some primitive tribes administer it as medicine. Even the Bible does not prohibit intercourse during the menstrual period. The line that refers to it, Leviticus 15:19, says, "And if a woman have an issue, *and* her issue in her flesh be blood, she shall be put apart seven days: and whosoever toucheth her shall be unclean until the even." Assuming "her issue in her flesh be blood" really means menstruation, intercourse is not actually condemned. A man who has intercourse under these circumstances is merely considered unclean until that evening. If a woman and her husband want to have intercourse during menstruation there is really no reason for them to hold back.

What if a woman doesn't want to have intercourse then?

Then she still doesn't have to go into sexual mothballs one week a month. If she has strong sexual feelings, there are other ways to reach a climax besides intercourse itself. It also makes sense for her to make sure her husband isn't marooned in the process. After all, *he* isn't menstruating. The same principle applies to pregnancy.

When should a pregnant woman stop having sex?

She never has to stop. Although most physicians solemnly instruct their patients to avoid intercourse during the last two months or so before delivery, many women keep going until the night they leave for the hospital to have the baby. Theoretically intercourse can cause all kinds of complications in the final weeks of pregnancy; actually few problems ever develop.

As in most sexual situations, it's a matter of individual choice based on sound information plus consultation with the family physician. For those who don't feel right about intercourse but still want sex, there are other ways. Masturbation, fellatio, and cunnilingus are reasonable temporary substitutes. There is however a word of caution about oral sex during pregnancy.

What's that?

The husband must be very careful not to force air into his wife's vagina in the process if she is pregnant. In rare instances it can find its way into the uterus and cause air bubbles (air embolism) to form in the bloodstream. While the possibility is remote the results can be disastrous—sudden death.

Is sex during pregnancy really so important?

Yes, it is—and in more ways than one. When they are pregnant a lot of women need more sex rather than less.

From time to time during her nine months of waiting around a prospective mother may feel awkward, unattractive, and unsexy—not to mention somewhat overweight. To her, sexual intercourse takes on an additional and important meaning. It emerges as undeniable proof that her husband still loves her, wants her, and needs her.

Some women go even further. Pregnancy for them sets off a tremendous surge of sexual desire unlike anything they have ever experienced before. Everything is suddenly intensified—all the way from fantasies to sensational orgasms. Many of those women who purr, "I just *love* to be pregnant," look forward more to the "love" than to the pregnancy.

Of course there is the exception to every rule.

What's the exception?

The few women who have the opposite reaction. From the moment of their first missed period, they are totally indifferent to sex in any form. Like the queen bee, once they are fertilized, they couldn't care less about sex. While that may be a reasonable reaction in the case of unwed mothers, it doesn't do a thing for the father of the child. For most husbands nine months of enforced abstinence is not the reward they expected for their part in the project.

What should a woman do?

It's up to her. But a compassionate wife will be sure to make some provisions for filling her husband's needs. Most men have a hard enough time adjusting to the idea of fatherhood without having to worry about where their next orgasm is coming from. Besides, no pregnant lady wants to have a sexually-starved husband wandering the countryside. A foresighted woman will look to the future as well. After the baby arrives her own sexual feelings will return and hopefully her husband will repay her generously for her help in his time of need. By then she may need him more than ever.

Why?

Because many women experience a dramatic increase in both sexual desire and enjoyment of intercourse after the baby arrives. The higher sex hormone level and ample blood supply to the sexual organs during pregnancy may have something to do with it. If a woman enjoyed sex before she got pregnant, there is a good chance she will enjoy it twice as much after her first child.

One pregnant lady who heard that information said, "Doctor, I'm going to write that on my jar of prenatal vitamins."

"Why?"

"So when I get to the ninth month and feel like a

herd of hippopotamuses, at least I'll know it's all going to be worth while."

What's the most common cause of sexual marooning in marriage?

Malfunction of the most important sexual organ of them all—the human mind. If the penis and vagina were somehow disconnected from the brain, copulation would be mechanical, uninteresting, and probably very efficient. Erection, ejaculation, and simultaneous orgasm could occur automatically according to schedule. But it wouldn't be any fun. The only part of sex that has any potential for human happiness is the part that goes on above the eyebrows. Ironically that's the same place that sexual satisfaction can be sabotaged. When the sexual function of human beings is taken over by the unconscious mind (and sometimes the conscious mind) and forged into a weapon, any chance of happiness goes down the drain. If the penis becomes a sword and the vagina becomes a bear trap, then sexual intercourse becomes a case of making war, not love.

How does something like that happen?

Insidiously. For some women sexual marooning in marriage begins long before the wedding day. The girl who never can bring herself to see marriage as it really is, can also never bring herself to see sex as it really is. The young lady who anticipates that wedding bells signal the beginning of one long Saturday night—lasting about twenty years—finds that Monday morning comes in about two weeks with a pile of dishes in the sink and laundry in the wash tub. Sometimes she expresses her shock and dismay in bed that same night. Lloyd remembers it well:

"I guess I just wasn't prepared for something like that, Doctor. During the engagement and the wedding and the honeymoon, Joy was wonderful. As long as we were splashing in the heart-shaped bath tub or making love in the king size bed, everything was perfect. From the time we moved into our new apartment, she lost interest in everything—especially sex. She even said, 'How do you expect me to be romantic when I have to wash your dirty dishes?' But, Doctor, didn't she know that I planned to continue eating after the honeymoon?"

Sometimes it isn't all the girl's fault.

In what way?

The kind of environment she lives in can play a role too. After two unhappy marriages, both based on sexual marooning, Luanne had this to say:

"You know, Doctor, looking back on it, I think a big part of the problem was the place where I live."

"How come?"

"Well, back in Missouri if you meet a fellow at a party and you hit it off well and both of you feel you might have something in common, the next weekend you go out on a date. Here in Beverly Hills, if the same thing happens, the next weekend you get married—for six months. Speaking from my own experience, for me, marriage has broken up some beautiful engagements."

Other women are so involved with themselves that there is no emotional feeling left over for anyone else. Although they never warn their prospective husbands about it, they consider marriage as simply an invitation for two people to worship at the same shrine—theirs. They look on sexual intercourse as just another opportunity for their husband to prove, as sensationally as possible, how much they appreciate the privilege of being associated with such exciting personalities as their wife. Strangely enough a marriage built on this foundation can be happy until something goes wrong. A bad performance or two in bed by the husband provokes massive retaliation by the indignant wife and his sexual privileges are suspended or revoked.

In these situations sexual intercourse is eliminated as an expression of love and turned into a commodity.

How is it used as a commodity?

For barter and exchange. Unless the husband is "good," he doesn't get any. An elaborate rate of exchange sometimes develops. If the husband doesn't cut the lawn or pick up a loaf of bread on his way home from work, his wife gets a "headache" at bedtime. If he has too much to drink at a party, the bedtime headache (or as one sarcastic husband called it, the "bedache") can last three or four days. A pay-off in the form of a box of candy or dinner at a restaurant can wipe out the debt and ensure an exciting night or two. Women who play this game run two big risks.

What are they?

Like any trader, they can be undersold by the competition. After all, they are not the only ones in the neighborhood who have the same merchandise in stock. Almost without exception the wife who plays this game finds that her husband eventually retaliates by taking his sexual business elsewhere. Trading in human emotions is a hazardous business.

The second risk is that treating sex mechanically *makes* it mechanical. When the feeling goes out of sexuality, sometimes the performance slumps as well. Then impotence and frigidity loom on the scene and little problems suddenly escalate into very big ones. The wife who turns off her own orgasm to control her husband may find it impossible to turn it on again when she feels like it. The woman who won't let her husband have an erection when he wants it may be unpleasantly surprised when suddenly he can't have an erection when *she* wants it.

What's the answer?

Because sexual marooning in marriage is a different problem for every wife, the specific answer is different for each individual. But there is an overall solution that applies to every married woman equally. The only way for a wife to find true sexual fulfillment in marriage is to make it her primary goal. She must be willing to cast aside everything else in life that might come between herself and her husband. She must constantly dedicate herself to him as completely as she did on the day of her wedding. If she does—and if *he* does—they will be rewarded with the greatest gift any human being can ever receive. In those spectacular fleeting moments of orgasm, their souls and spirits will fuse—and just for an instant husband and wife will become one. And that, after all, is the true meaning of love between a man and a woman.